C000242735

TAILS OF THE FORTIES

ANOTHER ANTHOLOGY OF TRUE AVIATION STORIES (MAINLY POSTWAR)

COMPILED AND EDITED BY
JOHN HAVERS AND PETER CAMPBELL

CIRRUS ASSOCIATES

PUBLISHED BY:
Cirrus Associates (S.W.),
Kington Magna,
Gillingham,
Dorset,
SP8 5EW UK.

ISBN 1 902807 23 5 (ISBN13 978 1 902807 23 2)

PRINTED IN ENGLAND BY:
Hobbs the Printers Ltd.
Brunel Road,
Calmore Industrial Park,
TOTTON,
Hants,
SO40 3WX.

DISTRIBUTORS:
Cirrus Associates (S.W.),
Kington Magna,
Gillingham,
Dorset,
SP8 5EW.

COVER PHOTO: The prewar Foster-Wikner Wicko (G-AFJB) has been completely restored recently by Ron Souch for Joe Dible, the latest in a line of owners which includes the ex-ATA pilot Lettice Curtis.

PHOTOS IN THE BOOK: We must apologise for any lack of clarity that you may notice in the reproduction of some of the photos, but in view of their age we felt that it was important that they were included.

PREFACE

The outbreak of war on 3rd September 1939 brought with it the promulgation of the Air Navigation (Emergency Restrictions) Order 1939, followed by the Air Navigation (Restriction in Time of War) Order 1939, which meant that all private and club flying was prohibited with immediate effect. At the same time the National Air Communications organisation came into being as a result of an agreement made in 1938 for a subsidy to be paid to UK internal airlines so that in time of war 200 aircraft of these operators would be at the disposal of the Government.

So it was that on 28th August that these 200 aircraft, ranging from the larger airlines of Imperial Airways to Puss Moths and other single-engined aircraft, were dispersed to airfields all over the country. This situation continued until May 1940 when the majority were impressed into the RAF, but this did not mean that civil-registered aircraft were no longer to be seen, for some internal and overseas services continued throughout WWII, and a number of light aircraft were permitted to be operated by aircraft manufacturers for liaison purposes.

The ending of hostilities in 1945 did not mean that private flying could resume, although a steady stream of new civil aircraft appeared from aircraft manufacturers. The *Aeroplane Spotter* reported in November 1945 that the ban on private flying was likely to be lifted in the December, but made the point that they didn't know if petrol would be obtainable, since petrol coupons were still required for motoring.

In the event the ban was lifted on 1st January 1946 and on that day civil flying training was recommenced by Marshall's Flying School at Cambridge; similarly, Cambrian Air Services Ltd. at Cardiff operated the first private charter when their Auster J/1 Autocrat G-AFWN, flown by Eric Symmons, carried a cargo of wine to Bristol (Filton). Hunting Air Travel Ltd. claimed to be the first air taxi service since the end of the war with Percival Proctor G-AGSX.

Avro Lancastrian G-AGWG of British South American Airways was the first aeroplane to take off from London Airport at Heathrow at the inaugural ceremony on this same day. Named *Starlight,* it was engaged on a proving flight to Buenos Aires via Lisbon, Bathurst, Natal, Rio de Janeiro and Montevideo in preparation for a weekly service to be flown by an additional Lancastrian (G-AGWH, *Stardust*) and three Lancasters.

It is with this background in mind that this volume was conceived in order to tell something of the years 1945 to 1949 in particular, when aviation was attempting to return to normal after six years of war. It also includes a few stories which extend into the fifties and beyond, as well as some wartime memories — which in most cases led the writers into a lifelong interest in all things concerned with aviation.

John Havers, January 2006

EDITORIAL & DEDICATION

With four books already in our range in which we have tried to sum up flying in the 1950s in most of its different aspects (but with an undoubted emphasis on private flying), it seemed like a good idea for 2006 to attempt to record various aviation experiences from the immediate postwar period whilst we are fortunate enough still to have with us a fair number of pilots and ex-pilots from that era.

On this occasion my colleague John Havers, an ex-CAA man and likely known to many readers, has kindly offered to act as co-editor; in fact he has also been the coordinator for much of the contents by kindly contacting various likely contributors and encouraging them to put pen to paper. I would also like particularly to thank Ambrose Barber (ex-de Havilland Technical School and Hawker Aircraft), who has persuaded several of his erstwhile colleagues to recall their memories before they fade, and also my chum Lewis Benjamin for his reminiscences of the immediate postwar period when he started one of the first Flying Groups.

I would also like to dedicate this new book to the memory of a dear school friend, Tim Foster, who sadly passed away in November 2005. It was Tim who, during our time at Lancing College in the early fifties, provided the impetus for me to start aircraft spotting at the nearby Shoreham Airport, and this hobby has remained an essential part of my life ever since (as will be readily apparent to anyone who has read *The Fifties Revisited*, my personal memories of that period!).

Tim has authored chapters in our previous books, so suffice it to say on this occasion that, although we lost contact during the period of his life when he lived in the US, we were both delighted to meet up again in 1996 unexpectedly after he had returned to live in the UK. This was on the occasion when I was at Shoreham Airport for the launch of Tim Webb's book detailing the history of the airport, entitled (not surprisingly) *Shoreham Airport, Sussex*.

It was the Fly-In associated with that occasion of still-airworthy aircraft with a Shoreham connection (as described in last year's book, *Shadows of the Fifties*) that then encouraged me to consider organising the annual event which has now become known as the Great Vintage Flying Weekend (or G-VFWE). Ten years later in 2006, this event, now recognised as the largest of its kind in Europe, is being held at Keevil Airfield in Wiltshire and attracts the very best of British Vintage & Classic aircraft along with a wide selection of European and American aircraft.

I would like to think that it was Tim's fond memories of his schooldays at Lancing that led him to make an unusual last request of his son Chris: this was that, after his death, his ashes should be scattered from a light aircraft into the sea off Shoreham. I was pleased (well, if one can be *pleased* under such circumstances — perhaps 'honoured' is a more appropriate word to use) to be able to arrange for this to be done on Thursday 17th November 2005, when Clive Ponsford and his son Mark flew over from Goodwood in their Tiger Moth G-ANNI specially to oblige.

Sadly, *tempus fugit* irrevocably, and both I and G-VFWE Operations Manager Terry Booker are due to consider standing down shortly now we are in our middle to late sixties. However we are both anxious to find an existing organisation with the will, aviation know-how, facilities and manpower to take over from us, so that G-VFWE can continue to thrive for as long as possible in today's very uncertain world, as a tribute to the great days of British civil aviation.

Peter Campbell, March 2006.

CONTENTS

CHAPTER 1

1946 IN RETROSPECT — A REVIEW OF CIVIL AVIATION IN THE PAST YEAR

by

STANLEY ORTON BRADSHAW

(originally published in The Light Plane *for January 1947)*

At the time of writing, the United Kingdom's first year of civil aviation is drawing near to its close. It is too soon yet to sum it up with any approach to adequacy, nor are the signs yet clear enough for probing the future. There is, on the one hand, much that is most encouraging: on the other, much more that is most gravely disquieting. If the achievements of the British aviation industry and the RAF in war were not enough proof of inventive skill and lavish display of the finest craftsmanship, the activities of the industry since the war's ending have given ample further proof that there has been no diminution in the practical expression of these qualities. In the all-important matter of jet engines alone we have what is authoritatively estimated as a three-year lead over our closest rival, the USA. Again the strikes, and other domestic setbacks which have convulsed those United States since VJ-Day, have at the same time and at a stroke done a great deal to level the pronounced disparities originally existent between the UK and the USA in their chances of trade recovery and reconstruction.

Obstructions

It must be said that no thinking person can find any fault whatever in the policy of planned reconstruction. The briefest glance at the contemporary American scene should convince the toughest reactionary. Nor may it logically be denied that certain reforms are long overdue, nor that some clearly specified aspects of nationalisation are obviously desired.

Nor can it be denied that a high degree of moral courage is necessary to carry through actions so far-reaching. But there is a distinct point where clear thinking ceases and blind bigotry borne of resentment begins, and that moment seems to have been reached some time back. The fact is abundantly clear at least so far as aviation in this country is concerned.

In possibly no other field have these dulling effects been noticeable more than in the light plane movement, all the sadder in remembering that Britain instigated this branch of flying and in it formerly led the world. Light planes and light aero engines figured before the war quite appreciably in our exports. Their excellence had given rise to subsidiary industries in most countries of the world. Our national reputation was enhanced by the many records and achievements of those aeroplanes and engines, and by their aid the country had built up a vast reserve of pilots and air-minded folk, who proved to be an excellent return for subsidy in our recent hour of need. Without them there would never have been an Air Transport Auxiliary, for example, and without that organisation there might well have been different conclusion to the Battle of Britain.

Airfields Released

On January 1st, 1946, the Government declared British civil aviation 'open'! The whole glorious picture of this 'openness' was somewhat as follows: in the whole of the United Kingdom there had been allocated for the private flyer, out of all the hundreds of aerodromes in existence and now largely derelict anyway, a grand total of 25. Of these, however, 13 were available only to operators of organised air services, and finally and in actual fact only eight were for the use of private and charter pilots. A study of the current air map of the United Kingdom showed that the whole thing was almost completely blotted out by warnings, obstructions and prohibitions.

On top of all this the Ministry of Fuel and Power now announced the fuel concessions that it was graciously pleased to grant civil aviators — outside the Government monopolies. Thus for charter and taxi services the allowance of fuel per month would be 60 gallons, and for club aircraft 50 gallons per month; so far so good. For the private owner enough fuel for four hours a month! Thus a London owner could fly, say, to Blackpool once a month and forget about his flying for the remainder of the period. For this pleasure he was evidently assumed to be demented enough to buy a new machine to the tune of £2,500 plus, or some RAF wreck off the junk heap for £40 or so and then spend several hundreds renovating and repairing it. Under the new regulations he is not now allowed to do the work himself, even if aided by a qualified worker. Last of all, the choice of eight aerodromes in all the United Kingdom!

Even that was not all. The Treasury, feeling that it had a right to the pickings of the corpse, promptly instituted a really handsome scale of landing charges made on State-owned aerodromes — which is most of them in any case. In moderation most people expect to pay for services rendered, but this scheme resolved in actual fact into precisely no service and precious little civility, a state of affairs which might be considered as sheer boycott, to coin a phrase. Heavy as these charges were, judged by prewar standards, they were raised in July to a crippling level, and no explanation given. Ordinary business circles would, one feels, term these practices as obtaining money under false pretences. For landing on a State-controlled, runway-equipped aerodrome, an Auster owner, for example, was liable to a landing extortion of 12s/6d. An aircraft in the Rapide class was assessed by the same token at £2-10s.

It is pleasing to be able to record that the increased landing charges were not long in force for in August, following the most energetic representations by the Royal Aero Club, the Aerodrome Owners' Association and so on, the Ministry of Civil Aviation reduced the scale of charges to somewhere within the bounds of reason. A little later on an increase in the fuel allowances was granted: that is, a private owner now gets six gallons of petrol per month as against the four of previously.

In all this where did the Clubs come in? Putting it precisely — nowhere. They had no equipment at all. Everything they possessed had been requisitioned or impounded at the outbreak of war and a move to remedy the matter was not made until later in the year. Finally it was decided that the Clubs that were able or plucky enough to restart should be allowed to tender for 100 surplus light aircraft. These worn-out wrecks were released at around £50 each, but all required an average expenditure of £500 to bring them back to a proper state of airworthiness. Before the negotiations were complete the RAF then threw a small spanner into the works by suddenly discovering that it wanted 19 of those poor waifs back again.

The Clubs Start Up
By May eight Clubs were functioning, though the Lancashire Club, true to tradition, had shown the first signs of returning animation back in January. Marshall's of Cambridge actually claimed the first 'A' licence on the 7th January, the soloist being Prince Birabongse of Siam. In the following month 18 Clubs were either in action or in the process of reorganisation. It was possible to refuel at 24 points in the United Kingdom, a state of affairs which called for a very elastic fuel tank with the average type of light aircraft. Flying charges, after some initial experimental fluctuation, had crystallised at £3-10s or so for solo flying.

The vigour and enthusiasm with which the majority of the clubs have faced their difficulties, and the degree of support which they have mostly gained from their members, even allowing for the falsifying effect of a postwar boom, has been very heartening. It must also be added that one or two Clubs at least — newcomers always — have a lot to learn about their business and should put their houses in order if they wish to survive when things normalise; nor is it right that they should risk bringing discredit upon the whole movement.

During the year there were several notable events. In a minor key there were the comings and goings of *Starlight*, *Aries* and the rest, and several trans-Oceanic Proctor deliveries by the ubiquitous James Mollison. Then, on the 10th February, the United Nations Organisation was invited to an aviation display at Radlett Aerodrome, Herts. With the exceptions of the Miles Aerovan and Gemini and the Auster V J/1, this shop-window show contained nothing else connected with light aviation. On the whole the display appeared to be designed solely to convince the organisers of peace what a mighty wallop the RAF could hand out to them!

During the weekend of the 10th & 11th August, the de Havilland Dove demonstrator, G-AGPJ, flown by its pilot Mr. I. S. Fossett, made a tour of 17 of the aeroplane Clubs, commencing at White Waltham and finishing at Elstree. Aboard were Air Commodore Whitney Straight CBE, MC, DFC, Col. R.L. Preston CBE, Lord Dunegal and press representatives.

Lympne Air Race

The first noticeable air race meeting of the year occurred during the weekend of August 31st & September 1st. It was held at Lympne under the auspices of the Cinque Ports Club and was very well patronised. The High-Speed race was a battle of giants, but the events of main interest were the Folkestone Aero Trophy race and the Siddeley Challenge Trophy race. In the former event, which was won by a Supermarine Walrus, pilot J. Grierson, at an average speed of 121 mph, the entries comprised a Percival Gull (once Miss Jean Batten's famous mount), one Messenger and five Proctors. The average speeds varied between 140.25 mph and 147.0 mph for the Proctors. The Siddeley Challenge Race was contested by two machines only, a Tiger Moth and a Miles Hawk, both the property of the Cinque Ports Club. The Tiger was the winner at 102.0 mph.

The most outstanding and impressive event of the whole year was undoubtedly the SBAC display, also staged at Radlett Aerodrome, on September 12th & 13th. As an exposition of what the aircraft industry could do when permitted, the display, both flying and static, succeeded 100%. On the other hand it emphasised the beggarly position of the light plane movement today. Once again some four or five diehard types were the sole representatives of this field. On Sunday the show was reopened for the RAeS Garden Party; at this display Geoffrey de Havilland (junior) made his last public demonstration before his tragic death.

On September 28th was staged an event of' great significance. The West London Aero Club at White Waltham aerodrome, the old HQ of ATA, originated, financed and staged a most outstanding event, namely a 'Display of Aircraft for the Businessman'. The underlying motive was to bring aviation and the businessman together for their mutual benefit. It was felt that if businessmen and their representatives were given an opportunity of meeting aircraft manufacturers and operators, and other commercial folk who actually operated aircraft for their business needs, they could thus gain at first hand a great deal of practical information about the subject, and in this respect the display certainly succeeded.

About 200 eminent persons attended the official luncheon, including the then Minister of State for Air, Lord Winster, who pledged his strongest support for the flying club movement. Altogether some 3,000 people attended the display and there were 70 visiting aircraft on view.

Final among the greater events of the year was the Paris Exhibition where, it has been universally agreed, the British section stole the show. Gratifying as this is, it is very sad to record that we had not so much as a bolt on view at the Cleveland, USA show. Why, when only a week or so later Sir Stafford Cripps uttered grave warnings about our future if we do not boost up our exports to the USA!

CHAPTER 2

1947 IN RETROSPECT — A REVIEW OF CIVIL AVIATION IN THE PAST YEAR

by

STANLEY ORTON BRADSHAW

(originally published in The Light Plane *for January 1948)*

In our issue for January last, which was number two in our first volume, we reviewed 1946, beginning with the following words: "At the time of writing, the United Kingdom's first year of civil aviation is drawing near to its close. It is too soon yet to sum it up with any approach to adequacy, nor are the signs yet clear enough for probing the future." A year later there is no difficulty about assessing the year now past, nor, if politics and economics were following different and clearer trends, would there be any ambiguity about the future.

The progress, both technical and social, that was so evident in 1946 has been even more marked in 1947, and but for the general obstructiveness of the so-called recovery plans and the quite unnecessary economic 'crisis', it is plain that the way ahead would be a steady surge forward of expansion and development. The British aviation industry is at heart as healthy and strong, as original and as skilled, as it has ever been, and the flying clubs have been working to capacity throughout the year. There has been no lack of interest and support; people want aeroplanes, they want to fly.

But in both cases unfortunate circumstances and misguided interference (official name 'control') are depriving our aviation of the proper means of just or self-expression. Already, mere weeks after the Radlett show, machines that could have added to our laurels in the world's markets and on the air routes are being withdrawn from production — or even contemplated production. This is due to lack of orders, even more to an absence of policy at the Ministry of Supply and the Government airline monopolies. One or two excellent firms are actually closing down, and others are known to be in difficulties. This makes the paradox all the stranger when our firms have, nearly all of them, one or more highly-saleable aeroplanes — aeroplanes, what is more, that are wanted by many people. There is one bright spot in all this; if care is taken now, the damage done in the long run to our industry may be less than that done to the US firms who oversold their market.

Many of the grumbles in our first review still stand. We are still wanting aerodromes, despite the hundreds of derelict ex-RAF stations which still scar the countryside. We learn that the RAF, notwithstanding the fact that these aerodromes are some time due to be returned to their original agricultural owners, are in many cases still maintaining runways at these places, the cost of same, we gather, around £2,000 per annum per runway — for nothing.

The petrol allowances we looked at rather askance last year, but in all fairness it must be said that they seem to have worked out pretty well. Of the latest cuts, well, it is better to control our feelings and say nothing. We do feel, to put it mildly, the cuts have been highly discriminatory. We shall not forget the enormous consumption of our precious petrol by Cabinet and other ministers on their alleged official comings and goings, or their highly gracious popping to and fro from their summer holidays to take a stray peek at the nation's affairs. The thousands of gallons of petrol thus consumed would probably have seen many flying clubs and all of our hundred or so private owners through next year, whilst the cost would have probably refunded many a postwar credit.

Aeroplanes? Well, we are still grabbing them off the junk-heaps, instead of being able to buy the many excellent new types that the manufacturers aren't allowed to sell us, or because overheads and taxes are beyond our impoverished purses. Of course, exports are all the thing, and quite right too. But that being the case, we do find it difficult to understand why some manufacturers are finding it hard to keep going when, so we are told, everything they produce can be instantly swallowed up in foreign markets. Perhaps, like Winnie the Pooh, we are only bears with little brains!

Landing charges are still with us and they still hurt. Less than they did, maybe, or in a different way. As we have said before, no reasonable person can object to payment for services rendered, but payment for precisely nothing plus rudeness renders most of us quite unreasonable.

Having reduced the emotional pressure, we can proceed more calmly with the aviation history of the year. Despite misfortunes there is an underlying motif of good, much of which we must assign to the appointment of Lord Nathan, late in 1946, to the post of Minister of Civil Aviation, no less to his happy co-operation with Mr. Peter Masefield and Mr. Whitney Straight, among others. From the first, Lord Nathan has adopted a kindly and helpful attitude toward light aviation, and would undoubtedly have done much more of practical good had circumstances been more fortunate and officialdom less preoccupied. We have personally heard — and like most others we have read — his reported words on several occasions, and always he has stressed his interest in, and his good intentions toward, civil aviation, very much including the Clubs. From his first meeting with the National Aviation Consultative Council on January 27th he has made these things evident. Very soon after his appointment he inaugurated the Informal Light Aeroplane Committee to deliberate and report upon the Clubs and our light aviation generally. Much of the good that this body might have done has been stultified by the belated issue of their reports in White Paper form coincident with the economic crisis and the panic plans for retrenchment.

It is possible, however, that the powers that be may be persuaded of the very serious results, in the long-term sense, of rejecting the report lock, stock and barrel, so that they may adopt it in part or in modified form.

Despite all the claims of modern planners and politicians, it is significant that, so far as light aviation is concerned, the only tangible and actual help it has received since July 1945 has still come from private benefactors. Two such instances may be quoted for 1947. One was the gift of £100,000 from Lord Kemsley, intended to help and promote light aviation and gliding in this country. The other was the kindly gesture of Lord Londonderry in placing the family town house, Londonderry House, at the disposal of the Royal Aero Club for 21 years at a moderate rental. Apart from being a much-needed annexe to the Piccadilly address, it also provides office accommodation for the Association of British Aero Clubs, the British Gliding Association, the Aerodrome Owners' Association, the British Association of Charter Pilots and the Guild of Air Pilots and Navigators.

Although the SBAC show at Radlett offered the proof of the pudding, we have seen ample evidence otherwise that in the technical, as well as the social sense, the movement has been productive of intensive thought. While much of it has been specifically generated by and for light aviation, some of the benefits have been entirely fortuitous, resulting from deliberations intended mainly for the 'heavies'. For example, conferences concerning accident prevention, radio developments, meteorology and flying control, to name some of them, have formed the core of these things, but much of this knowledge is applicable to the designer, pilot or operator of the light aeroplane. We gloss over, for the moment, the many possibilities (or threats) which are fulminating about the constitution of the 'A' licence of tomorrow. So far we know no more than common rumours, but if they contain any truth, then we fear the very worst.

Technical developments have not been backward either. The light aeroplane *côterie* have been spared, thank God, such problems as boundary layout control, sonic barriers and jet propulsion, though the gas turbine should have its uses one day. Other conveniences, mostly solved beforehand for us by the 'heavy brigade', are now in common use: for example the retractable undercarriage, variable-pitch airscrews and flaps. The crosswind undercarriage has received attention in the USA. Apart from these things the emphasis in design has been placed upon trying to provide the ideal form, or forms, in light aeroplanes. In spite of all this, the Clubs and private owners are still mainly compelled to equip themselves from junk-heaps. Possibly it was this very position of things which prompted the ABAC to compile and produce their report on the Servicing of Light Aeroplanes, which was accepted by the SBAC. A commendable attempt at rationalisation, but it might not be unconnected with the daily task of getting the best out of aged aeroplanes.

From the social and sporting angle, this year has been one of the busiest on record. Starting with the reunion cocktail parties at Redhill and Portsmouth on the same Saturday afternoon in late April, right up to the last display at Cowes in September, the season has been one long living proof of the vigorous life there is in the light plane movement (and the ultralight portion). It must be realised that so much good is done by these events. A breed of private and sporting pilots is maintained, aeroplane owners are generated, the general public are assisted in becoming air-minded and foreign friendships are made and kept. We defy any Treasury spokesman to prove that the cost asked to aid such a movement as this (actually one fifteenth of one day's expenditure in the war) is an undeserved burden upon the taxpayer. Apart from these considerations, the displays have paid good dividends in other directions. For example, the records gained during the Lympne races; these have more than mere prestige value, though we can do with a little more of that commodity these days. Readers scarcely need to be reminded that no fewer than four records were taken in that meeting.

If petrol allowances and other circumstances permit us to have meetings next year, it might be a good thing if the club committees and the Royal Aero Club could see fit to cooperate in organising the season's programme to avoid the unfortunate overlapping that often occurred this summer. On more than one occasion as many as three different meetings were held on the same day, which is hard on the enthusiastic type of supporter, and adds greatly to the difficulties of the Press.

Taken all in all, despite fuel and financial crises, growing foreign competition, and the stranglehold of the civil servants upon producers and users alike, it has been a very good year indeed. Next year could see the promise upheld and our enthusiasm justified, if only our natural energy and initiative were free to get on with it. Quite apart from overriding factors such as the national finances, there is a steady infiltration of smaller, but none the less harmful, influences insidiously creeping into our affairs. Let me quote a case.

It appears that MCA is getting itself organised, which means making itself larger and larger, and there is now a recently formed department whose job it is to go more deeply into the 'A' licence medical forms as they are received from the candidate's doctor. Recently, an 'A' licence pilot of many, many years' standing went through the usual motions of renewing his licence. He has, I may add, a large number of flying hours, wide experience and has carried many passengers. After a long delay he was summoned to attend the officials of this new department. He was informed that his eyesight was not satisfactory. Now he has one eye somewhat below par, it has been like this since birth probably, and all his flying has therefore been done with it so. This would not do, he must be properly examined by the RAF. He submitted himself to this examination, and the MO said that he would advise the said department to renew the licence, at the same time advising them that glasses were *not* to be recommended, as they would actually affect the candidate's flying detrimentally. The sequel is that when the victim duly received his renewed licence it contained the typed proviso: "This licence is renewed subject to the aforesaid wearing corrections when flying." So presumably these penpushers know better than the medical experts! We can, and *must*, do with a very great deal less of this sort of thing.

CHAPTER 3

MY MEMOIRS

by

CLIVE ABBOTT

(The author writes: "My career in aviation was short-lived; it started in the school summer holidays of 1947 when I volunteered with Brian Stead to sell pleasure flight tickets for Monique Agazarian of Island Air Services in the public enclosure of Croydon Aerodrome. Their Proctor Vs accommodated three passengers and, when there was an empty seat, Brian and I took it in turns to make up the load. During the fortnight we worked for 'Aggi' I managed this on eight occasions, which included a round trip to Luton for spares.

Although Island Air Services got the pleasure-flying contract at London Airport in 1948 and 1949, I was out of luck as the older 'spotters' cornered the market. However, when they were called up for National Service in 1950 my luck changed and, whilst at art school, I worked for 'Aggi' for four years at weekends and during the summer holidays as part of the ground crew and occasional aerial guide to London landmarks. The first year was the best: there was still a barnstorming atmosphere, London Airport was developing fast, airlines were arriving from all over the world and I was a very, very small part of it. Imagine what a fantastic experience this was for a teenager, working with aeroplanes and charismatic pilots, flying regularly, sometimes six times a day — absolute bliss.

It was then my turn to do National Service. I volunteered to fly in the RAF, with a logbook containing 293 passenger flights to support my application, but spent two years in the Royal Army Service Corps — and that was the end of my aviation career. I got married in 1957 shortly after leaving the army and worked in advertising as a visualiser/art director until October 1968, when I lost my job and started freelancing. My connections with aviation were few and far between: occasional flights in naval helicopters when working for the Royal Navy, plus designing and illustrating stamps with aviation subjects for the Post Office, Guernsey and other small Commonwealth countries.

In 1985, I was reunited quite by chance with my boyhood friend Gordon 'Ginger' Bedggood after a lapse of 30 years. He was then a flying instructor with the Met. Police Flying Club at Denham, having recently retired from BCal. Whenever possible I flew with him: we joined the Croydon and Shoreham Airport Societies, I joined the de Havilland Moth Club and aviation became a major hobby again. My one regret is that I never leaned to fly.")

In retrospect it seems hardly surprising that I developed a lifelong interest in aviation. I was four years old when my parents moved into a new house at Wallington in 1937, separated from the western boundary of Croydon Aerodrome only by the houses in Foresters Drive. There was a gap between these houses at the end of runway 12/30, and from my bedroom window I had an excellent view — through this gap — of aeroplanes landing. The typical airliners of this time — the Handley Page HP.42s, Douglas DC-2s and DC-3s, Junkers Ju.90s, Focke-Wulf Condors, Ensigns and Albatrosses — were slow and low enough for me to see even the waving passengers. My mother often took me to Roundshaw Park to watch the aeroplanes, and after the war started she was convinced that the solitary man we had seen taking notes was a spy; but I suspect that he was just a prewar 'spotter'.

At the start of the war, most houses in Foresters Drive were requisitioned for the RAF, and Spitfires and Hurricanes were dispersed around the airfield boundary at the back of the houses. The pilots, who included many from Canada and occupied Europe, gave sweets to us kids and we were allowed to have a close-up look at their aircraft whilst the ground crews serviced them and patched up the damaged ones. I was nearly seven years old and immediately decided that I wanted to be a Spitfire pilot; sad to say, this wasn't to be, but I did finally get the opportunity to fly in Carolyn Grace's two-seater at Duxford on 10th June 1996.

Unfortunately there were a number of aeroplane crashes at the aerodrome during the war, and I vividly remember the Blenheim that crashed on 45 Foresters Drive on the evening of 24th February 1940: the flash as it exploded was visible through our thick blackout curtains. On another occasion a fighter crashed into the allotments in Roundshaw Park after performing a 'victory roll'; Rex Nicholls and I still cannot agree as to whether it was a Spitfire or a Hurricane and, although he has researched squadron histories, he has been unable to find any record of this crash. For a short time black-painted Defiant night-fighters were a regular sight, standing on their noses in the middle of the aerodrome.

The war started in earnest at Croydon when, in the early evening of Thursday 15th August 1940, there was an unannounced air raid on the aerodrome. A lot of factory workers were killed at the Waddon Industrial Estate, particularly at the Bourjois and British NSF factories; the terminal building was damaged and the western end of 'C' hangar was destroyed. My father was in the back garden when he heard the sound of many aircraft approaching, so when he looked up and spotted the German crosses he immediately bundled us into the cupboard under the stairs.

Our family was evacuated after the Battle of Britain for 18 months in 1941/42 during a relatively quiet period, but returned in time to witness the onslaught of the Doodlebugs. One sunny afternoon in the summer of 1944, I was with a group of mothers and children picking fruit on a smallholding at Woodmansterne when I saw 21 flying bombs, one of which exploded just half a mile away amongst the fruit bushes. Another one landed alongside Wallington County Grammar School that afternoon, and this greatly extended my summer holiday whilst the damage was repaired, as I was due to start there in the autumn.

Later during the war, an Oxford crashed onto a house in Plough Lane South and finally, on the night of 21st April 1944, there was a tragic accident when a disabled Lancaster bomber attempted to land at Croydon. During the subsequent overshoot its undercarriage clipped the roof of our family doctor's house in Foresters Drive and then the aircraft crashed into houses in Lavender Vale. When I went to Bandon Hill School the following morning there were bricks and tiles on the road and the recognisable remains of a Lancaster perched on the houses behind the school. To a 10-year old boy, the bombs and accidents were very exciting, but fortunately none of my friends or family were injured or killed, and my parents ensured that I was shielded from the horrible reality of civilian and aircrew deaths.

Whilst Croydon Aerodrome was a fighter station, at various times Gladiators, Hurricanes, Spitfires, Defiants, Tomahawks, Mustangs and Blenheims were based there; but by 1943 BOAC had returned to run the aerodrome in conjunction with RAF Transport Command. However, there were still many interesting military aircraft that I remember seeing: Wellingtons with magnetic hoops for exploding mines (although, at the time, I didn't know that that was what they were for), the occasional USAAF Mustang, Thunderbolt, Fortress and the all-silver USAAF P-38 Lightning which overran and ended up on its nose in the Foresters Drive gap in about 1943; then there was the arrival of a flight of Vultee Vengeances, later in 1945/46 a French Air Force Martin Maryland and Douglas Dauntless, silver RAF Stirling transports (possibly for servicing by BOAC), Czech Air Force Dakotas and Junkers Ju.52/3Ms, then the dramatic arrival of about half a dozen Russian Air Force Li-2s (licence-built DC-3s), carrying the Russian national football team — the Moscow Dynamos — which I witnessed from my back garden as they flew in line astern in an anti-clockwise (I think) direction around the aerodrome perimeter at rooftop height. Lastly, in 1946, I watched the large Air Ministry Junkers Ju.352 take off towards me from my vantage position at the top end of Purley Way: it only just made it!

However, it was the return of civil aeroplanes — when BOAC started to overhaul their fleet at Croydon — which persuaded me to start a spotter's log. This came about on 13th May 1944 when a camouflaged Avro York (G-AGJA) thundered low across our garden on take-off. By the end of 1945 I had recorded 11 Yorks, 17 Lancastrians, 42 Dakotas, two each of Hudson IIIs, Mosquitos and Liberators, plus a single Lancaster and Warwick, all sporting the BOAC Speedbird emblem. A lot of them were camouflaged with registrations in black outlined in silver and underlined by a red, white and blue bar. All the Lancastrians, most of the Yorks and some of the Dakotas were silver but still with the red, white and blue bars under the registration and the RAF tail flash. An exotic exception in 1945 was when a BOAC York was repainted in South African Airways' colours, registered ZS-ATR and named *Impala*.

In November 1944 the Associated Airways Joint Committee (AAJC) restarted internal air services at Croydon, initially operated by Railway Air Services, West Coast Air Services (WCAS), Air Commerce and Great Western Air Services (GWAS), using camouflaged Dragon Rapides and four DH86/86Bs. Later, in 1945, Scottish Airways and Channel Island Airways operated with Dragon Rapides and Railway Air Services introduced silver Avro XIXs.

At about the same time as the internal services started I recorded a DC-2 and four DC-3s of Swissair and four DC-3s of ABA (Sweden). If my memory isn't playing tricks, the Swedish aeroplanes were painted orange overall during hostilities. By the middle of 1945 other foreign airlines started to reappear and up to the end of the year I saw the following:

Air France: four Bloch 220s, two Dewoitine D.338s, 19 Amiot AAC.1 (French-built Junkers Ju.52/3Ms), five Lodestars and a solitary DC-3
Aer Lingus Teoranta: DH.86B and DC-3
LOT, Polish Airlines: DC-3
SABENA: five Lodestars

The Bloch 220s and Lodestars were silver overall with French Air Force markings and only the last three letters of their civil registration. The Blochs were soon civilianised but I didn't see any of the Lodestars with their complete registration. (One of the Lodestars still exists and I recently saw it at the USAF Museum at Dayton, Ohio, displayed in an American military colour scheme). The SABENA Lodestars were all camouflaged.

In 1944 the late Gordon 'Ginger' Bedggood became a neighbour and firm friend through our shared interest in aviation. We spent a lot of our childhood making model aeroplanes at my house, as it had a better view of the fascinating aircraft that visited Croydon than that afforded from his house. We became enthusiastic aeroplane spotters, and by the summer of 1945 were given permission by our parents to cycle to the other side of the aerodrome, by which time Purley Way had reopened. Our favourite spotting location was the bombed site of the former British NSF factory, which was being used to store large, wooden cable drums. Sitting on these gave us an unobstructed view of the tarmac in front of the terminal building and we spent many a happy hour there. As we got older and bolder, we climbed through gaps in the railings to get a closer look at the aeroplanes and had fun and games evading the airport police, not always successfully.

It was on one of these forays that we discovered the remains of five camouflaged BOAC DH.95 Flamingos (G-AFYF, 'G, 'J, 'K and 'L), some of them in giant packing cases, in the derelict workshops behind 'C' hangar. Another wreck was the Lockheed 14 (G-AGAV) parked at the southern end of the BOAC hangars by Purley Way, where earlier, in 1943/44, an unidentified Albatross had languished.

A DC-2 (NL203) and two DC-3s (NL202 and 204) operated by the Dutch Government appeared by Plough Lane North in the summer of 1945, where they were overhauled and repainted as G-AGBH, 'GBD and 'GJS.

Other interesting visitors in 1945 were as follows:

Miles Falcon Six (G-ADTD, camouflaged), Stinson Reliant (G-AFHB), Avro XIXs (G-AGNI and 'GPG), the second prototype Viking (G-AGOL) — reputedly for a compass swing —, Messenger III (G-AGOY), Aerovan prototype (G-AGOZ) — on 12th October —, Hunting Air Travel Proctor V (G-AGSX), Caudron Goeland (F-BAIO), Nord 1000 (F-BAKD), Nord 1101 Noralpha (F-BBJC), Lockheed 14 (YR-BPL).

Also seen were new aircraft on delivery:

Dragon Rapides (CS-ADI, 'ADJ and 'ADK), YI-ABD (for Iraqi Airways) and PH-RAA (for KLM), and Proctor V (CS-ADN).

The Ministry of Civil Aviation also based their fleet at Croydon, consisting of Proctor III (G-AGLJ), Auster Vs (G-AGLK and 'GLL), Anson XI (G-AGLM), Proctor V (G-AGPA) and Tiger Moths (G-AGRA & 'GRB).

From 1st January 1946 I started keeping a daily diary of aircraft I hadn't seen before and for a short period kept a record of every aeroplane seen and the time it arrived or departed from the aerodrome. From this log is a list of movements that I saw on a typical day, Friday 12th April:

Channel Island Airways: Dragon Rapides G-AGPH, 'GUF and 'GSK (twice)

Air France: Bloch 220s F-AOHC and 'OHE

Amiot ACC.1 (French-built Ju.52/3M)I: F-BAKP

KLM: DC-3s PH-TBA and 'TCA (twice)

SABENA: DC-3s OO-AUL and 'CBB

Railway Air Services: DH.86B G-AENR, Avro XIXs G-AGUD, 'GUX and 'GVA (twice); Dragon Rapides G-AGLR, 'GUU, 'HGG, 'HGH & 'HGI

Scottish Airways: Dragon Rapide G-AGOJ

Morton Air Services: Dragon Rapides G-AGWR & 'HIA

ABA: DC-3s SE-BAB *Hoken* and 'BAC *Falken*

Aer Lingus Teoranta: DC-3 EI-ACE

Swissair: DC-3s HB-IRE and 'IRO

West Coast Air Services: DH.86B G-ADYH

DNL: DC-3 LN-IAI

British American Air Services: Dragon Rapide G-AGZJ

Aeroplanes that were regularly parked were: Autocrats G-AHAT and PH-OTO, Proctor I G-AHBS, York G-AGOC and Dakota G-AGKF of BOAC.

As 1946 progressed, more and more scheduled services operated, charter companies proliferated, British aeroplanes were delivered overseas, military aeroplanes were civilianised, private owners from home and abroad visited, and BOAC still overhauled Yorks, Lancastrians, a Liberator and an Anson. It was the most interesting year of activity at Croydon.

RAF Transport Command Dakotas had the monopoly of regular British airline services to Europe, with the exception of those to Sweden, Spain and Portugal, which were operated by BOAC Dakotas. Air France, SABENA, LOT, CSA (Czechoslovakia), DDL (Denmark), ABA, Aer Lingus Teoranta, Iberia, Swissair, DNL (Norway) and KLM were the foreign competitors. Internal air services still operated under the AAJC banner but gradually reappeared in BEAC colours. All the foreign airlines used DC-3s, a lot of them camouflaged and still showing evidence of RAF or USAAF markings, with KLM having the largest fleet: I logged 29 of them. Junkers Ju.52/3Ms were operated by Air France, SABENA and CSA, and in November were introduced by BEAC. A second Swissair DC-2 and Aer Lingus DH.86B appeared briefly, but some rarer types ceased operating. The last Dewoitine D.338 I saw was in January, and Bloch 220 on 26th April. The fledgling BEAC mainly used Dragon Rapides, Avro XIXs, Dakotas and the occasional Viking, possibly on diversion from Northolt.

Prewar British-registered aeroplanes gradually resurfaced, with de Havilland, Miles, Percival and Taylorcraft well represented. Rarer types included two Foster-Wikner Wickos and Tipsy Trainers, Monospar ST-25, BA Swallow, Airspeed Envoy, Hillson Praga, Cessna Airmaster, Piper J-2 Cub, Stinson Reliant, and Beech 17s. New British-built aircraft were increasing in number, with Autocrats (61 in total) leading the way, this tally including exports to Uganda, Holland, Belgium, Switzerland, Sweden, Denmark and Egypt. Proctor Vs were nearly as prolific and I logged 44, which included one for Zambezi Airways. Dragon Rapides passed through on delivery to operators abroad including Iraqi Airways (4), Central African Airways (2), Southern India Steamships (3), Arab Airways Association (5), South Africa (4) and Denmark (1). Avro Ansons went to South Africa, Belgium and Southern Rhodesia, Avro XIXs to Misr Airwork (3) and Belgium (2).

Foreign light aeroplanes became frequent visitors, neutral Switzerland leading the way with three Leopard Moths, Taylorcraft Plus D, Alfred Comte AC.12 Moskito, Koolhoven FK.50A and FK.50 Mark III, Whitney Straight and three ex-RAF camouflaged Fairchild Arguses on delivery. From Denmark came SAIAS KZ.III Larken, KZ.IV, DH.60M Metal Moth and Miles Hawk Trainer. France was represented by five Nord 1002s, Nord 1101 Noralpha, Nord 1203 Norécrin, ex-RAF Bücker Bestmann and Whitney Straight, and Belgium by two Beech D-17s, Piper Super Cruisers, Fairchild Forwarders, Stinson Reliant, Noordyn Norseman, Cessna Bobcat and Miles Aerovan, Czechoslovakia by Benes-Mraz Sokol, Siebel 204D and Bobcat, and Iraq by Leopard Moth (YI-ABI) — which later became G-AIYS.

Charter companies mainly used Dragon Rapides, Consuls, Ansons, Avro XIXs, Proctors and Autocrats, plus the occasional Bristol 170 and Aerovan; and the first de Havilland Dove appeared. Foreign charter companies from South Africa used DC-3s of Pan African Air Charter, Anglo-Vaal Air Transport and Suidair International, and eight Caudron Goelands from France were regular visitors.

Other visitors of interest included the first American-registered civil aeroplane, a Beech D-18S (NC80014), a South African Lodestar, a British and French Lockheed 14, three Lockheed 12As, an NC.701 Martinet (French-built Siebel 204), a Liore et Olivier Leo.45 Rouland, two Lockheed 14s of TARAS (Romania), two ex-military Dakotas on delivery (CX-AGD and PP-VBB), the third prototype Viking and the exotic, pale blue Handley Page Halton G-AGZP reputedly operated for the Maharajah Gaekwar of Baroda by British American Air Services.

The urge to fly in an aeroplane was very strong by this time, and by July 1946 I had saved 10 shillings, which wasn't easy on sixpence-a-week pocket money. In those days the milkman, baker and coalman delivered their wares with horse-drawn vehicles, and I enhanced my savings by being paid three pence a bucket from my father for collecting the manure whenever the horses obliged. This was quite competitive in our cul-de-sac, but, being young and agile, I usually beat the older residents to the treasure.

So, on the morning of Saturday 13th July 1946, at the ripe old age of 12¾ years, I went to the aerodrome with my friend of long standing, Brian Stead, and clutching my precious ten-shilling note. At first, the policeman on gate duty wouldn't let us in — maybe he recognised us from one of our previous escapades — but somehow or other we finally persuaded him and then presented ourselves at the Air Taxis desk in the booking hall. With our pilot, Kingsley N. Cubitt, we were in the aerodrome — legitimately for the first time! — and helped push a brand-new cream and red Autocrat (G-AGVS) from the hangar. Brian, being the older by a few years, commandeered the right-hand seat, and I sat in the odd sideways-facing seat in the back. We had estimated that our 10 shillings would pay for 10 minutes' flying, so we were delighted when we found we had had 25 minutes. We proffered our 10-shilling notes to the pilot but were informed that we should pay the boss in the office. Brian and I can't agree as to who the boss was; he reckons it was Jock Adie, but I thought it was Charlie Allen, however, Brian was more likely correct. Much to our delight, whoever it was wouldn't take our money, saying that it was only a test flight. You can imagine the reactions of our spotter friends who were waiting outside with their noses pressed to the railings in Purley Way when they heard the news.

CHAPTER 4

FLYING IN THE AIR TRAINING CORPS IN THE LATE-FORTIES

by

GRAHAM LEWIS

(Graham Lewis [born December 1931 in West Dulwich] was educated at Alleyn's School, Dulwich 1943-1949. He joined de Havilland Propellers at Hatfield in 1953 as a Trainee Design Draughtsman, and later, in 1974, gained a BA Degree in Science and Technology with the Open University. He became a member of the Royal Aeronautical Society in 1977, and finally retired as Senior Design Engineer with British Aerospace at Stevenage in 1992.

He joined Air-Britain in 1961 and is proud of the fact that he soloed in Tiger Moth G-APCC with the Surrey and Kent Flying Club at Croydon Airport in 1958 [the year before it closed]. He is currently a member of the East Herts Flying School at Panshanger — Ed.)

My enthusiasm for aircraft and flying started before World War II, when my parents took me to the RAF display at Hendon in 1937 and the Empire Air Day at Northolt in 1938, plus occasional visits to Croydon Airport. Of course the war provided endless spotting opportunities. Like many other young boys my ambition was to join the RAF as a fighter pilot, and the first step to achieve this was to join the ATC. However, you had to be 16 years old before you could enrol, so I had to wait until the end of 1947 before joining No. 1481 Squadron (Norwood). The ATC offered so much in those days (as I am sure it does today): air experience flights in Service aircraft, training in all the flying subjects, drill, shooting and summer camps at RAF Stations. With the war over, one might have expected the ATC to be run down and its activities reduced, but this was not the case as the Cold War was gaining momentum and the Korean War was on the horizon. Belonging to the Corps had three great advantages:

1. Provided you gained your Advanced Proficiency Certificate and were medically fit, you were guaranteed entry into the RAF when you were called up for your National Service.

2. Your National Service basic training (square-bashing) was reduced by two weeks.

3. Most important of all (in my opinion) was that it gave you an insight into service life, which proved invaluable when it came to National Service.

Of course the great attraction was the flying. For me, this was carried out mainly at Kenley and the summer camps at Manston. From my logbooks, I see that I averaged six flights a year in the following aircraft: Ansons W1731, EG228, MG629, MG901 and VM366, Tiger Moths DE412 and DE744, and Dominie NR679.

The Ansons and Dominie were being operated by the No.61 Group Communications Flight, and the total flying time for these flights amounted to 10¼ hours. In addition to the air experience flights (which were available to all), there were a limited number of other flying activities: a gliding course, a powered flying course, and a trip abroad on a RAF Transport Command aircraft where one acted as a supernumerary crew member. Not all such flights were by the RAF: a friend of mine had a trip to the USA in a Constellation, courtesy of the USAF.

In 1948 I was fortunate to be selected for a gliding course with No.125 Gliding School at Langley. This was a grass airfield situated east of Slough and operated by the Hawker Aircraft Company. It contained a factory which had manufactured a considerable number of Hurricanes during World War II, and some Typhoons and Tempests, but due to its close proximity to Heathrow its days were numbered and it closed when Hawkers moved to Dunsfold – I think in 1950. Gliding was carried out at the weekend, and the thing that surprised me then – and even more so now – was the apparent complete lack of security; I cannot recall if there was a security guard on the entrance, but once inside I never saw another soul apart from our ATC Unit personnel. The factory was closed up, of course, but we had complete freedom to wander around the airfield as we pleased (happy days!). During the period between November 1948 and January 1949 I recorded the following aircraft at Langley:

Airspeed Consul G-AIUT
Avro Lancastrian G-AGWL, G-AKFF, G-AKFG, G-AKMW, G-AKTB
Avro Lincoln RF342 (currently stored at Sandtoft)
Avro York G-AHFB, G-AHFF, G-AHFG
Bristol Freighter VT-CGW
DH Tiger Moth G-AHRV
DH Rapide G-AESR, G-AGDP, G-AJFJ
Hawker Sea Fury FB.11 VW634 coded '113' (awaiting delivery to RN)
Hawker Tempest II (several awaiting delivery to India)
Lockheed Constellation G-ALAK
Percival Proctor G-AGTH
Vickers Viking EI-ADG, G-AGRP

Unfortunately I photographed only a few of these, and all the prints were of poor quality. If only – but how many times have we heard that? I assume Hawkers had a contract to maintain or refurbish the airliners seen there.

I commenced my gliding course for my 'A' Licence Certificate on 30th November 1948, and gained my Certificate on 9th January 1949. Strangely enough, I cannot recall any weather during this period bad enough to stop us flying. I have heard many present-day PPL holders being a little disappointed when they receive their Licence, which is a computer print-out. My gliding Certificate, issued by the Royal Aero Club and the Fédération Aéronautique Internationale, was quite posh: it was a small booklet similar in size to the old driving licence, which contained the holder's photograph and signature, instructions to assist the holder in six languages and the Certificate Number.

The aircraft used on this course was the single-seat Slingsby T.7 Cadet Mk.1. All flights were winch-operated. Initially you started with ground slides, where the glider was just pulled along the ground and you had to keep the wings level and hold a straight course. From here you progressed to 'low hops', about 10-20 feet off the ground, and finally to 'high hops' up to and above 100 feet.

To gain your Licence I think you had to complete two 'high hops' of over 100 feet and a flight time for each of at least one minute. The technique for 'high hops' was to hold back on the stick until the winch disappeared below the nose, ease the stick forward, pull the cable release and land straight ahead. There were no instruments in the cockpit to worry about, and the only real concession to safety was a releasable coupling mounted externally on the nose, which automatically released the winch cable if you reached an unsafe angle during launch. I was never quite sure if this was in the interest of the pilot or the winch operator, who was installed in a protective cage ahead of you.

Because of my small stature and weight I always had to fly with a large bag of nuts and bolts under the seat for ballast — always a good joke for the other members of the course! My only major mishap was when landing from one 'high hop', when the skid under the glider dropped into a deep vehicle rut and broke off. It is interesting to note from my flying log that all flights were classified as solo times. Not once during this course did I have a reassuring instructor next to me, or any dual time in a two-seater glider. Today, I think the Health and Safety experts and the CAA would disapprove completely of this course. On reflection, I think I must have been mad, as you can do yourself a lot of damage from over 100 feet – but such is youth! I flew in the following Cadets at Langley: VM537, VM502 (see photo), and VM507.

In late 1949, my next big adventure was the allocation of a trip to Germany with Transport Command in a RAF Dakota, which I looked forward to with excitement. Then disaster struck – I went down with (of all things) German Measles and was unfit to fly, which was a great disappointment. However, this turned out to be a blessing in disguise, as when I had recovered I was then allocated a flight to Singapore; this trip was scheduled to last 11 days, five days out, one day in Singapore and five days back, but in fact my trip lasted for just over 5 weeks! It was necessary before embarking on this journey to take suitable precautions against disease, and from my records I received a total of nine injections against cholera, yellow fever, smallpox, typhoid and tetanus.

The great day eventually arrived, and we left RAF Lyneham for Luqa in Malta on the 16th February 1950 in Hastings TG583 (see photo); this aircraft was sadly to crash at RAF Dishforth 5 months later. The Hastings was on the strength of No.241 OCU, but I believe that during my trip it was being operated by No.511 Squadron. The Hastings had only recently been introduced into RAF Transport Command, and was beset with teething troubles in its early days. Standing between the two pilots on approach to Luqa we appeared to drop below the level of the runway, then a surge of power restored our approach, but on landing we cracked our tailwheel casting, which necessitated a two-day wait for repairs prior to our next stage flight to Fayid in Egypt. During the short stay in Malta the crew took me on a tour of Valetta, which included the 'Street of a Thousand Lights', a notorious red-light district. We all kept strictly to the centre of the road to avoid being molested by the 'ladies', and the experience was at that time quite an eye-opener for an 18-year-old.

On our flight across the Mediterranean I was sitting in the pilot's seat admiring the view, with the aircraft on automatic pilot, while our gallant Captain was discussing a navigation problem with our navigator in his little office behind. Aircraft of this period were fitted with a deployable trailing aerial with a weight on the end, which was wound out of the aircraft by the wireless operator and trailed many feet behind the aircraft. As I sat in the front watching the approach of some cumulus clouds, we were struck by lightning: I can still recall seeing the lightning coming out of the clouds and hitting the nose of the aircraft with a loud bang. On hearing a cry behind me from our wireless operator, I turned round to see him with his arms in the air and a ball of blue static electricity around the exit point for the aerial beside him. When he came to wind the in aerial it had been reduced in length to a few feet – with a very charred end!

On arrival at Fayid there were more problems. The aircraft had to be checked for the effects of the lightning strike, compass swing etc., but in addition the actuators that controlled the engine cooling gills had gone unserviceable and needed replacement. This was a common fault at the time and actuators were in short supply. In the end it was nearly three weeks before the aircraft was fully serviceable and we could leave. The Officers (the two pilots) were catered for in the Officers' Mess, but the rest of us were billeted under canvas. The days were spent by the Great

Bitter Lake swimming, sunbathing and sightseeing locally, while the evenings were spent at a local bar, the favourite tipples being a locally-brewed beer by the name of Stella and a John Collins (rum and lemonade, I believe). These activities always included the whole crew, but we always dressed in civilian clothes.

We would arrive back at camp late at night or early morning, where there was a large parade ground that we had to cross surrounded by large stones (painted white, of course), plus the odd circular machine gun post constructed of sandbags around the perimeter. For reasons that escape me, the crew delighted in depositing as many white stones as they could across the parade ground and filling in the odd machine gun post with its own sandbags — all very irresponsible! I am still amazed that we were never apprehended by the Military Police.

During our stay at Fayid, we carried out two air tests, and on one of these we took a Mosquito pilot along for the ride. Climbing to 18,000 feet (the highest I had ever been) our intrepid Captain shut down two engines and feathered the propellers. The Mosquito pilot then rashly suggested he would like to see a third engine shut down, whereupon our Captain complied: our rate of descent was rapid, to say the least!

With repairs complete we were ready to depart, only to find that some of our windows had been removed. Apparently, an iron lung case was being flown home from the Far East and the authorities wanted to check the access for equipment via a Hastings's windows, and our aircraft happened to be available at the time. Needless to say, our pilot was none too pleased but we finally got under way, our next stop being Habbaniya, just west of Baghdad in what is now Iraq. On arrival at Fayid we had lost our status as a passenger aircraft and only carried freight, all seats having been removed, and from memory most of this freight consisted of spares for other Hastings which had become unserviceable along the route. Much to my surprise the aircraft was unloaded at Habbaniya by rather well-built Iraqi women. The flight itself was over miles of featureless, uninhabited desert, not a place to come down in. During this stage one engine was playing up, but our Captain decided to press on to Mauripur in West Pakistan, not wishing to be stuck in Iraq. Not long after starting our journey the engine had to be shut down, and we proceeded on three engines for the rest of the trip. By the time we arrived at Mauripur another engine was in trouble, so we now required two engine changes. At this point the crew decided they had had enough and returned to the UK on the first available flight. I was given the choice of returning with them or continuing on another aircraft, so I chose the latter and transferred to an Avro York, PE104 of No.51 Squadron.

The next stage of the flight was to Negombo on the west coast of Ceylon (now Sri Lanka). What a change it was from miles of desert to a beautiful sub-tropical island with lush green vegetation. On the return journey home I bought three or four pineapples at a halfpenny each; these were still a luxury at home, in short supply and expensive, and rationing was still in force for many items. Finally we arrived at Changi, Singapore in the middle of a thunderstorm; it was the first time I had seen a complete circular rainbow visible from the air and below the aircraft. We had a short stay of two days, during which I managed a flight in KJ932, a Dakota of RAF Far East Communication Squadron which was carrying out an air test.

As for sightseeing, I did *see* (but not frequent) the legendary Raffles Hotel and the Changi Jail. The return trip to the UK was uneventful and on schedule, arriving back at Lyneham on the 25th March 1950. The total flying time was 81¼ hours, but unfortunately during this time I made very few notes of aircraft seen. Regrettably, having long since run out of film and money, I never took any photographs of the York or Dakota and have not been able to obtain photos from other sources.

CHAPTER 5

POSTWAR COMMUNITY FLYING

by

LEWIS BENJAMIN

To be honest, postwar flying in the late forties was very little different from that prewar or, for that matter, the early sixties, but there was no question that that period was for us, the merry participants, an unforgettable time. The reason of course for the blurring of the decades both before and after centred on the machines we flew and a hang-over thirties' bureaucracy still reeling from the return to their ranks of enlightened ex-servicemen, and we were to benefit from this delightful confusion. That is until a sterner civil service management began rebuilding their hierarchy in their own image rather than the public's, who, poor fools, still believed them to be their servants.

There was no fanfare of trumpets, for 'community flying' was born out of necessity, the practical outcome of a determination to fly cheaply. Perhaps the idea was not new; after all, men had shared possessions before. Most had at one time part-owned an ancient car or motor bike, so why not an aircraft? This form of ownership was nevertheless new, for aircraft were expensive both to fly and to maintain. It was soon realised that *a few* enthusiasts could not afford it: it had to be *many*. Thus clubs were formed, but clubs with a difference, and to help proclaim this difference, some called themselves 'groups': perhaps they felt that 'club' sounded too conventional.

Community flying, though, was a one-off, bearing no resemblance to the conventional flying club. The concept was born in 1946 and died a quiet death from natural causes in the early fifties. To my knowledge only two such 'communities' existed; our one, the Brookside Flying Group formed down at Shoreham, was beaten by a year by Jill Donnisthorpe (who, it is rumoured, is still around in the West Country — if you read this, Jill, please make yourself known!).

Without question the history of postwar flying was enhanced by their presence, and the enjoyment they offered may now only be remembered by the few, and with a considerable degree of glee.

The background to the birth of 'community flying' arose out of the difficulties of the established clubs when they reopened for flying training in January 1946. Most did so from the bases they had occupied prewar, using the same licensing, the same aircraft – if somewhat older – and the same order of instructing. But these flying clubs faced two new factors that nearly drove them to extinction.

The clubs weren't to blame, but with 'the war to end all wars' behind them, the new Labour government had little option but to withdraw the prewar subsidies and the exemption from fuel tax. Now much of the prewar growth and success of our flying clubs was built on the flourishing and heavily-subsidised pilot flying training scheme that existed to encourage pilots to train to 'A' level: war was looming and a vast RAF expansion was essential, and needs must. Indeed many clubs were also founders of EFTS units, so all in all the through-flow of revenue ensured a thriving club.

Now the same clubs, but without government support, faced not only a fraction of their prewar income but also a dearth of *ab initio* applicants into the bargain. Flying costs in 1946 rose to a fiver an hour (three times the prewar figure), and a fiver was at that time a weekly wage — not good.

A third factor, albeit a one-off for that period, was apparent, but knowing it didn't make the clubs' existence any the better. The country was awash with fully trained pilots, all were current, and civil licences were available for the asking. Even the flying test — at the best a 10-minute event — went by the board provided the applicant had RAF flying experience behind them.

Back in 1948 I wrote: "The critics had long decried the idea of 'community flying,' and those individual flyers were to prove the critics quite wrong. The idea of part-ownership caught on, and experienced ex-servicemen were hauled out of retirement. The RAF, Navy and ATA men, wise in the ways of instructing, found in 'community flying' an infectious enthusiasm. Their old line: 'If I never take off again it will be too soon' fell by the wayside. The way they gathered up the reins of their old job belied their studied indifference towards instructing, and as for their pupils, there was no conscription here, just men and women grasping their first chance to learn to fly with experienced instruction given free. 'Community flying' owes a great deal to those men for, by their generous example, groups were able to operate at cost, thus creating the hallmark of 'community flying' — flying everywhere on a non-profit basis.

It was once shrewdly observed that an Englishman worked at his hobby and only played at his work. The writer *had* something there: with no spare cash for decorating and furniture, the owner-members made every effort to render their clubhouse comfortable. But thanks to some enterprise, clubhouses benefited by some odd items of furniture scrounged, no doubt, from unsuspecting families. Many of the accepted club amenities went by the board; since all help was given voluntarily there could be no permanent bar, no restaurant, although some appetising meals were often prepared over a primus stove!"

But back to that first essential — the aircraft we flew. Everything we touched had previously been through the hands of the RAF/ATA training and communication units. I tell a fib, that's not entirely true. There had been many aircraft that had remained in civilian hands, for not every source was commandeered for war service. Believe it or not, a limited amount of buying and selling did go on throughout the war. You only have to see the 'For Sale' and 'Wanted' columns in both *The Aeroplane* and *Flight* to arouse your interest. And yes, they were flown, positioning flights and air tests were permitted, plus of course the inevitable bit of flying on the side, but fuel was tight. The prepared answer of "Oh, it's fuel we still had in the tank" must have worn a little thin as the years went by. The chances were that most of the fuel was scrounged from the service aircraft that often shared in common both servicing and hangar space.

The belief that wartime servicing left a lot to be desired was far from the truth. Aircraft released at the war's end were usually in top-line condition with log books right up to date. When one considers their war years' utilization, the aircraft available in 1946 when civil flying first restarted were in excellent trim. Even the pre-1939 examples seemed none the worse after six years of impoundment. Their airworthy condition, indeed their very existence, owed a great deal to regular maintenance from the RAF and ATA. Put to rest the myth that the servicemen fitters and riggers were a slapdash lot, believe me there was a high standard of ongoing maintenance on all machines, and it showed on every ex-service machine I ever saw or flew. Mark you, I speak of light aircraft. If there were surplus service types available on the civil market just after the war, and I believe there were, they would have been hideously expensive to run. Consequently they didn't figure in our thinking, which was inevitably how much and how cheaply. Nothing changes!

But let's go back to the commencement of postwar club flying and see it through my eyes — a small personal window into one club and how they operated, for in outlining the conditions and costs of getting airborne in 1946 leads to a better understanding of how and why the 'community' concept emerged.

In July of 1946 I joined the South Coast Flying Club at Shoreham, which was much the traditional sort of club. I was still in the RAF, but I lived nearby in Hove and on my leaves I would go to Shoreham and do the one thing the RAF wouldn't let me do — take my civilian friends flying. The Club fleet consisted of Tiger Moths, and the CFI was the most remarkable of men. Cecil Pashley, or 'Pash' as he was known far and wide, was a legend in his own lifetime, and about the most famous of all flying instructors. He'd been around a long while too. He had built, and flown with his brother, his own aircraft before the first World War, and in 1946 had around 18,000 hours instructing to his credit. Even with my current flying practice — and I was actually doing a refresher course on Tigers at Brough in Yorkshire — 'Pash' insisted on showing me around the Tiger as though it was the first aircraft I'd ever seen. When I offered to swing the propeller for him he was horrified.

"No," he said firmly, "always leave things like that to qualified engineers, never do it yourself."

We climbed in and awaited the engineer. When no one turned up 'Pash' began to fret. Impatiently he climbed out of the front cockpit, his long leathers flapping in the wind (I thought irreverently of Grumpy of the Seven Dwarfs for he was scarcely five feet tall), snorted around to the front and reached on tiptoe to grasp the propeller.

"Contact," he shouted.

The engine caught first swing and the Tiger nearly ran him over: he'd forgotten the chocks.

"Let that be a lesson to you, Benjamin," he barked, as he disappeared back into the front cockpit. He was a great man and loved by everyone.

Flying was quite unrestricted immediately after the war. There were almost no recognisable regulations, and even getting an 'A' Licence, as the private pilot's licence was then known, presented no problems. Eight hours' solo was all the experience needed, a simple oral exam plus a flying check which was observed from the ground.

Just to hold my first 'A' licence turns my clock back 60 years. With its stiff RAF blue 6" x 4" cover, it reminds me that this series of licences was first issued in 1919, and was still going strong in its original form when I got mine. The mind boggles — at least mine does!

But let's begin with the black lettering on the cover:

CERTIFICATE OF COMPETENCY
AND LICENCE TO FLY
PRIVATE FLYING MACHINES

Then, inside, and right across the top pages, was the legend:

NOT VALID FOR FLYING PUBLIC TRANSPORT
OR AERIAL WORK FLYING MACHINES

Then, beneath, details of me, of course, finally declaring that I was hereby licensed to fly the following types of flying machines:

ALL TYPES OF LANDPLANES

I cherish it — but I digress.

Civil flying officially began again on January 1st 1946 and the first postwar licences were issued that very week, mine being amongst them. Since I was RAF-trained I was allowed to skip the flying test; all that was needed of me was to take the oral exam. I presented myself for this at the Royal Aero Club premises in Piccadilly on January 6th 1946, in company with a fellow RAF pilot. The Secretary General had a bit of a cold that day, so his second-in-command, Colonel 'Mossie' Preston, officiated.

We stood before Mossie's desk like recalcitrant pupils before the Head. Needless to say we hadn't a clue what questions he was going to ask us. We'd swotted up on a prewar publication, and had an idea about the positioning of lights on a balloon cable, but little else.

He first turned to Dicky and snapped: "What's a Customs Carnet?"

Dicky was game for a try. "Isn't it something you need if you leave the country?"

Mossie growled and then turned to me. "And you, Benjamin?"

"I agree with Dicky," I said loyally.

He looked at both of us for a moment or two, gave an imperceptible shrug and a shadow of a smile appeared. "I can see you two know bugger all about it. Here, give me the papers." We were in and out in five minutes.

We left behind a pound, I think it was, and came out with the prospect of a licence soon to be in the post, and clutching an aviator's certificate, which cost us five bob. I still have that little blue book with its behest in several languages that all who read this give the holder of this document every help. And all written in the most beautiful copper plate, it was worth five bob of anybody's money. An idiotically earnest boy looked out from the accompanying photograph.

I stayed with the South Coast Flying Club for over a year. They were a jolly lot and led by Duncan Davis, surely one of aviation's most irrepressible and cheerful stalwarts. Duncan was known as 'Drunken' Davis among the regulars. I expect if he knew his *soubriquet* — and he probably did — he'd have approved.

I remember one evening when Duncan was really drunken he decided to go flying with two pretty girls. The Club manager was in despair, and shot out ahead of him to urge the engineer to fix the Proctor so that Duncan couldn't fly. Anxious to help, I held up the cowlings with one eye on the club doorway whilst the engineer, doing the best he could at short notice, hurriedly opened up something or other and inserted a piece of paper between two contacts. "That'll never start," he muttered. But we had no sooner fixed the cowlings back than Duncan staggered out, pushed his giggling passengers into seats and clambered in after them. "Clear," he shouted to the world at large, pressed the starter and the engine roared to life; and before anyone could stop him — were that even possible — he rushed away and took off. White-faced, stunned, we watched him fly, tensed against the enormity of what could happen, but the engine continued heartily and Duncan came back safe and sound, as good a pilot drunk as sober. Greatly shaken, the other two went inside, presumably to get as drunken as Duncan.

Once again I pass on an observation from those early 1948 scribblings, with a weak conclusion that only a 23-year-old could hold with conviction. I added hopefully:

"Many were the teething troubles with 'community flying,' including unhappy encounters with the established clubs, who feared in this new sort of flying, not something to be welcomed for fostering airmindedness, but a rival who would offer flying for a third of their prices. The new groups at first denied they were rivals, although they were unable to draw upon past experiences to strengthen their sincere belief, but in time, the case was proven, and both types of club expanded side by side. Those who could afford it preferred the added comfort and attention of an established club, but those who would never have flown at all without the support of the community groups joined together to help themselves, although in somewhat austere surroundings, and with no bar, although — as some wit put it — with the right spirit."

Now with the gift of hindsight, the real reason for the death of 'community flying' was nothing more than a lack of continuity. All was well whilst someone kept an eye on things at the airfield, where honesty and integrity was taken for granted, but to ensure continuity — that was the rub.

As we grew older, had families, moved away, there were many times when our Maggie, the Clubroom, the cash box and records were unattended. The established clubs won through for the simple reason that it wasn't treated as a hobby, but as a business; for the community flyers it wasn't a business, and we folded.

Our youthful naïvety showed through, yet our enthusiasm wasn't wasted, for all that vitality and eagerness with which we strove to fly surely echoes today in the PFA. After all, the Brookside Flying Group was part of the original Ultra Light Aircraft Association, which was later renamed the Popular Flying Association. So there is a link, and one that I'm proud to have been part of.

CHAPTER 6

PICNIC WITH AUNTIE

by

MARY DE BUNSEN

(Reproduced from Light Plane and Private Owner *magazine for February 1948.)*

The other day two nephews, recently demobilised, suggested that the writer should fly them to Land's End, sharing expenses, just for a picnic. It seemed a good idea, and an excellent way of finding out whether casual air travel is practical nowadays, or whether it is really better to go by train.

White Waltham provided a Fairchild Argus at £12 per day, plus fuel expenses. Air-Met gave us weather information we wanted. The Argus has a range of about 400 miles, but nobody wants to fly for four hours nonstop if they can help it, and it was necessary to find out which airfields *en route* would welcome us, which would merely tolerate us, and which would take penal action in the event of our alighting within their sacred precincts. Well, the appropriate Notice to Airmen revealed that the best bet for refuelling in the West Country is Exeter, and that the only suitable bolthole for weather etc. between Exeter and the Home Counties is Thruxton, near Andover, where there is a flying club. The Southampton area, over which we intended to make a detour, is well provided with airports available to private pilots. Land's End (St. Just) does not offer refuelling facilities.

Armed with this essential information, we took off and headed a little west of south. Near Farnham, we circled and enjoyed, with the godlike detachment of the skilled escapist, the chaotic spectacle of the rest of the family moving house – cars, dogs, trunks and impedimenta all round the front door, plus a few antlike figures running in small circles. Resisting the temptation to land at Worthy Down from force of habit (it used to be the checking-in point for the Southampton controlled zone in wartime), we reached the Solent, which was looking as lovely as we have ever seen it, glittering through the last of the lifted fog, with a sharp false horizon to the south-west where a temperature inversion had trapped the Portsmouth smoke. Lymington to Portland Harbour we timed at 27 minutes. We got quite a kick out of this, as on recent occasion it had taken the writer 27 *hours* to cover the same route in the reverse direction in a small, engineless yacht. And how much safer one feels in an aeroplane! It was fun looking down upon a certain tide-race where the wind had failed, leaving us in great jeopardy just as the kettle boiled for elevenses.

By the time we got to Exeter, we were hungry and a little cramped and decided to land on one of the runways. It is a good airfield now, and a great improvement on the little field of 1939 off which we once staggered in a Praga Baby, accompanied by a 17-stone instructor. But there was no sign of life, no landing tee out, and the red panel in the signal area was occupied by two dirty yellow bars which were lying in a non-committal pattern, neither a cross nor a diagonal. So we were relieved at our welcome, which was friendly. They proffered petrol, but the writer, underestimating the distance to Land's End and remembering that the airport at St. Just is very small, decided to defer refuelling until the return trip, so as to take off from St. Just lightly loaded.

"No," we replied, "we don't want anything, thank you. We've just come for a picnic."

Jaws dropped, eyes opened wider, and we were left to eat our sandwiches and regarded curiously from a distance, as by natives in the bush. The Argus is a civilised aeroplane. Having eaten, we pulled the starter knob and took off without further assistance.

Exeter to Land's End took much longer than we expected. The Mk. 2 Argus is excessively slow. and cruising at about 90, we arrived at St. Just in an hour and a quarter and plopped in over the hedge with 70 on the clock and plenty of engine, landing nice and short.

Once again, the natives were friendly, but a problem arose. There was not enough petrol to get back as far as Exeter with a comfortable margin and we had noticed "landing prohibited" crosses on the runways at Plymouth, where we had hoped to refuel on the way back, as there was supposed to be a club there. A telephone call to Plymouth might have set our minds at ease. but time was getting short, so we took in the few gallons which British European Airways are kind enough to issue in emergency, and handed over two of the coupons with which White Waltham had provided us. The passengers went off to pick bedraggled specimens of typical local flora for their mother while the petrol was put in and we paid a landing fee of five shillings.

They have a twelve-volt starter battery at St. Just, but the plug did not fit our socket, which was probably a non-standard American one. However, once again we started up easily on our own battery. I once saw a man start a Fairchild Argus by hand-swinging the prop, and get away with it, but later somebody else was killed doing the same thing.

We taxied out, considering the take-off. It is really, of course, quite easy, but we were perhaps right in not attempting it with full tanks. It looks short to anyone accustomed to big service airfields, and it was necessary to decide whether to take off uphill (the longest way), a little out of wind, or a shorter way, into wind, starting from the top of a little mound. Whilst we dithered the Scilly Isles Rapide taxied out, briskly climbed the mound and took off; so we followed its lead and unstuck not much more than halfway across, crossing the boundary with a comfortable 80 on the clock. (The DH Dove has been in and out of St. Just, with an unspecified load, but the DH Drover, a 3-engined type which is being designed in Australia for bush flying, is probably more suited to this class of work.)

Back at Exeter, taking in the rest of the 25 gallons for which we carried coupons, we realised that we should only just make it. But they refuelled us very quickly, leaving an hour and a quarter to get home, with a slight tailwind.

It became very smoky on the way, and we really got down to a little navigation, minutes being precious. There was a familiar and almost nostalgic feeling about plugging home in a Fairchild in hazy twilight, just a little anxious about last landing time. This is the sort of occasion when a few more available airports would be assuring. However, we had been asked to be back a few minutes after seven, and we were — just. Total time in air — 5 hours 45 minutes. It had been a good day.

POINTS WORTH NOTING
1. *Notices to Airmen* are a fair guide, but the only reliable aerodrome information is obtained by ringing up the place before you start.
2. Do not trust the advertisements of flying clubs alleged to be in operation.
3. Nowhere on the route was there a battery with a plug to fit our Argus, but it started up five times on its own battery without showing signs of fatigue.
4. There are not enough airports in the West Country.
5. It's a long, long way to Land's End.

CHAPTER 7

A WARTIME APPRENTICE

by

RON COOPER

Since leaving school I had been working as a junior clerk in a large office at a nearby Central Ordinance Depot, although I could not see me doing this job for ever. Nevertheless it was a job and, after all, it was obtained for me by my parents who both worked at the same place, so I could not really grumble. I was not happy though for, apart from all the paper shuffling — which I thought such a waste of time — most of the folks in the office smoked, and I hated the constant smoky & smoggy atmosphere that I had to work in. Some mornings I would get there early and throw open all the windows to let in some fresh air, only to see them all closed one by one as the rest of the staff arrived.

In my break times my thoughts would wander back to the day I rode my new Hercules pushbike on a six-mile ride cross-country to see the opening of the new Derby Aerodrome at Burnaston in the fall of 1938. From my position outside the perimeter fence I watched all the goings-on in wonder; there were aeroplanes all over the place, both on the ground and in the air, and the Handley Page HP.42 sitting over by the new hangar seemed huge.

I was really enjoying it all, but for some reason I turned away from the aerodrome and looked into the sky, and there I noticed a sleek white aeroplane coming in to land. As it got closer I saw it was a real racy-looking machine and its lines sent a tingle up my spine; what I did not know was that it was Alec Henshaw in his Percival Mew Gull. There and then I made up my mind that I was going to be a part of this exciting thing of flying machines: to me they were just fantastic.

So my determined move from a smoky office to be with aeroplanes began, and I eventually convinced my parents and Air Schools Ltd., the operator of the aerodrome, that I wanted to be an apprentice aircraft engineer. My apprenticeship papers were finally signed and stamped in April 1943 — success!

In the meantime the family had moved from Woodville to Burton-upon-Trent to be closer to their work, which for me meant that I had to push my trusty old Hercules six miles each way each day to work; but who cared, I was keen! I must admit though that charging along the road to get to work at a certain time was a little different from cruising the country roads as I had done before. But who cared about all the energy being applied? I was now working with aeroplanes, and that to me was everything. Little did I know at that time that aviation was going to occupy a large lump of my life.

The Early Years
It was to be a different kind of aviation over the next few years to what I originally saw in 1938, for Burnaston Aerodrome was now operating as No.3 Elementary Flying Training School (No.3 EFTS) producing young pilots to enable the Air Ministry to meet the demands of the war now raging in Europe. The school had at least 70 de Havilland DH.82A Tiger Moths which were being operated almost around the clock.

I was placed with a foreman-cum-mentor whose every move I followed, and thankfully he did not mind being asked questions: in fact he encouraged them. With all those aircraft needing maintenance to keep going, my experience came fast.

One experience I soon collected was how to swing an aircraft propeller to start the engine. The particular Flight that I was working in operated around 20 aircraft, each going up throughout the day on around two-hour details. This meant, of course, that around every two hours 20 or so propellers had to be swung, this task being shared by myself and two other apprentices: I often wondered why my right arm seemed longer than the left! At the peak of the training the aircraft in use rose to just on 108, these being a mix of the DH.82A and the wood-constructed Miles Magister two-seat trainer.

Keeping the whole operation going was serious work and this was realised by all, from top management down to the apprentices, but now and again a few things did happen that raised a few smiles on faces. One such case was when the aircraft being operated were mainly the DH.82A Tiger Moths. A gaggle of these was parked on the tarmac immediately in front of the main hangar, awaiting the next detail of young trainee pilots to go up for instruction, when a young Air Force Officer appeared on the balcony on the small control tower, which formed part of the office block at the end of the hangar, and fired off a 'recall' flare into the sky which, to his horror, after reaching the top of its trajectory proceeded to come down heading right for the rear cockpit of one of the aircraft standing on the tarmac! Needless to say quite a fire ensued and, before the fire engine people could dowse the flames, around 10 aircraft had been lost, mainly due to them being so tightly packed on the tarmac.

One other such case was on a non-flying day in winter when aircraft were all stowed in the hangar, a work of art in itself, especially that area within the hangar we also used for maintenance and overhaul of the aircraft. However one keen young apprentice was in the front cockpit of one of the Magister aircraft doing his best to clean down the area down front by the rudder pedals. Not much natural light gets down there so he had with him an inspection light, but then the inevitable happened and some of the cleaning fluid splashed onto the hot bulb: a fire started, from which he fortunately extracted himself in seconds, but there we were with an aircraft on fire and a packed hangar of aircraft all neatly 'jigsawed' in place!

Staff in the hangar were immediately galvanised into action when they saw what had happened and, while some stayed to put out the fire with extinguishers, the rest leapt into action and in less than no time the hangar doors had been opened wide and aircraft were spewing out at a fair rate onto the tarmac. All this happened within minutes with no damage to the aircraft: curious this, because the aircraft push-out normally took about 45 minutes!

At one period there was a real purge to get Army people trained to become glider pilots, the training to last 10 hours including the first solo flight. The main body of the trainees that we had were drawn from the Guards, who have strict traditions, one being that they wore highly polished hobnailed boots which they wore even when under flight instructions.

An aircraft rudder and its controlling rudder-operating bar in the cockpit are pretty sensitive things in terms of movement, but unfortunately feet inside hobnail boots do not have the required touch and feel, so many were the occasions when one would see an aircraft speeding along towards take-off swinging violently from side to side. The Magister aircraft being used at the time, though well built, did have a rather spindly undercarriage which did not suffer gladly these violent changes in direction; as a result undercarriage legs were sheared off or very much bent, and the aircraft came to a grinding halt on the grass, leaving a few furrows where it had ploughed along. These incidents got so bad that a directive came out for all Army trainees to fly in their stockinged feet!

The method of getting up to the front cockpit of the Magister aircraft — the rear one being used by the instructor — was up and over the wing, where the designers had provided a narrow reinforced walkway. Again the hobnailed boots did not really fit in with the designer's intentions and many were the boot-clad feet that went through the thin plywood skin of the wing before the 'socks' directive appeared!

It was also during this somewhat pressurised period that we had a number of aircraft literally land on top of one another; miraculously some of the crews survived, but some did not.

There was no doubt that the Air Traffic Control people were having a hard time keeping the hundred or so aircraft operating each day and under some form of control, especially with the restricted vision from the small control tower at the end of the main hangar, and these Army types didn't seem to care much about this thing called Air Traffic Control. Something had to be done, so one day a small black & white chequered cabin-on-wheels was moved out to a position by the fence at the allocated take-off and landing point for the day. As it was summer, a couple of controllers were outside on the grass sitting in chairs, equipped with an Aldis lamp connected to a 12-volt battery which they used to light-signal aircraft both on the ground and in the air — a green light to commence take-off or continue to land, and a red to hold any take-off or to forbid a landing.

The operation went well with the initial first flights of the day, but when all the aircraft started to return from their details the poor controller on duty was presented with a sky full of aircraft all wanting to land, some not even bothering about a clearance to land and seemingly coming at him from all directions. For a while the controller made a good effort to sort it all out in an orderly fashion, but after a few aircraft had skimmed by him his nerve seemed to break and, dropping everything, he made a mad dash for the sanctuary of the cabin. This resulted in pure bedlam as even more of the approaching aircraft decided to 'have a go'. Needless to say the idea was dropped and the controllers were moved back to the safety of their tower.

Just over the southern boundary of the airfield was a rather large sewerage farm, nothing like the modern processing plants of today as it covered a good 40 acres or more. Like moths around a light the farm seemed to have a fatal attraction for aircraft, and on a number of occasions they would land either short or overshoot *into* it. It became the job of the hangar Chief to detail a team to go and collect the crumpled aircraft, understandably not an easy job as everyone would either be doing something that could not be left or just could not be found anywhere. Even after a good wash-down, and sometimes even after repair and new paintwork, the distinctive odour remained: good job they were open cockpits!

It was after an accident repair job that I was given a ride on the test flight after signing the required 'blood chit' to indemnify the company. It was not long before I was being strapped in the front cockpit of a Magister, pulling on a helmet and goggles and seeing the engine burst into life. Every minute of that flight I savoured and enjoyed, even the part where the pilot threw the aeroplane over the sky in hopes of getting me to go 'green'.

"This was the life," I told myself: "one day I will fly one of these machines."

In the meantime, though, I had my apprenticeship to concentrate on, although this was going well as I had now graduated from engine drip-tray and aircraft cleaning and was being given jobs to do on the aircraft on my own under the supervision of the tradesmen I worked with. One was a cabinet-maker by trade by the name of Bert Marples; he had been redeployed into aircraft work from the cabinet making trade and was an absolute wizard with wood, so with the Miles Magisters, which were entirely of wooden construction — mainly sitka spruce, the odd bit of ash and lots of 2 mm birch plywood — Bert was in his element.

Many was the day when I watched and assisted Bert replacing wing leading-edge panels (which always seemed to be colliding with something) and saw him gently persuade and mould the birch ply round into position. Where the new panels joined the old ply on the wing front spar a 1:10 splice was required where the two surfaces joined, and this on a plywood material only 2 mm thick called for a feather-thick edge, an art within itself. It was routine for Bert, though, as with his woodworking skills his tools were kept immaculate with chisels and cutting blades honed to perfection.

Apart from helping Bert another of my jobs during these repairs was to make up the glue. The whole of the Magister structure was glued together with casein glue (manufactured from a by-product of milk) mixed with water. The glue, once mixed, had a fairly long working time, so during the day a number of batches were mixed, and then after each batch was mixed two pieces of timber of a set size were glued together and later tested to destruction to see if the glue strength was sufficient. Thankfully I never mixed a dud batch and hate to think what would have happened if I had!

There were about 14 other apprentices apart from myself, and it seemed that at least half of us ended up meeting in the washroom sometime during the day after making up batches of glue for our supervising 'chippies,' carpenters or cabinet makers like Bert. For us it was an ideal time to swap yarns of the day's events and for general teens 'chat,' as little went on in the hangar without it being noticed by the apprentice gang.

Time rolled by and the day came when Bert thought I might 'have a go' with putting on a short section of new leading-edge ply skinning. I was cock-a-hoop and did well with the preparation of the new ply skin but, during the fit and moulding to the leading edge I thought I would never make it in time before the glue started to go off, and that's when Bert had to come to my rescue. I might mention that to help the ply around the profile of the leading edge warm water was applied to give the ply added suppleness. Needless to say the news was soon around the washroom that yours truly had "mucked up the job," but thankfully the next repair I was offered came out alright.

The 'gang' generally thought our taskmasters real slave drivers and somewhat a 'bolshie' lot but, looking back, we ourselves were not an easy lot to handle and were always getting up to something, and in the main did not take things too seriously. With these facts, together with the constant pressure on the hangar staff to provide the maximum number of aircraft each day to meet that ever-increasing demand for trained pilots, it was no wonder that from time to time some of us would get the 'heavy end of the stick' from the bosses.

There was one period I remember where, much to the annoyance of our taskmasters, we were forever disappearing, eventually to be found in a corner listening and gyrating to swing and jazz being played on a radio charmed away from its usual place. The American Forces Network programme was our favourite with Glen Miller, Harry James, Artie Shaw and the like: we thought they were just fantastic.

One particular apprentice had the habit of going missing from time to time, until one day he was noticed curled up fast asleep in a rear fuselage in among the control cables: he didn't stay long after that!

There could have been a possible reason for this, as in the main, workers had to find their own way to work, most living at least six miles away either in the Derby and Burton areas. The main road between the two towns passed by the end of the airfield, but even so there were very few buses that ran along it and the ones that did were either during the early morning or evening time. So it meant almost a dawn start to be sure the early bus was caught. I know that the young apprentice I mentioned had to get three different buses to connect with the main road bus, so to me no wonder he was tired.

The airfield had no permanent crash and fire rescue crew, so when the 'crash alarm' bell sounded a duty driver, usually someone from the hangar who could cope with the tender, would dash out to the fire/rescue tender sitting at the edge of the main hangar apron, followed by a 'bore' of other bodies out of the hangar who leapt aboard the old Crossley tender as it moved away. The tender was large and very much underpowered so it seemed to take for ever to get anywhere. Most of us had had little or no training in crash, fire and rescue drill, so we were lucky that most of the crashes we had were not major — that is, but for one.

This occurred on one of those soft misty night-flying sessions when a Air Force Handley Page Hampden light bomber attempted, for some unknown reason, to land on the airfield — which was far too small for it — and ended up smashing into one of the small dispersal hangars in the north-eastern corner of the field, completely wrecking the hangar and the aircraft. It was a real mess, as became apparent the next morning when I was able to go along with others to view the scene. The fire rescue crew had done their best to save the crew and the aircraft but it was a little out of their league. Looking at the mangled wreck made me realise how plucky the underbelly gunner must have been, for lying there under the aircraft just to the rear of the bomb-bay, he would have stood little or no chance of survival in any landing accident. I wonder if the aircraft designer ever thought of this fact, and memories of that accident stayed with a number of us for a long time.

As the days went by some of the luckier ones of our apprentice gang managed to get themselves motorcycles of some sort or other. Having these new 'toys' made it hard not to slip out of the hangar to where they were parked and either sit fiddling with the machines or just sit there admiring them, again much to the annoyance of our taskmasters. However their annoyance was tempered to some degree: the occasional one himself had a motorcycle so, after all, were we not fellow motorcyclists and members of the 'brotherhood'?

One such person was a Mr Scott, a senior in the engine shop, who, funnily enough, rode an immaculate Scott Squirrel water-cooled twin cylinder two-stroke; this had a fantastic exhaust noise nothing like the 'putter-putter' of the little Francis Barnet two-stroke I had at the time. I was to learn a lot about engines from this man, who gave freely of his knowledge.

Later, as I moved around the various tradesmen, I found them most happy to pass on their knowledge and skills, which was lucky for me. One particular person I think of immediately was a man by the name of 'Speedy' Felts, the Deputy Chief Engineer; not only would he freely pass on his knowledge but he would push me all the time to ask questions as to the why and wherefores, a habit I developed which paid off in my later career.

Getting to and from work had its interesting moments, due to the vagaries of the English weather. Riding a motorcycle in the summer was great and exhilarating, but not quite so much so with pouring rain, fogs and icy roads, and I wondered at times why I'd ever bought the thing. Even with a heavy rubberised and specially designed Bellstaff motorcycling coat, leather helmet, goggles, gloves and a thick woolly scarf, the cold and wet still managed to get through. Rain seemed to delight in running down the petrol tank and in under my coat, ending up with me sitting in a puddle of water. On rainy days too, should I omit for some reason or other to strap the coat tails to my legs, the flapping coat tail would eventually contact the top end of the spark plug, resulting in a high-voltage reminder that there was something I had forgotten to do.

The thick claggy fogs that often used to descend on the local countryside in the latter part of the year were not the choicest of conditions to be riding a motorcycle in, with even getting off the airfield being a hazard in itself as the there were no roadside kerbs to follow. The case was similar on the side roads, but once on the main road it was a case of deflecting the headlight downwards to follow at a crawl the road kerbstones and grass verges, straining one's eyes for the road ahead and hoping to pick out in time the various unwanted side turnings. Inadvertently a motorcyclist would end up with a queue of other cars and trucks tagging on behind his tail light!

It was on such a thick 'pea-souper' night that I fumbled my way and bore left instead of going straight on, and it was not till a few minutes had passed that I realised I was on this old narrow side road that ran to an old stone bridge over the river Dove, after which it eventually joined the main road again a little further on past the new main road bridge. To stop people using the old bridge large concrete blocks had been placed in the road — no worry for me as I could easily get through with a motorcycle or pushbike — so I pressed on. It was as I wove my way between the blocks that I heard the screeching of brakes and some very loud voices shouting some unsavoury comments: I'd forgotten completely about the cars and trucks trailing behind me! I didn't stop to find out what happened from then on, but there would have been a few problems a moment later as the road was narrow and only just wide enough to turn a car around.

I recall one winter, that of 1944, I believe, when the countryside suffered heavy falls of snow which closed most roads outside of town due to heavy drifting that had continued during the night. Even so I set off to walk to work, along with many others from the town, but once clear of the town I was 'on my own', an odd feeling. It was a long tiring walk scrunching along in the thick snow which in places had built up to hedgerow height. When I eventually arrived at work it was surprising how many other folks had turned up for work, and in fact the management showed their appreciation by letting us off from work mid-afternoon. By the next day great efforts had been made by the County Councils to clear the main roads, so I was able to climb aboard my old Franny Barnet and have a 'slip-sliding' ride to work. Luckily for me there was not much traffic on the road.

It was during this period of heavy snow that Rolls-Royce Aero Engines offered the Derby County folk a jet engine strapped aboard a truck to try and clear snow from the main roads, although if I remember rightly I don't think it achieved much!

Some days during the warmer and more pleasant times of the year, light mists would form in the early mornings, and they seemed to come up especially over the Derby Corporation Sewerage farm about a mile ahead of where I turned left off the main road into a side road that led to the airfield. On this particular length of road was quite a dip where the road ran over the Derby-to-Stoke railway line, and the mist, as you can imagine, also held the smell coming off the farm, so it was a stretch of road that you got through as quickly as possible. It was bad enough having to take a deep breath before going down into the dip and up the other side, but it was even worse if the crossing gate happened to be closed, as there was nothing for it but to sit gasping until the train had passed through and the gates were reopened. You got to know the train times so always made the effort to be through before the train arrived, but there was always the morning when it was not on time and then, apart from getting 'gassed', the delay would also mean that you were late clocking, in which further underlined the situation.

You're in the army now!

Away from work I was busily attending to my social life and fitting in a couple of evenings at night school and one evening at Army Cadet activities. The odd weekend was also spent on Army Cadet activities, which I had taken to earlier after not being too impressed with the Air Training Corps; it didn't take long for an old school pal, now an officer in the Army Cadets, to convince me to join them. It was not long before I found myself training to be a Signaller, being instructed in the use of signal 'Flags' and to tap out the Morse code. This I really got into and enjoyed, but the thing that really drew my attention was the instruction on motorcycle and car engines and the weekend camps at places in the country where we did courses and training aimed at getting us through our 'War Certificate.' We also used to get some hands-on training on motorcycles and cars brought there by the Army instructors. It was not very long before we were given an examination and practical test in regard to our signals capability, all of our small class getting through and being awarded our Signals Badge.

A matter of three months later our Commanding Officer was approached by the Local Home Guard Company Commander with a request for some of the newly-qualified signallers to share duties with some of their regulars on their local Head Office switchboard, and also to help out in their signals. They did not go far for volunteers, even if it did involve some night duty, for apart from other things, the move gave us access to their social club — icing on the cake as far as we were concerned.

On one weekend a band of us were invited to spend a day at an American Forces camp near Litchfield, just south of Burton. We had great time being shown around by our American GI hosts, about three cadets to one GI. The lunch in their canteen was to us just 'out of this world' and I was really amused by the way they plonked everything — including desserts — on one big tray. The lunch was made even more enjoyable for there in the canteen was a biggish swing band playing all the current favourite tunes that I listened to on the American Forces Network radio. Towards the end of the meal I asked our host what the fantastic band might be, and a look of amazement came on his face.

"Jeez, boy, you do not know what that is? Why, that is our one and only Glen Miller band of the Allied Expeditionary Forces!"

Wow! I thought I had recognised the style but was a little nervous of making a suggestion as to whom it might be, hence the question. So, for me, prime news for the gang back at work in the washroom!

Another camp I well remember was at Longcroft Hall, a Georgian-styled house around 20 miles north-east of Burton. There were just on 20 of us travelling there and the main purpose of the camp was for us to complete the remainder of the training for a 'War Certificate A', a bit of paper that allowed one to progress up through the ranks. The final training and tests included things like taking apart and reassembling a Sten automatic gun, followed by a firing test at targets and an assault course. We had done the Sten gun exercise a couple or so times already, so didn't see any problems there, but what the assault course was going to be like we just did not know: all we knew was that we had 30 minutes in which to complete it. So there we were, all kitted out in overalls and army boots and nothing much else, standing in line behind the Sergeant in charge of the course, who was releasing one of us every three minutes or so to go off into the course. Then came my turn and the command "go, go, go" rattled into my ear, so off I went at full speed down the woodland track.

From watching the cadets ahead it was obvious that the first obstacle was around 100 yards or so down the track just round a corner, for not too soon after disappearing around the corner there was often a yell, let out as you do as you hurl yourself to get over something. I soon found out what the yells were for when suddenly I was presented with a 12-foot drop into a muddy morass below. I reckon my "yow" beat the lot! The first obstacle set the standard for the rest of the course, as it was full of tortuous surprises and a lot of mud!

Nobody made the course in the allowed 30 minutes, my time being just on 45 minutes. One final test was when the Sergeant gave us each a bit of Sunlight soap, pointed us towards the ablutions and indicated he wished the overalls to look as good as new! Later that evening at dinner we were all awarded our 'War Certificate A' by a very happy Commanding Officer.

Life on the whole, irrespective of the fact that a war was going on, was for me getting more and more interesting as I set about 'peopling' my life. I was also bidding farewell to people I had got to know well as they walked off down the road to do their bit for King and Country, having been called up for National Service. It was inevitable that one day it was going to happen to me, and it did in January 1945, starting with that ominous brown paper envelope with a letter inside asking one to attend for a medical grade assessment examination as required under the National Service Act. A few weeks later another brown paper envelope arrived inside which was a little brown printed card telling me of my medical grade; this turned out to be Grade 1, so it would not be long now before I would be joining the other lads down the road.

Eventually the next brown OHMS envelope arrived with its instructions for me to present myself to HMS *Royal Arthur* at Skegness on the East Coast. Yes, believe it or not I was being called-up into the Navy — or the Fleet Air Arm as it eventually turned out to be! How about that? I had had experience in the Air Force way of life through my work and the short time with the Air Training Corps, and I'd gathered experience on the Army way of doing things through the Army Cadets, but some Civil Service cleric in the Ministry of whatever had decided I'd do better in the Navy. I reckon that square pegs in round holes must have been his speciality!

CHAPTER 8

AFTER THE WAR WAS OVER

by

EDWARD W. MASLEN-JONES MC, DFC, MA

Had the Japanese not surrendered on the 15th August 1945, the following recollections, and the account of my last sortie in the Far East, would not have qualified for inclusion in an anthology of postwar aviation stories. In the event 656 Air Observation Post Squadron RAF/RA had completed their task of supporting the 14th Army in Burma some six weeks after the recapture of Rangoon in May.

The task itself had been both arduous and eventful throughout the two years it had lasted. We were the only AOP Squadron that had been made available to the Burma theatre, and were greatly overstretched throughout the campaign. Our last tour of action alone lasted for 10 months, during which time a number of major battles took place, including the recrossing of the great rivers, the Chindwin in December 1944 and the Irrawaddy in the middle of February the following year. Replacement equipment of all kinds, especially aircraft, did not exist, and it was a case of 'make do and mend'. Maintenance of all kinds took place 'in the field', and that included the re-covering of at least three Austers. The performance of our artificers and ground crews was quite amazing, and I cannot recall a single occasion when I was unable to undertake a sortie, from the point of view of either flying or communications.

The number of sorties flown by the Squadron during the 7-month period up to May 1945 was in excess of 6,700, in something over 5,700 flying hours. In his final report before leaving Burma, our Commanding Officer, Major (later Brigadier) Denis Coyle wrote, rather wearily: "The Squadron has undertaken the work of three for the last two years . . ."; the situation was that, in the middle of July, he had received a directive to take his Squadron back to India to prepare for the amphibious assault that would lead to the reoccupation of Malaya. Codenamed "Operation Zipper", this would have been an opposed landing with the Japanese well aware of our intentions.

Denis Coyle had roughly six weeks to get his Unit from Rangoon to Madras by sea. All aircraft had to be crated, and a suitable maintenance unit had to be found in Southern India. He found very little help when he got there, but as a result of desperate individual moves he succeeded in finding generous support from the Royal New Zealand Naval Air Service at Coimbatore, who billeted us and provided all the necessary facilities. The Auster Mk.V also appeared at this time, and Denis accepted four of them as replacements for those Mk.IIIs that had become unserviceable.

In addition, all our vehicles had to be modified for the seaborne landing, and that meant taking them to Bombay, this apparently being the only place in India that could carry out the work. Then, in addition to all this, he had to ensure that his men had at least some leave. The war ended while all this was taking place, and even now I can hardly believe the situation that this man found himself in. I have always thought of Denis as one of "Kipling's men"; he had a sensitive insight into what makes individuals 'tick', which he combined with powerful leadership qualities, and was quite unflappable. In the exceptional circumstances that we had been through, we were most fortunate to have had him in charge.

On the 6th and 9th of August 1945 the two atom bombs were dropped on Japan, which led to their surrender; this prevented, literally by only a matter of days, what would have been an opposed landing. With the benefit of hindsight it greatly improved the chances that I would, one day, get back to the UK, for the landings, when they came, were an absolute shambles.

The assault on Malaya (Operation Zipper) by allied forces from Burma involved 250,000 troops and took place down the western coastline, and the central thrust was towards the capital. But it transpired that the beaches had not been fully reconnoitred: troops and equipment, which had been delivered by Royal Navy landing craft at low tide onto sandy beaches, were unable to proceed ashore when they encountered mangrove swamps, and were overcome by the incoming tide. Huge delays ensued, following which craft were diverted, some as far as Singapore. Our own Squadron personnel became widely dispersed, some of them being requisitioned locally to assist with disarming the Japanese. It took nearly three weeks for our Commander to assemble his unit at Kuala Lumpur, where we were to use the golf course as our airstrip.

The original plan had been for all the aircraft to be ferried onto the Royal Navy Escort Carrier HMS Trumpeter from Trincomalee to the Malacca Strait, and to fly ashore from an agreed position to a variety of destinations. This had to be changed so that we could be despatched from the carrier in groups of four over a period of time. I was in the first group and the first to go, with instructions to fly directly to Kuala Lumpur. It was an exciting prospect, and a completely new experience. Our aircraft had been winched on board outside the harbour at Trincomalee and stored below the flight deck until the Commander (Flying) briefed us the evening before departure. I was due to leave the ship at first light the following morning on a compass bearing of 102°. The flight path would cover 75 miles of sea, with landfall at Port Swettenham, and then a further 25 miles to Kuala Lumpur and its golf course, and an RN destroyer would act as escort over the first part of the flight.

Only one Auster would be on the flight deck at a time, and *Trumpeter* would adjust her speed so as to ensure a manageable headwind for take-off; if necessary she would steam aft! I was transported by lift to the flight deck, and manhandled into take-off position by a team of eight crew who had been carefully instructed as to the delicacy of an Auster as compared to the Barracudas that normally occupied the ship.

I became distinctly apprehensive as I opened the throttle and contemplated the short take-off run with nothing but sea beyond. Furthermore, I was loaded with my own gear and other equipment that I was required to take. I was just about airborne when I ran out of deck, and so I made full use of the height above the sea to gain airspeed. After those first few moments it was quite straightforward and I set about enjoying the new experience of flying into a new country from out at sea. After landfall it became a question of pressing on into the unknown and identifying my golf course. My flight, over a distance of just over 100 miles, took me something over 75 minutes, and I landed my Auster IV, MT358, on the 18th fairway at around 0900 hrs on the 10th September 1945.

The three other Austers joined me at intervals during the morning. There were very few facilities, and we settled for the Clubhouse as a billet, parking our aircraft in the close vicinity so that we could take turns at looking after them at night. We literally had to fend for ourselves, as there was hardly anyone about, and we had no idea when the ground crews would get through to join us. As it turned out, it was four days before anyone from the Squadron reached us, after which they arrived in groups, depending upon where they had eventually come ashore. The Commanding Officer flew in on the sixth day; he had landed at Port Swettenham, where he was able to assess the situation and begin to take control. Communication was particularly difficult but, after he had made contact with Administration in Kuala Lumpur, a number of residential properties in Bukit Bintang Road — adjacent to the golf course — were made available; they became our HQ and remained so for the next four years.

In the meantime, a Civil Affairs Officer, who had been behind the lines with Force 136 throughout the occupation, had heard about the aircraft that had landed on the golf course. He paid us an early visit, during which he took care of our immediate needs and arranged for a supply of fuel. On the 11th September he asked me to fly him on a "flag-showing" visit to the east coast, first to Kota Baru in the north-east corner of Malaya and then to Kuala Trengganu, some 80 miles down the coast.

This was to be some flight! The only maps available were 'dodgy', there would be no air-to-ground communication, and it was clear that it would be unwise to follow the shortest route, which would be over jungle most of the way. However Brigadier Thompson was familiar with much of the landscape, having been there for the past three years, and had also been able to send word that we were coming. We set off with overnight bags and plenty of spare fuel in cans. It was very much a 'seat of the pants' trip; we flew east towards the coast, and turned north when the jungle gave way to open country. We were continually looking for possible landing sites in case of trouble, but reached Kota Baru in the late afternoon. It was then a question of deciding where to land, but during a square search of the town we saw a large gathering of people assembled on a small airfield, which the Brigadier correctly assumed to be his reception party; this group turned out to include the Sultan and his Elders, together with most of the town's population. We were greeted with enormous excitement, and my passenger was clearly in his element. He gave a rousing speech at a banquet — which lasted into the early hours — and the following morning our departure was just as enthusiastic as our arrival had been.

At Kuala Trengganu things were less exciting. The Chinese Communists, who throughout Malaya had been disrupting the Japanese occupation, had more or less taken charge. British troops would not reach the east coast for some time, as they were in the process of rounding up prisoners ahead of the anticipated order regarding their movement. Two days later I flew Brigadier Thompson again, this time to Kuantan on the east coast and some 80 miles from Kuala Lumpur. Kuantan was the home of the Japanese puppet government, and had been subjected to continuous guerilla activity throughout the occupation, principally by the "Malayan People's Anti-Japanese Army" (MPAJA), who had now taken charge. The town had been a hotbed of violence for the past three years; the occupants had had a wretched time, and we found terrible evidence of atrocity on the beach — a great pile of corpses told the story. An English lady we met confirmed this; she and her husband had hidden in the jungle since 1942, and she herself survived to tell of almost nightly selection of someone in the town for summary execution. The MPAJA themselves also carried out executions of those they judged as being collaborators.

I was able to log a fair amount of information regarding navigation and likely landing places as a result of these two trips, and this was passed to Squadron HQ as they established themselves in Kuala Lumpur. Almost immediately we began to disperse: 'C' Flight went north to Ipoh in support of 25 Indian Division, 'B' Flight went east to Trengganu in support of 23 Indian Division, and I went with 'A' Flight to Jahor Bahru in support of 5 Indian Division. We settled into a nice billet in the residential area just north of the causeway into Singapore, where a Chinese family called Wong looked after us in style. Our airstrip was again on a golf course, this time in the grounds of the Sultan of Jahor's

Palace. It soon became clear that exciting flying would be a thing of the past; it does not seem possible that one would ever say that about flying, but we had become used to sorties with urgent objectives, and searching for targets at lowest levels: now we became virtually a taxi service. I found myself flying individuals from A to B with hardly a word said; this was particularly the case with senior members of the Chinese Communist Party whom I picked up and took to 'important' meetings. It was noticeable that they were the only force that did not lay down their arms, and they were particularly concerned to place armed sentries outside their meeting places. At the time we did not notice that this was the beginning of what was to become — several years later — the Malayan Emergency.

At the end of September the Squadron Commander took 'A' Flight to Java to support the 5th Indian Division in putting down Sukarno's uprising. They were to find themselves back at war for several months until things came under control. As my repatriation was imminent, I was left behind, together with my close friend and comrade Mike Gregg, and we were given a task that was to take nearly a month to complete: the Administration required an up-to-date aerial survey of Singapore Island, and this involved continuous flying along each grid line at a height of 2,000 ft. Mike had become proficient in the use of the hand-held camera which had been so valuable in Burma. We plotted each sortie to enable us to take overlapping pictures at planned intervals. The only satisfying aspect of this work was that it was creative and that the final result looked impressive, but it was tedious and demanded intense concentration.

Soon after we finished, Mike returned to his native Bermuda. It was a thoughtful parting, as we had been through a great deal together over the past two years. Before he left we presented each other with a Malayan pewter tankard inscribed with the signatures of all the pilots in the Squadron; these tankards have now come together again and are on display in the archive at HQ 656 Sqadron AAC.

Early in November I was given the post of 'Squadron Captain', an unattractive task similar to that of Adjutant, and basically a desk job. There were few opportunities to fly, although at least I could intercept any order for me to return to the UK. However, on the 24th November I received instructions to carry out what would be my last sortie.

General Seishiro Itagaki had been the Japanese 7th Area Commander, and responsible for all their troops in Malaya, Java and Sumatra, over 700,000 men in all. He had signed the surrender documents in Singapore on the 12th August 1945, and in due course he would be returned to Japan to stand trial for war crimes, with probable execution in due course. In the meantime he was given the task of placing the 26,000 Japanese prisoners in the Malayan theatre on one of the archipelago islands off Singapore; the name of the island was Rempang, and I was instructed to fly him on a reconnaisance so that he could make his plans.

It was arranged that we would *rendezvous* with the Japanese party at midday on the 25th November, using our own airstrip on the Sultan's golf course at Johor Bahru. It was a hot, cloudless day and I had estimated a round trip of 90 minutes; this was the most I could do in the way of planning before I met the General.

Conscious of the need to be 'in charge of' the situation, I arranged with my ground crew to receive the party and await my arrival: this enabled me to make an entrance at H hour plus 5. When I got there my lads had already lined up the General — who was accompanied by his Air Commander, an interpreter and five assorted soldiers — and were taking photographs of them beside my Auster. After a bout of saluting and bowing I was presented with a beautifully-drawn map which contained all the information that I needed: location, distance and, more particularly, a number of clearly-marked places around the island that the General wished to inspect. There were two messages in English. The first said: "When reaching spot marked X, kindly swing your wings so that the General knows you are at the spot". The second one said: "Thank you very much for flying me over Rempang Island and safely back," signed "General Seishiro Itagaki, 7th Area Commander."

What faith! I admired the map for its precision as well as its beauty, but I did treat it formally by indulging in a bit of a show in making notes; it was, I felt, necessary for me to establish a superior position. At the same time I placed my revolver handily inside my belt, and we climbed into the aircraft.

It was a strange feeling to be in such intimate proximity to this man who had been responsible for so much atrocity, and who would already be aware of his likely fate. We flew south over the Causeway, Singapore Island, and out over the Straits. Rempang was quite easy to identify: it was a small round feature some 4-5 miles across, well out to sea and a few miles north of a much larger feature called Butan, and entirely covered with trees. We now spread the map on our laps between us. Communication throughout was by hand signals: I would nudge him and point, and in reply he would either nod or grunt. After circling the island twice at a height of 500 ft, I decided to concentrate on the "spots marked X"; this provided a welcome opportunity to dive to sea level each time, and to fly backwards and forwards so that he could assess the area. All the places marked turned out to be inlets, and seemingly possible landing places.

By now I was thoroughly enjoying myself, but I was not so sure about my passenger, as I had no way of knowing. However there was a high degree of turbulence and he did lose his cap at one point, as well as showing an inclination to hang on, occasionally to *me*! Nevertheless he must have felt his responsibilities: it was clearly going to be a major task to get 26,000 of his countrymen onto this island in quick time. I was not around to see the result, but I was told later that, with typical efficiency, it was achieved in the space of three weeks, and that much of the felled timber had been used to build accomodation.

We returned to base without incident. After landing there was, once again, a great deal of bowing while the interpreter made a short speech of thanks. Strangely, as they all returned to their Jeeps, he came back and addressed us all.

"The General forgot to say one thing. The war is not over, it will go on for a hundred years."

As far as I was concerned the General had not said a single word during the whole visit, so we concluded that the little man had had his own reasons for the outburst.

As the convoy disappeared in a cloud of dust, I flew back to HQ to resume my desk job. Two months later I returned to the UK to continue my further education at Oxford University.

CHAPTER 9

MESSENGER TO CAIRO

(The diary of a flight from Woodley to Almaza by Walter Hutchinson, reprinted from the Miles Magazine *of January 1947.)*

Saturday
Leaving Woodley at about midday, with the weather fairly warm and visibility improved to eight or nine miles, we soon passed over Brooklands race track, still camouflaged, and looking forlorn in the watery August sunshine. From 2,000 ft the South Coast was sighted, and approaching Lympne ships could be seen out in the Channel. After landing at the airport we parked in the company of a Whitney Straight, a Hawk and a Messenger.

Airborne again after lunch and Customs check we noticed Lympne racecourse below, the surrounding countryside looking green and fresh. Soon the cliffs at Dover came into view, unusually white against the background of sea, with the French coast visible through slight mist. Crossing the French coast at Boulogne many sunken ships could be seen in the harbour, and a great deal of bomb damage in the centre of the town, where huge areas were laid waste. In contrast to this scene, prefabricated houses were being built on the hillsides, but beyond these the ground was still pockmarked with thousands of bomb craters. Abbeville also had much damage and there was evidence of gun emplacements and probably flying bomb sites.

At 1605 hrs we sighted the Eiffel Tower and the river Seine winding through Paris, with Le Bourget Airport coming up on our left. As we prepared to land, once again we could make out Miles aircraft on the tarmac — a Messenger and a Whitney Straight. Although we did not voice the platitude we thought that "the more miles one goes, the more Miles one sees."

After dinner we walked about Paris, surprised at the scarcity of goods in the shops and at the high prices. As it was a Saturday, the sidewalks had the usual French style of pavement stalls where the majority of Parisians do their shopping. It seemed that, slowly, France was returning to her prewar mode of living.

Sunday
During the night there was a thunderstorm with heavy rain, but the weather improved by breakfast time and, having cleared Customs, we took off. Heading south over Melun and some fine chateaux in Fontainebleu Forest, we shortly passed over the town of Fontainebleu. There appeared to be a good harvest of wheat and corn in the fields, but

few sheep were seen and only small herds of cattle, a reminder of the very urgent need for sending out livestock from England to the war-devastated areas of Europe. Towards St. Étienne the country was more undulated, the river Loire winding in and out of the hills making a very fine picture. Visibility improved as we headed for the Rhône Valley, with the hills rising to 4,500 feet round about us. Flying down the valley we saw several bridges which had been demolished during the war, in particular that at Avignon. Soon we sighted Lake Berre, which runs into the Mediterranean west of Marseilles. Towards Marignane, our next landing ground, we saw many airfields and landing strips ploughed up by bombing, with hangars in a badly damaged condition.

Monday

Leaving the BOAC hostel at Marignane after enjoying a comfortable night, we took off from the airfield in fine weather, with good visibility and temperature rising. Flying over Marseilles and heading along the rugged coastline towards Toulon, we saw many islands, and soon, in the distance, Toulon itself. Passing over the town and harbour, the remains of the French battle fleet and the many boats scuttled there could be seen, also much damage in the dock area. Now came the prospect of one hour's flying over the water to Ajaccio, on the northern point of Corsica.

The sea was quite rough, with white-crested waves, but at 3,000 ft we cruised smoothly at about 120 mph. Through the haze we soon sighted the Corsican coastline, and our course now lay from Ajaccio across the Straits of Bonifacio to the Gulf of Oristano and on to El Mas aerodrome at Cagliari in South Sardinia.

Nearing the coast we could see the waves breaking on the rocks, the high mountains in the distance making a vivid contrast. Cape Rosso and Cape Feno soon came into view. It was pleasant to be near land again, although our engine was running perfectly and flying was calm. Ajaccio, a fairly large French naval base, looked clean and modern, most of the buildings being five storeys high. Within five minutes of leaving Corsica, and flying towards the Straits of Bonifacio, we could see the high rocky point of Sardinia in the Gulf of Asinara. Sardinia as a whole looked a much smoother country than Corsica and had more cultivated land.

Crossing the coastline again east of Port Torres, and heading for Cape Caccia, we saw Sassari — a typically Italian town where no house has a chimney-stack and where fires of charcoal are lighted in the street and carried indoors in braziers.

Within three hours we were flying inland and parallel to the Gulf of Cristano, heading straight down the valley towards El Mas, where we landed in the early afternoon. This airport, in RAF hands, showed signs of some war damage, and out in the bay we could see wrecked aircraft under the water where they had been shot down.

After refuelling and a meal, we took off at 14.15 hours and, flying over Cagliari, crossed the coast and set course for Tunis. From 3,000 ft we could soon see the North African coast, but in fact we were only halfway across the water, actually crossing the coast at 15.35 hours. In the harbour at Bizerte were many ships sunk during the German retreat at the end of the North African campaign. At Tunis, where we landed at about 16.00 hours, everyone was most attentive, the Shell people organising our clearances and arranging for hotel accommodation.

Tuesday
Early morning we headed out over the sea again for Sousse and the much-mentioned Mareth line, towards Sfax and Gabes, where the country looked dried-up in the heat. Small areas near the coast could be seen divided into orange grove estates, but the marshes beyond Sousse looked like huge salt pans. Sfax, laid out in true Italian style, had each house with its own piece of land.

From Sfax to De Djerba the sea was beautifully calm, a mist obscured the horizon and at 3,000 ft it was very hot. The aircraft touched down at Castel Benito, Tripoli, just before noon, and after a good meal (which included fresh white bread) we were airborne again, headed for Benghazi.

The battlefield at Marble Arch, now symbolised by a marble arch built over the main coast road along which Rommel retreated, was clearly visible. We noticed, too, that the runways at the old airport were in good order although the buildings had been demolished.

On the ground we recognised a Proctor, which we had been passing and repassing all the way from England. We circled the machine twice and saw that nothing was wrong; the pilot waved to us and threw sand into the air to give us wind direction, but we decided not to land, continuing instead towards Benghazi, crossing the coast again at Agheila. Two hours later we landed at Benina aerodrome, Benghazi.

Asked immediately for news of the Proctor, we were able to report that we had seen it at Marble Arch. We were pleased to know that the RAF pilots were prepared to go out to find the aircraft, but it was now dark and we assumed that the Proctor had gone on to El Adem.

Wednesday
We took off from Benghazi and flew across the old battlefields. Before leaving, we were relieved to learn that our friends in the Proctor had landed at El Adem the previous evening and there was no need therefore to keep a look out for them *en route*. Setting course in a straight line across the desert towards El Adem, inland from Tobruk, there was no opportunity to see Derna or the villages along the coast but, crossing the

desert, tank tracks were still visible in the sand where the fiercest fighting and the following up of the enemy took place.

We refuelled at El Adem, had a quick meal and took off again at 13.47 hours. Soon after leaving the airport we noticed dozens of crashed and burnt out aircraft along the desert as we headed for Bardia and Salum. Reaching Halfaya ("Hellfire Pass") and recrossing the coast south of Sidi Barani we could see thousands of bomb craters. Along the coast road on each side there were hundreds of demolished and burnt-out tanks, transports and aircraft which, from 4,000 ft, could be clearly seen for miles.

We flew along the desert railway and in the distance could see Mersa Matruh, fast becoming the favourite holiday place of Egypt on account of the natural lagoon-like harbour. Along the coast we could see El Daba, and after crossing the El Alamein battlefield we turned our nose slightly and made towards Cairo.

Soon after 17.00 hours we were over Cairo West Airport where Mr. Churchill, Mr. Roosevelt and many other VIPs landed during the war. Course was now set for the Pyramids, which could be seen looking very majestic in the late afternoon sun. To the east, the river Nile, flowing away towards the Delta, looked much fuller than usual on account of the floods in Upper Egypt.

Flying between Cheops and Giza, the two largest Pyramids, and then over the Sphinx, we wondered what the Pharaohs would have said if they had seen this easy, modern way of travel. We then passed over the Misr Picture Studios, the Egyptian 'Denham' or 'Hollywood'; on towards Giza and the Kasr El Aini Hospital, and looking towards the island of Gezira we noticed its four bridges linking the two sides of the Nile with the Island.

Our route took us over Abdin Palace, the home of King Farouk, and on towards the Citadel and the Mokatam Hills, beyond where part of the stone was quarried for the Pyramids. We flew over the Dead City known as the Tombs of Mamaluka and Khediva, and away in the distance we could see Heliopolis aerodrome, and beyond, that of Almaza. After circling the airport we touched down at 17.44 hrs, making a total of 26 hrs and 7 mins actual flying from Woodley to Cairo, the Messenger, as we expected, providing for us an easy, trouble-free and swift journey.

TIMES OF FLIGHT

Woodley to Lympne	1.00
Lympne to Le Bourget......	1.40
Le Bourget to Marseilles ..	4.00
Marseilles to El Mas	3.40
El Mas to Tunis	1.40

Tunis to Tripoli		3.30
Tripoli to Benghazi		5.00
Benghazi to El Adem		1.50
El Adem to Almaza		3.57
	TOTAL	26.07 flying hrs.

(This was G-AHXR on delivery to the Regent of Iraq, which left Woodley on 24th August 1946 flown by Sqdn Ldr. Charles Dugdale Harris-St. John, DFC and bar, DSO, accompanied by Walter Hutchinson (who left the trip at Almaza), on the first leg of the delivery flight to Baghdad via Lympne to Le Bourget, and from there to Marignane on 25th, then to El Juina via El Mas on 26th, to Benina via Castel Benito on 27th, to Almaza via El Adem on 28th, to H3 Pipeline via Lydda on 30th, finally arriving in Baghdad on 31.8.46. The total flying time for the delivery flight was 34 hr 10 min.

The Messenger concerned was c/n 6333, a Mk.2A, 'Messenger No. 4' and second of only three Mk. 2As known to have been fitted with square rear windows. First flown with 'B' mark U-9 on a date unknown. Application for C. of A. and registration made by Miles Aircraft Ltd. on 10th April 1946 and registered G-AHXR to them that day. First test flown by Hugh Kendall 10.8.46; C. of A. No. 8077 issued to Miles Aircraft Ltd., Woodley 12.8.46. On 19.8.46 Sqdn Ldr. Harris-St. John made a 1 hr local flight in G-AHXR from Woodley, followed on the 21st by a 2 hr 20 min 'consumption tests' flight. UK registration cancelled as sold abroad in Iraq 15/2/47 where it became YI-HRH for His Royal Highness the Emir Abdul Illah, Regent of Iraq. C. of A. renewed in Iraq 9/11/47. Returned to England and re-registered G-AHXR to Airwork Ltd., London (based at Heston) 26/5/48; cancelled 27/9/49; C. of A. renewed 21/10/49; re-registered to Major The Hon J.B. Fermor-Hesketh, Bletchley, Bucks 3/11/49; C. of A. renewed 13/11/51. Cancelled 9/6/53 and re-registered to Mrs. Barbara Weininger, Sywell 15/6/53; C. of A. expired 14/1/62 and WFU; cancelled 5/7/65 on sale to person(s) unknown. G-AHXR was removed from its hangar at Sywell on 10/7/65 and taken away by road on 25/7/65 to an unknown destination; registration cancelled 20/12/65 as WFU; no further details.
(History courtesy of The Miles Aircraft Collection).

Messenger 2A YI-HRH was used in 1947 by the (late) Regent of Iraq.
Photo: Dennis M. Powell.

The Junkers D-AUAV used at Woodley postwar as the HQ for the
Reading Sky Observers' Club. Photo: Noel Collier.

The Cirrus Minor-powered BA Swallow 2 G-AEWI seen at Croydon during the late forties. Photo: Don Conway.

Proctor IV G-AJTP runs up at Croydon during the late forties. Photo: Don Conway.

CHAPTER 10

HITCHHIKING BY AIR

by

DON CONWAY

Thinking of the tight security at many of UK airfields these days often reminds me of my early aviation enthusiast days, when visits to London's Croydon airport in the late 1940s following WW2 were not a problem.

In those days, I made many trips by bus from my South London home to Croydon Airport, to see aeroplanes such as the Caudron Göeland, Bloch 220, de Havilland Rapide, Airspeed Consul, Avro Anson, Douglas Dakota and Miles Gemini, to name a few. Local 10-minute pleasure flights were made in 1947 & 1948 in de Havilland Dragon G-AECZ and in the Island Air Services' Percival Proctors G-AHDI and G-AJTP; I had by now caught the flying bug!

Aviation enthusiasts and I were accepted by the airport authorities and issued with passes by the Aerodrome Manager, on behalf of the Ministry of Civil Aviation, enabling us to visit Croydon Airport and its hangars. From this our aerial hitchhiking adventures began. Visiting pilots (many ex-RAF) noted our enthusiasm when reporting in at the airport's landing office and, on my asking if there was a spare seat available, it was often a case of: "yes, hop aboard!"

My first aerial hitchhiking flight was recorded when we flew in Airspeed Consul G-AHFS on 8th January 1948 from Croydon to nearby Redhill aerodrome in Surrey, an 8-minute flight. I hastily entered the flight in my 'Passenger Personal Flying Log Book', purchased from the W.H. Smith kiosk at Croydon, which the pilot duly signed. The Consul was one of a number owned by British Air Transport for charter flights and early morning delivery flights of London newspapers to the Continent and Channel Islands.

On 13th November 1948 we hitchhiked by road to Gatwick for the first time to visit the Ministry of Civil Aviation Flying Unit. In the following months we flew in the Unit's Airspeed Consuls G-AJXE, 'JXF, 'JXG & 'JXH and in their Avro 19s G-AGPB, G-AGZT, G-AGWA & G-AGWF as well as in their two de Havilland Doves; for instance, on 22nd January 1949 we flew in Dove G-AJLV from Croydon to Gatwick, a 15-minute flight, flown by Capt. B. Marshall, while on 24th September 1949 we flew with pilot Capt. Geoffrey W. Stallibrass (much later Controller, National Air Traffic Services, CAA) from Gatwick to Northolt in Dove G-ALFT. This was a 25-minute flight, landing there at 1255 hours, but ten minutes later we were airborne once again, flying from Northolt to Stansted in 45 minutes. The MCA Flying Unit moved from

Gatwick to Stansted at the end of 1949, where their fleet of aircraft continued to give sterling service in the work of testing radio aids such as Standard Beam Approach systems at airports. An additional task was instrument rating and other checks for professional pilots.

A cycling trip to Elstree aerodrome in Hertfordshire during February 1949 resulted in a flight aboard de Havilland Rapide G-AEAL on an air survey flight between Elstree and Luton. After 2 hours we landed at Luton Airport before flying back to Elstree, just a 20-minute flight; the 1936-built Rapide was owned by Hunting Aerosurveys Ltd. Another flight was in March 1949 when Miles Gemini G-AJKS, piloted by Mr. Ray Jeffs of British Aviation Insurance Co., flew us from Gatwick to the Hawker-owned airfield at Langley near Slough, taking 30 minutes.

On 14th April 1949 we were airborne once again from Croydon when wartime pilot Wing Commander O.V. ('Titch') Holmes asked us if we would like to accompany him and his wife on a flight over London that evening to see the lights from the air. Of course "yes, please!" was our answer, and so we were airborne at 1925 hours heading for London in the cream-with-red-trim Airspeed Consul G-AIUS of Stewart Smith & Co. Ltd. I flew again with 'Titch' Holmes on 1st April 1950 when he carried out a 15-minute circuit of Croydon airport in Piper L-4H Cub G-AKAA.

On the lighter side was a trip on 21st May 1949 with a Mr. D. Doughty; this was in his BA Swallow G-AEWI from Croydon via the Gatwick overhead to Shoreham in 35 minutes, then returning in a similar time, for once not a case of hitchhiking home! Later I recorded another swift — for a Swallow — flight of 10 minutes from Croydon to Redhill; we must have had a strong tailwind that day!

Two of my most unusual flights were, firstly, one in May 1950 in Westland-Sikorsky S-51 Mk.1A helicopter G-ALIK owned by Westland Aircraft; at the time this was based at Croydon, and would fly daily to Barnes Common near Chiswick to ferry passengers from Barnes to the British Industries Fair being held in Birmingham. This was my first helicopter trip and took just 15 minutes from Croydon to Barnes. The second was in the Short Sealand demonstrator amphibian G-AKLO in the summer of 1951, when the aircraft had been fitted out to carry seven passengers and two crew. We left Croydon at 1215 hours with friend John Havers and myself on board bound for the River Medway, the pilot Don Tanton demonstrating the feathering and restarting of the starboard engine *en route*. After 25 minutes' flying the pilot carried out a touch-and-go on the Medway before landing at nearby Rochester aerodrome. We got the Green Line bus home!

Many of our aerial hikes from Croydon were non-return flights, so we often found ourselves hitchhiking home by road from airfields such as Fair Oaks, Hanworth, Cambridge, Eastleigh, Stansted, Blackbushe, Hastings, Heathrow, Thruxton, Denham and even from as far away as

Staverton (Gloucestershire) and Ringway (Manchester): our parents rarely knew when to expect us home!

An example was when we flew in Miles Gemini G-AJFD of Bees' Flight Ltd. during August 1950 to Lea on the Isle of Wight. This turned out to be a one-way 40 minute journey, as the pilot decided at the last moment not to return to Croydon that day, although later in the afternoon we joined a pleasure flight around the island, taking in Cowes and the Needles during a 40-minute flight in the Gemini. Late that evening we were made comfortable on a makeshift bed for the night in the airfield lounge, and then the next morning we were awakened at 0700 hours to be informed by the pilot of de Havilland Rapide G-AKMH (also owned by Bees' Flight) that he was flying to nearby Eastleigh (Southampton) and then to Paris to collect a stretcher case for hospitalisation in London. So we flew in G-AKMH on a 15-minute 'hop' to Eastleigh, where we thanked the pilot and took to the road. We were soon hiking our way back to Croydon before returning to our homes, and were amazed on reaching the airport to find G-AKMH landing there from France just 10 minutes after our arrival!

This story covers some of my aerial hitchhiking days from January 1948 to August 1950, but by mid-1952 these came to an end on my joining the Royal Air Force. During my period of National Service I was airborne again as a passenger aboard types such as a Handley Page Hastings, Avro Anson and de Havilland Chipmunk, but that's another story!

CHAPTER 11

CRUISER VP-KFR AND BARBARA DUTHY

(This chapter is reproduced, by kind permission of the author, Joan Wedekind, from our very recent publication Keith Campling and the Story of Aviation in East Africa *— Ed.)*

Several Piper Cruisers were imported into East Africa by CBV (Campling Brothers & Vanderwal) during 1947, but perhaps the one that had the most interesting and longest career of all was VP-KFR; this belonged to Barbara Duthy, later Mrs. Sandy Simpson, and stayed in Kenya until 1967 when it was flown to England.

Barbara Duthy was born in India in 1914 and came to Kenya as a child with her family, who settled at Makuyu. Her sister was Isolde Ann Duthy, who had been a receptionist at the Outspan Hotel while Keith Campling (founder of CBV) was there in the thirties. Barbara started her education at a small school in Nyeri but was later sent for schooling to England, and it was as a teenager in England that she had her first taste of flying with Cobham's Flying Circus; this was a scheme whereby Alan Cobham, financed by Lord Wakefield, gave English schoolchildren the opportunity to fly, as Cobham felt that, in the event of war, Britain would need pilots and that the scheme would help develop enthusiasm for flying. And in fact flying with Cobham made such an impression on the young Barbara that after that she could not wait to take it up!

But her chance to fly did not come until June 1947, when she was working for the Veterinary Laboratories at Kabete outside Nairobi and was able to save sufficient money to commence flying lessons. She learnt to fly in CBV's two Cubs, VR-TAK and VR-TAL with Bill Duirs as her main instructor, but she also took lessons with Arthur Appleby and Wally Brown. In addition to flying the Cubs she made several flights in the Luscombe 'KDD, mostly cross-country flying to Thomson's Falls and Gilgil. Barbara was just crazy about flying and loved every moment of it; she was always one of those people with a great enthusiasm for life and a capacity to really enjoy it, and earned Private Pilots' Licence Number 138 at the end of August 1947.

In 1948 she bought the Cub VR-TAL, which was one of the first three Cubs to be imported by Keith Campling; then in 1949 she sold the Cub and replaced it with a Piper Cruiser, VP-KFR, which was a three-seater (the Cruiser has a front seat for the pilot and a seat for two passengers immediately behind). That same year Barbara joined Mike Bearcroft in his Cruiser VP-KFS, and together with Peter Hoosen they flew in 'KFS to England. While in England Barbara bought an Auster 5, G-AKWH and, after some flying in England to familiarise herself with the aircraft, she decided to fly it back to Kenya. At this stage Barbara had a grand total of only 169 hours' flying time, but she had tremendous enthusiasm and a lot of guts. For company she took a young Australian with her who claimed to have some experience in aircraft engineering, and she thought he could be of some use as map-reader and navigator on the flight.

Leaving England on the 30th October 1949, they headed across the English Channel to Le Touquet. Then they crossed from Nice to Tunis, and made their way down through Africa without any problems until they arrived at Juba in Southern Sudan on the 13th November. From there they headed for Soroti, west of Lake Kyoga in Uganda, but something went wrong with their navigation and they found themselves lost over Lake Kyoga; by the time they had crossed the lake they were running low in fuel and Barbara looked for somewhere to land. The roads were narrow and overhung by trees and the countryside filled with sugar cane, but she eventually managed to find a small clear space between some anthills and landed safely, sustaining damage only to an elevator.

It was 4.15 pm and, as always in what seems to be remotest uninhabited Africa, it was not long before several Africans appeared, including one with a bicycle on which Barbara managed to get a lift to the nearby railway station. This was Namwendwa, south of Lake Kyoga and some 50 miles south-east of Soroti, and she was able to make a phone call to Entebbe from the station there.

When she returned to the Auster she found to her horror that her companion had completely dismantled the aircraft and removed the wings, so that was the end of any hope she may have had of completing the flight to Nairobi. They spent the night in the home of an accommodating African policeman and later made their way to Entebbe and on to Nairobi. The Auster meanwhile was loaded into a lorry and eventually found its way into CBV's workshops, but by then it had sustained considerable damage due to the rough way with which it had been handled and the jolting over bad roads. In addition Keith found that the wings had not been unbolted but that the fuel lines and steel cables had been sawn straight through, making the Auster virtually a write-off, so any ideas Barbara might have had of selling it and making a profit out of it were gone. Nevertheless the Auster was eventually bought by Caspair and repaired later.

Barbara's Auster 5 (which finally became VP-KID) was one of two Auster 5s that were imported into Kenya and sold to Caspair; the other was VP-KGD. VP-KID was written off when it was hit by a vulture, and VP-KGD came to grief during a flight back to the UK. Meanwhile her companion disappeared. One rumour had it that he had headed for Arusha in Tanganyika and then further south under a changed name, while other rumours linked him with some sort of a crime, possibly even a murder case, in England!

Barbara still owned the Cub VP-KFR, which she found she was able to use in the course of her duties on behalf of the Vet. Lab. She made a further saving in the running costs of 'KFR by letting Denis Zaphiro of the Game Department have a share in it; he had been another of CBV's pupils under Roy Marsh. On one occasion, when flying for the Veterinary Department, Barbara landed at Aitong on the Loita Plains, and the following morning she discovered a tear in one of the wings. So she found someone with a large linen handkerchief, and with a needle and thread she made a very neat repair, to which she later applied some dope, and this lasted until 'KFR's next C. of A. Barbara was a very competent needlewoman and over the years won many prizes for her beautiful embroidery and handwork.

In 1951 Barbara took 'KFR to Cape Town together with Mike Richmond, ex-Royal Navy and a well-known pilot, and 'Sammy' Clayton, the famous female cartoon artist, who had had some flying experience ferrying aircraft during the war while a member of the Air Transport Auxiliary; at one stage she had owned her own Auster, VP-UAL, but Barbara found Sammy a bit weak on navigation and with a tendency to veer off course.

With Barbara at the controls the three of them left Nairobi for Zanzibar on the 31st July, and thereafter they headed for Moçambique, flying via Lumbo, Quilemane, Beira, Lourenço Marques and Inhambane before crossing into South Africa and flying on to Durban. They nearly found themselves in trouble in Moçambique, as Sammy Clayton did not have a valid yellow fever inoculation certificate, but she managed to forge the date on the old one. However this was spotted when they reached Durban and caused a heap of inconvenience, and Sammy had to spend a night in an isolation and quarantine centre. The remainder of the trip round South Africa was trouble-free and very enjoyable. While in South Africa, Mike Richmond and Sammy Clayton took delivery of a Piper Cruiser, VP-KJA, and they flew this back to Kenya while Barbara returned on her own with 'KFR.

They made the trip north through Bulawayo via the Victoria Falls and on to Lusaka, Ndola and Kasama and Tabora before finally both arriving in Nairobi on the 17th August. Here Barbara encountered more officialdom, concerned that 'KFR had returned from an international flight when, according to their records, it had never been on one. In fact Customs were so concerned with this that they totally overlooked all the items in the well-packed 'KFR that could have been dutiable!

Back at work with the Vet. Lab., Barbara continued to enjoy flying all over Kenya on veterinary and tsetse control work, landing in all sorts of remote places and every type of airstrip, and her log books filled with names like Narok, Namanga, Kajiado, Amboseli, Sotik, Macalder's Mine, Lokitaung, Njoro, and Nanyuki. But Barbara's flying was not always connected with her work; she always loved the coast, especially landing at Jadini, Malindi or Lamu, and she was a regular visitor to Jadini and Malindi for the air rallies that were sometimes held there.

When Barbara married Sandy Simpson she taught him the basics of flying in 'KFR and, after he obtained his licence, he often took 'KFR in the course of his work as a District Commissioner or Resident Magistrate. Finally in the mid-1960s the day came to retire, and Barbara and her husband went to settle in a beautiful spot on a ridge overlooking the sea at Watamu Beach, south of Malindi. Here they found they did not need an aircraft (and indeed could not really afford one), so with much sadness they parted with 'KFR to Dave and Viva Maculoff, who later flew her to England.

At about this time Keith was looking for materials with which to build a hangar in Nairobi, so Dave Maculoff sold him a warehouse in Mombasa which, after dismantling, was sufficient to build a hangaer in Nairobi, and also one in Malindi on the airport that was opened there in 1961 to replace the old Carberry airfield behind the Eden Roc Hotel.

VF-KFR was re-registered as G-AXUC by the Maculoffs in England and kept until about 1990, when they sold her and returned to live in Kenya. To the best of Barbara's knowledge the Cruiser was still flying in 1994, and in fact the aircraft is still current in 2005 with J.J. Bunton in Kent and has a brand-new British C. of A. valid until July 2008!

Barbara kept her flying licence valid until December 1971 when she made her final flight in a Cessna 150, 5Y-AER, but while she may have retired from flying she certainly did not retire completely; she then threw her enthusiasm into boating and the study of seaweeds, on which she and Sandy wrote a book. She also devoted time to her hobby of bird-watching and the study of indigenous plants, and then after Sandy's death she turned her home into a very popular little guesthouse, being still a very busy lady into her eighties! Unfortunately she was gradually crippled with arthritis, and was also almost blind by the time she died in Watamu in 2002 at the age of 87.

CHAPTER 12

OLD ENGLISH AEROPLANES

by

MARTIN BARRACLOUGH

(Martin Barraclough was out in East Africa postwar working for Steel Brothers [Tanganyika Forests] Ltd., based in the Southern Province of Tanganyika. Although his contribution does not strictly concern the postwar forties, nevertheless it provides details of that period in general (and of several well–known aircraft in particular) which will be of great interest to anyone who remembers those times. Martin now lives in Hampshire and has recently published his memoirs, from which this extract is reproduced with his permission — Ed.)

Verney Lovett-Campbell was at the time Managing Director of Steel Brothers (Tanganyika Forests) Ltd., and also a member of the Royal Aero Club, at that time enjoying delightful premises at 119 Piccadilly, next in line to the Cavalry and the Royal Air Force Clubs. Whenever he returned to England he would frequent the Club, enjoying the company of Colonel "Mossy" Preston, the Secretary General, and the stalwart members of 'The Throttle Benders' Union', who propped up the bar and who lived for the National Air Races. Verney had already persuaded Steels to purchase a Miles Gemini, as they believed that their Managing Director should fly in the safety of a twin-engined aircraft. But when a crankshaft sheared in one of the Blackburn Cirrus Minor engines, he was unable to maintain height on the other and made a spectacular forced landing on the main forest road leading up to the Rondo Plateau, writing off the aircraft but without doing any damage to himself or his passenger. Despite this misadventure, and because he was staunchly British, he was determined to buy and fly British aircraft and not to do what every sensible flyer in East Africa did, which was to buy a suitable American aircraft, of which the products of Piper, Cessna and Beech were in the great majority!

So when a Miles Messenger was offered for sale by Noon & Pearce Air Charters in Nairobi, Verney jumped at the opportunity and traded in the Piper Cruiser that he had had to use since the demise of the Gemini. Having flown the Cub and the Cruiser, both high-wing aeroplanes, I was excited at the prospect of flying a new type and a low-wing plane to boot. It also had four seats and a spectacular short field performance, so was likely to be a step in the right direction. VP-KJL was a M.38 Mk.4A Messenger with a de Havilland Gipsy Major engine, considered to be more reliable than the Cirrus Major engine which powered the majority of the earlier Messengers. However, as all pilots of Gipsy-engined aircraft know, the impulse starter in the starboard magneto tends to stick, effectively preventing the magneto from delivering the heavy initial spark needed to fire the engine into life. The only way to deal with this irritation is to bang the coupling between the magneto and the engine housing with a suitable implement such as a spanner or heavy screwdriver until a click is heard, which signifies that the offending mechanism has come unstuck. The Messenger's Gipsy Major was no exception and many were the embarrassing times that I had to explain this alarming corrective action to visitors from London. To be flown off a beach by a teenaged pilot must have been startling enough for some of my elderly London-based passengers. To have to witness the pilot, after failing to start the Messenger's engine, reach under the seat for a stout metal bar and then proceed to leap onto the sand, unbutton the starboard engine cowling and pound the starboard side of the engine, must have made their hair stand on end! But the alternative method of travelling to the Rondo was a three-hour Land Rover trip over really ghastly roads, so they had to sit, tight-lipped, while this whippersnapper went about his business.

The Messenger was silver with black registration and was a delight to fly, but was no faster than the Cruiser. In fact, with the original fine-pitch propeller she was even slower, cruising at about 90 mph. Now anyone who has flown in Africa will know that the best time to fly is early in the morning. At this time of day the cumulus clouds are light and fluffy and are at around a few thousand feet above ground level, but as the sun rises and the heat of the day builds up so the clouds rise and thicken. Flying above them is calm and delightful; flying below them is rough and hot. By midday the base of the cumulus clouds is around 10,000 ft and below them it has become very hot and very turbulent. As the afternoon wears on the cumulus turns to cumulo-nimbus and the great thunderheads form through which no sane pilot ever flies! So any flights we made after about 10 o'clock in the morning were perforce below the cloud level and were hot, bumpy and — in the Messenger — excruciatingly slow!

I was to spend hours and hours flying between Dar es Salaam and Lindi or Rondo, being bumped around in the turbulence and getting hot and sweaty, bad-tempered and fed up. We had no radio — another unnecessary aid as far as Lovett-Campbell was concerned — so there was nothing except miles and miles of bloody Africa to engage one's attention! After six months I began to dread those trips to Dar es Salaam, but I piled on the hours, and by the first anniversary of my first solo I had clocked up over 200 hours. Despite her three massive tail fins the Messenger was always prone to ground-loop, the cable-operated differential brakes having little effect once the swing got under way, and this was to be the undoing of VP-KJL. Alan Kenyon, a low-hour pilot and sawmill assistant from Lancashire, who had only learned to fly on his last home leave, landed on the new airstrip at Rondo, ground-looped and ran into a deep water ditch which ran alongside the strip. Both undercarriage legs were smashed backwards and, although they were intact, they broke the front spars to which they were attached. The Messenger was painstakingly rebuilt on the Rondo by a Kenyan engineer, Bill Trollope, and sold to a Kenyan farmer, Buster Cook, who flew her back to Nairobi. This was the end of Steel's association with the Messenger, but not — as I shall recount later — mine.

In 1954 Lovett-Campbell took leave and bought, for his own account, a unique aeroplane, the Miles M.7A Nighthawk G-AGWT. This aeroplane had been built by the Miles brothers for their own personal transport during the second World War, and consisted of a Nighthawk fuselage with Mohawk wings. Lovett-Campbell bought her from Group Captain C.M.M. Grece, who was tragically killed only a few weeks later when his replacement aircraft, a Percival Proctor, crashed. Grece had taken off from Southampton to fly back to Middle Wallop, where he was CO. Despite a magneto having failed on his pre-take-off engine run, Grece said that it was only a short hop to Wallop and that he would risk it on one magneto, but the other magneto failed on take-off and, as he turned back to the field, the Proctor spun into the ground — he made two of flying's classic mistakes and they cost him his life.

The Nighthawk was typical of the last prewar Miles aeroplanes. The occupants sat low in the four-place cabin with the pilot peering out at eye level throught a triangular moulded windscreen. The fixed undercarriage was set in a thick-section Miles wing and was tightly faired into a trouser which ended about three inches off the ground. If a heavy landing was made, the undercarriage, whose suspension consisted of two undampened coil springs, would bounce up into the trousers, which hit the ground and split. After a year of beach landings in Tanganyika this undercarriage became so worn by the sand that it had to be replaced with a Proctor undercarriage and spats. The control column was positioned between the front seats, ending in a hinged section in front of the pilot, at the end of which there was a large yoke shaped like two triangles joined at their apexes. By pulling a knob on the column the yoke could be swung over to the person in the right-hand seat to let him take over control. The Beech Bonanza incorporated a similar, more modern version of this yoke. The flaps were hydraulically operated by a two-way lever and a manual pump on the left side of the cockpit. An incurable twist in the port wing caused the plane to fly 'left wing low'; we could never fly 'hands off' and constantly had to prop up the bottom left corner of the yoke to keep the wings level! The aeroplane was reputed to have unpleasant and difficult stall characteristics, so we never stalled her, and always landed on the main wheels — never on three points.

Grece had repainted the aircraft and won the Concours d'Élegance at the 1954 Jersey Air Rally before he sold her. Lovett-Campbell then flew her in the National Air Races that year, winning the hideous Norton-Griffiths Trophy for the fastest aircaft — the Nighthawk beat all the Proctors by a good 20 mph. He then flew her out to East Africa by the old Imperial route and she was re-registered VP-KMM. Although made entirely of wood and held together with the old casein glue she gave Steel's wonderful service until long after I had left Tanganyika. She was eventually flown back to the UK, and the last time I saw her was at a race meeting at Thruxton in the early 1960s just before her final owner tried to fly her to Singapore; he was halfway down the Rhône valley in France when he had some sort of accident, and the last that was known of this lovely old aeroplane was that the fuselage was languishing in a children's playground somewhere near Lyons!

Steel Brothers' rules, enshrined in a leather-bound book, dictated that the first overseas tour for an assistant should be four years, the second was to be three years, and thereafter tours would be two and a half years, each followed by six months' home leave. I was only signed on to the London staff in 1954, and so it was to be 1958 before I was allowed the treasured home leave. Lovett-Campbell, however, returned to England for another spell of home leave in 1957. Once again he decided to buy a British aircraft and, unphased by the misadventure with the old Blackburn Cirrus-engined Gemini, he bought a second Gemini, but this one was a Gipsy Gemini powered by two de Havilland Gipsy Majors each of 150 hp, and none other than Nat Somers' King's Cup-winning aircraft G-AKDC. This was a lovely aeroplane to fly, with each engine producing 50 horse power more than the Cirrus Minor and with the added reliability of the de Havilland design and manufacture. It could even — just — stay up on one engine, and although this may seem to have been a bit pathetic, it must be remembered that the first twin-engined aircraft produced by Piper, the Apache, had a hardly better performance. Lovett-Campbell flew G-AKDC out to Tanganyika via the West African route, ending up crossing the forests of the Belgian Congo to enter East Africa at the south-west corner of Tanganyika. His co-pilot on this trip was a young Englishman who was to be my co-assistant, Shaun O'Connor-Parsons; he had only obtained his PPL at CSE Oxford a month earlier so it was a major cross-country for him!

The Gemini was re-registered VR-TBP on the new Tanganyikan register (the Nighthawk had been eventually re-registered VR-TMM), and after only a brief 10-minute flight and two landings with Lovett-Campbell at Mzungu Bay (another of our beach landing strips) I flew my first twin solo off the beach. Although a delight to fly, the Gemini was an absolute pig to maintain as the Gipsy engines had been shoe-horned into tight nacelles and nothing was accessible without special tools. She eventually came to grief in December 1958 at the hands of Shaun, who suffered an engine failure on the way into Mtwara, lost control in the circuit, and failed to make the airstrip, plunging into the thick bush which cushioned his crash, saving him from anything worse than a cut on the head, but putting an end to the aircraft.

Although the Nighhawk flew on for the next few years, on the demise of the Messenger and Gemini we resorted each time to hiring an aircraft from Campling's, the first time our faithful old Cruiser, VP-KFY, and the second time a delightful Pacer, VP-KKE. When I eventually left the Rondo in 1959 Steels were still operating the Pacer and the Nighthawk.

Hastings TG583 seen at Luqa, Malta on 17th February 1950.
Photo: Graham Lewis.

Slingsby T.7 Cadet VW502 with the ATC at Langley, 14th November
1948. Photo: Graham Lewis.

Gemini VR-TBP (ex-G-AKDC) at Ngala. Photo: via Mike Barraclough.

The ignominious end of Gemini VR-TBP (ex-G-AKDC).
Photo: via Mike Barraclough.

Mike Barraclough, Mike the dog (a spaniel-dachshund cross) and Messenger VP-KJL. Photo via Mike Barraclough.

A young Mike Barraclough stands by Messenger VP-KJL on Lindi beach. Photo: via Mike Barraclough.

The Miles Nighthawk VR-TMM (ex-G-AGWT) at Lindi beach.
Photo: via Mike Barraclough.

Servicing the Nighthawk VR-TMM (ex-G-AGWT).
Photo via Mike Barraclough.

CHAPTER 13

RACING A SPITFIRE POSTWAR

by

LETTICE CURTIS

(This account has been adapted, with the author's permission, from a chapter in her recent autobiography, published by Red Kite Publications, which describes Lettice's experiences in racing a Spitfire postwar. The Foster-Wikner Wicko G-AFJB, which Lettice owned during the late forties — and which has recently been restored for Joe Dible by Ron Souch — adorns the front cover of this book.)

Just postwar, Sir Peter Masefield, who a couple of years previously had been posted to Washington as British Civil Air Attaché, had been allowed to take a Proctor with him (possibly G-AHMG). His opposite number in London, Livingstone (Tony) Satterthwaite, was somewhat envious of this and sought permission from his government for an aircraft to use in Britain and Europe. The US Government however, were unwilling to ship an aircraft from the States for him and asked him to apply to the Air Ministry for a surplus Fairchild Argus. But Tony, unimpressed by the low performance of this aircraft, asked instead for a war-surplus Spitfire.

On leaving the RAF the aircraft went first to 33 Maintenance Unit at Lyneham, where military equipment was removed, and was then sent to Vickers to be prepared for civil use. On 27th January 1948 the aircraft was ready for handover and Tony was asked to collect it from Eastleigh, Southampton. Now an American aircraft, the Spitfire was to be held by the American Embassy Flight at Hendon, where informal arrangements had been made with RAF Hendon for servicing. Hendon then was where, after handover, it was required to go, but Tony, although he already had use of an Embassy Harvard, did not feel happy about making his first flight in a Spitfire to Hendon which, even for those days, was a small airfield. Now Tony was a good friend of mine and, in a rash moment, although I had flown only light aircraft since leaving the ATA over three years before, I volunteered to fly it to Hendon for him. Thus on a dreary January day we motored down to Eastleigh and, the presentation over, I had no option but to get in and start it up. No radio was fitted — the military one would have been removed at Lyneham — so it was a question of map-reading.

Hendon at the time had two runways: one, 1,000 yards long, ran from north-east to south-west, while the other, from east to west, was just 800 yards long and approach from the east was over a railway embankment.

Arriving at Hendon, therefore, I was more than a little relieved to find the 'T' on the longer runway, but it was with considerable trepidation that I made my approach, and in the event, managed a reasonable landing.

Next day Air Marshal Sir John Boothman, KBE, CB, DFC, AFC who, as ACAS Technical Requirements Manager, had been involved in the transfer of the aircraft to Satterthwaite, rang him at his office; he, it so happened, had been at Hendon when the aircraft arrived and he was now ringing to congratulate him on what he took to be his first Spitfire landing. Inevitably he was somewhat shaken to be told that the pilot had in fact been a woman.

But Tony was still not happy about taking the Spitfire in and out of Hendon. So when he wanted to fly I would take half a day's leave to take it initially to Bovingdon, where there was a longer runway. It was not until 25th February 1948 that, from there, Tony made his first flight, after which I returned the aircraft to Hendon.

But at the end of the month I was due to change my job in London for one at Boscombe Down. Ten days before the move I borrowed the Spitfire and flew down to Boscombe to tie up loose ends. I have often wondered what people there thought about a junior future employee — and a woman at that — arriving for an interview in a Spitfire! On 11th April I again took the Spitfire to Bovingdon, where it must have gone unserviceable because my log book shows that I returned it to Hendon after a test flight on 1st May. It was 22nd May before Tony flew it again, this time from Hurn. He picked me up from Boscombe in the Harvard — in which for some reason I would take over the flying — and we flew back to Hendon to collect the Spitfire. At Hurn there were again serviceability problems, and it was 9th June before we picked it up again and took it to Bovingdon, from where someone from Hendon had taken over flying it in and out.

From Bovingdon we flew back in the Harvard to Thruxton, a Club airfield close to Boscombe, and whilst we were there we learnt that an Air Day was being arranged on August 15th, which was to include a handicapped race open to all types of aircraft. In another rash moment I suggested to Tony that he enter his Spitfire, to which he somewhat surprisingly replied that if I would race the Spitfire he would himself enter in the Harvard. Thus on 12th August Tony collected me from Boscombe and took me to Hendon to collect the Spitfire, which I flew back to Thruxton. But before racing it the engine would have to be thoroughly checked and the racing number painted on. I therefore sought permission from our Air Officer Commanding at Boscombe, Air Commodore — later Air Vice Marshal — 'Sam' Patch, to bring it in there, as there were Rolls Royce representatives available and the CATS engineers had volunteered to help with polishing and painting the race number.

Permission given, the following day I moved the aircraft over to Boscombe Down. In those days aircraft were handicapped against their full-throttle performance, but on becoming a civil aircraft the Spitfire engine had, mercifully, been de-rated from +18 psi maximum boost to +12 psi which would have to be held at 2,850 rpm for around half an hour; however the Rolls Royce reps told me that this should cause no problems. ATA's recommended cruise was 2,000 rpm and zero boost so, for me, racing was going to be something different from what I was used to!

The race was from Thruxton to Totland Bay in the Isle of Wight and back, and all other aircraft in the race were light club types. On handicap therefore I had a 30-minute wait from when the first Auster took off until my turn came to be flagged away. As I waited on the starter line I had to decide when to start the engine; if I started it too early it would overheat but if I left it and it didn't start immediately I would miss my starting time.

By the time I took off some light aircraft were already on the way back. Immediately after getting airborne I made a climbing turn to 2,000 feet so as to be above the rest of the field. Whilst still on the ground engine coolant temperature had reached the maximum and the needle remained at maximum throughout the flight — my only worry. An 180° turn round the marker at Totland Bay and I was on my way back, but it was only after I dropped the nose to gain speed over the finishing line that I saw other aircraft below me, so before landing I made a couple of circuits to cool the engine. Also in the race was Bruin Purvis, Chief Test Pilot of the Civil Section in which I worked, who had flown a Proctor he had entered with Sandy Powell, another test pilot. He told me afterwards that he had been convinced that he was winning, and was not at all pleased when within seconds of crossing the line, the Spitfire shot past him. One can but congratulate the handicappers!

On the strength of this win Tony was asked to enter the Spitfire for the prestigious Lympne high-speed handicap race later that month. The 1948 High Speed Handicap Air Race was run from the Cinque Ports Flying Club at Lympne. In those days aircraft firms would enter military types they were developing, hiring them for the day from the equivalent of the Ministry of Defence. The aircraft were raced by their test pilots, and the course was over four circuits of a 20-mile course from Lympne to the Capel airship hangar near Folkestone Harbour pier, then along the sea front to the Hythe gasholder and then back to Lympne.

The course involved two very sharp turns. Participants in this race included J. Colqhoun in a Spitfire Mk.VIII Trainer (which proved the winner of the race), John Cunningham and John Derry in de Havilland Vampires, J.O. Mathews from Fairey's in a Mk.4 Firefly, W.J.G. Morgan from Vickers-Supermarine's in a Spitfire Mk.24, and T.S. Wade from

Hawker's in a Mk.1 Hawker Fury. In addition Bill Waterton had entered a Meteor VII but in the event he did not take part in the race. To me, ill-prepared and an amateur who had only flown a Spitfire at full power on one occasion on a there-and-back course, this was a daunting experience and, on behalf of Tony as well as myself, I was seriously afraid of making a complete fool of myself; but it was too late to pull out now.

At this time Lympne had no hard runway and the run was not all that long for Vampire jets, especially on grass. The wind was light and there was some indecision as to take-off direction. In the event we all started up and taxied to the west, taking off towards the sea. Then at the last minute the Vampires, which were being given priority, requested take-off east to west, so we all had to taxy to the other side of the field. This was where my Spitfire put me at a disadvantage. The radiators on this model opened automatically when the coolant reached a specified temperature and, as no manual control was provided, remained open until the temperature dropped again. During the extended taxying the radiator flaps had opened, giving a perceptible increase in drag, and they remained open for the first three of the laps, the fourth showing an increased speed of some seven mph. This increase, if applied to the other three laps, would, with a very favourable handicap, have won me the race — in spite of the fact that my turns could not compete with those of the professionals.

But as it was, the honours went to Colqhoun in the Spitfire Trainer, while John Cunningham, who came second, averaged (according to next day's press) 521 mph over the last three laps. I came fifth, which could have been worse! Throughout the race Tony stood under the Control Tower keeping a check on the Spitfire and talking to celebrities such as Douglas Fairbanks junior and the Parliamentary Secretary to the Ministry of Aviation (Lingren), who later invited me to lunch in the House of Commons where, I recall, we had whale meat. We spent the night in Folkstone celebrating and I flew the Spitfire back to Hendon the next day. It was the last time I flew it as Tony was posted back to the Department of State in Washington. Before he went we spent many hours discussing the possibilities of flying the Spitfire to America but, under the terms of the gift, it appeared that the aircraft could not be domiciled outside the UK.

Tony Satterthwaite in due course became First Secretary in the US Embassy in Copenhagen, where once I spent a very happy holiday. In October 1959 he was killed in a helicopter accident whilst visiting his 'parish' in Greenland, and with his death Great Britain lost one of America's most ardent Anglophiles.

CHAPTER 14

WEST COUNTRY MEMORIES

by

NOEL COLLIER

The year 1945 opened with great anticipation by all that the end of World War II was in sight. As 14-year-old aircraft spotters my pals and I took a certain pride in that we were able to identify over 60 types of aircraft. Thanks mainly to the publication since 1941 of the now legendary *Aeroplane Spotter* by Temple Press Ltd., we were kept abreast with the latest developments in the air, whether friend or foe. Of the latter we had even seen a Junkers Ju.88, Messerschmitt Me.109 and Dornier Do.217, as well as a profusion of many RAF and US types. However the most common type to be seen over East Devon skies were the PB4-Y1 Liberators operating from nearby Dunkeswell under the command of Fleet Air Wing Seven, US Navy, outbound on their anti-submarine missions in the south-western approaches and the Bay of Biscay. Dunkeswell was the only American Navy air base commissioned on UK soil during WWII.

The 3rd January 1945 brought with it warm sector conditions over south-west England during gathering darkness; consequently Dunkeswell, being 850 ft above AMSL, was below minima, so three returning Liberators were diverted to Exeter. Unfortunately number two, 38497, extended its downwind leg too far and, on turning base leg, struck the ground 50 feet below the top of Fire Beacon Hill just west of Sidmouth and slid 175 yards before coming to rest with tragic results: five of the crew on board suffered fatal burns injuries and four were in severe shock. The scene next day was still of carnage, with just the rear end of the Liberator undamaged: the smell of burning was still prevalent and there was wreckage everywhere.

For several years afterwards ammunition could still be found in the undergrowth, whilst after another 30 years a local farmer selling cider surprised the writer by showing him a pilot's seat in use in the barn as a resting place for local workers! After a certain amount of pleading, the owner reluctantly exchanged this seat for a new chair from our furniture store, and the pilot's seat now resides in its rightful place at the Dunkeswell Memorial Museum. As a postscript, the farmer never failed to remind me when I returned for more cider in later years that they much preferred the old Liberator seat to my new chair from the shop!

We cycled the 17 miles to Dunkeswell more than 15 times to view the activity at the base from the best advantage point near whichever runway was in use on the day. Our efforts were often rewarded by being able to observe regular movements around the airfield, which on one occasion included a detachment of amphibious Catalinas recently arrived from North Africa and looking rather ungainly out of their natural habitat. Lockheed 12A 33615 would arrive and depart about its daily business, and amazingly this aircraft, which had been used by Sidney Cotton earlier during the war on aerial photography missions, became G-AGTL postwar and still exists in France as F-AZLL. Another surprise was a bright yellow Naval Aircraft Factory N3N-3 Canary, reputed to be the Base Commander's pride and joy!

But above all was the chance to see the Liberators close up for the first time in our lives. As youngsters the Americans took us under their care in no uncertain manner and provided us with ice cream of all flavours, as well as early editions of *Batman* and *Superman* comics which I'm sure would be very collectable today.

A day's logging in March 1945 would include Liberator, Corsair, Norseman, Spitfire, Hurricane, Master, Dakota, Typhoon, Walrus, Lightning, Fortress, plus such rare types as Henley, Hotspur, Hamilcar, Welkin, and even a Curtis Owl.

Despite the imminent end to WWII in Europe being within sight, the spotting possibilities continued unabated. A short-lived society named The Sky Observers' Association of Great Britain was formed, which I thought fit to join, and my father, noting my enthusiasm, purchased for me a pair of 6 x 30 prismatic binoculars from Gamages' mail order in London which duly enabled me to win first prize from the above association for logging more types in a single day than any other member! I still treasure the two volumes of *Aircraft of the United States* by R.A. Saville Sneath, which was the prize awarded.

At the termination of hostilities in Europe, Dunkeswell was handed back to the RAF, with Fleet Air Wing Seven having the distinction of sinking five U-Boats and being credited with the partial destruction of a further five. History was also made when B-24 32282/'M' took the surrender of U-249 on 9th May 1945 after it hoisted a black flag. By the end of May 69 Liberators were awaiting repatriation to the USA, but of these 34 were broken up on site as being war-weary, including two that had destroyed U-Boats. The remainder were ferried back to NAS Clinton, Oklahoma in July. Unfortunately 38948 caught fire while being refuelled on 18th July and was struck off charge the next day, although the fuselage could still be seen by the writer as late as October 1946.

Having reached the age of 15, my school pals and I decided to join the local No.1064 Air Training Corps Squadron, in which we enjoyed our baptism of the air from Exeter Airport in DH.89A Dominie NR671 (later in life to become G-AJHP of Brooklands Aviation). A second flight of longer duration that year was with the RAF No.16 Ferry Unit, based at Dunkeswell, in Avro Anson NK168. My reward for the privilege of sitting next to the pilot was the legendary chore of winding up the undercarriage after take-off, a mere 169 turns of the handle, I recall! Another member of our squadron made himself thoroughly unpopular with the ground staff by inadvertently opening his parachute whilst trying to enter the aircraft!

A sure sign that the postwar era of civil aviation had arrived was when a Boeing 314A (believed to be G-AGCA), escorted by a trio of Curtis Seagull floatplanes, visited the airfield, the vision of which is still imprinted in my memory. On 21st February 1946 a PanAm Constellation was observed overflying Lyme Bay; this was possibly en route to Hurn from La Guardia, New York via Gander, a service which the airline had inaugurated on the 3rd of that month.

On 24th March 1946 Oxford AB754 crashed into the side of the Muttersmoor escarpment just west of Sidmouth in very low cloud and mist; the two occupants fortunately survived the incident after a very cold and damp night. The control column from the Oxford, which I retained in my possession until recently, has now been passed on to Joseph Thomas at the Branscombe private airstrip for a planned new museum there.

During August 1946, 1064 Squadron ATC attended a week's summer camp at RAF Locking, Weston Super Mare. Most of us cadets had never been away from home before, so this event was viewed with great excitement. We were not to be disappointed for, apart from various lectures, airborne experience was gained in either Dominie X7370 or Anson N4948. This Anson always seemed to follow us wherever we went on later airfield visits, and we longed to ride in a different one! The icing on the cake from a spotting point of view was a visit to the Air Electronics School, where a compound of aircraft in various stages of disrepair were to be seen. These were Barracuda BV706 (badly burned), Lancaster 1 PD418 (minus wings, and later 5736M), Meteor 3 EE228 'XL-P' of 616 Sqdn., Spitfires W3707, 5544M and 5932M, Avenger FN911, Corsair JT207, Catalina 3435M (nose section only), Blenheim 3980M (in a poor state), Halifax 3677M, Beaufighter 5340M/'KZ-R', Oxford 5353M/'VG-A', Sea Hurricane 5373M (ex-NF686 of 800 Sqdn.), Hurricanes FB.2C 5367M (LF765), 5368M (LF656) and 5370M (LF718), Martinets 5775M, 5882M, 5636M and 5367M, Typhoons 5641M, 5643M and 5648M. Back on the airfield the resident aircraft appeared to be Avro Tutor K3125 (all yellow and later to become G-AHSA), Cessna Airmaster G-AFBY, DH.87B Hornet Moth G-AFDT, Percival Q.6 G-AHTA, DH.89A Rapides G-AERN and G-AGUU, plus a pair of unmarked Supermarine Walruses.

Evenings drew many of us to the famous Weston Pier for our leisure, mainly chatting up the local talent! Come the weekend and most left for home with fond memories of Weston and a few heavy hearts of enduring puppy love!

With 1947 came a marked increase in civilian air traffic in the skies of East Devon, mainly in the form of manufacturers' test aircraft. The ill-fated Avro Tudor was no exception, as Tudor 2 G-AGSU passed over Sidmouth on January 17th, only to crash on take-off at Woodford on the 23rd August, a short life of seven months! Tudors Mk.1 G-AGRD and G-AGRE were similarly logged in March and February respectively, the latter lost somewhere over the Atlantic near Bermuda on 17th January 1949. A real treat came in the form of Lancastrian CF-CMV, while Bristol 170 Wayfarer LV-XIP flew south on delivery to the Argentine on 1st April where it soon became LV-AEX. On the lighter side, Avro Club Cadet G-ACHP was seen on numerous occasions. The 8th April was a unique day, when a Curtiss Helldiver was seen which, according to the Sidmouth Royal Observer Corps Post W/4, was a type never before logged over the area!

A short family holiday later in April to my sister's new home in Reading provided an ideal opportunity for me to catch the local bus service to Woodley aerodrome, home to Miles Aircraft, where access was no problem and we were free to wander at will around the airfield. Parked out were no less than eight Miles Monitors awaiting an uncertain future, including NP410, NP412, NP424, and NP425, Martinet Trainer JN275 with an enlarged rear cockpit, the second prototype Marathon G-AILH, Gemini VH-GGG, and an all-blue Aerovan with no signs of a registration. The Nighthawk G-AGWT was giving joyrides with Hugh Kennedy at the controls, and so I spent my hard-earned 7/6d pocket money for a most enjoyable 15-minute flight around the area.

June 11th saw a nationwide tour from Marham by nine B-29 Superfortresses of the USAF, and what a grand sight they made in perfect summer skies! For the record they were 42-7308, 42-84124, 44-84094, 44-8100, 44-89096, 44-86257, 44-86298, 44-89098 and 44-86246. Group marking on the fuselage side in each case was 'BE-' followed by the last three numerals of the serial numbers (details courtesy of *The Aeroplane Spotter*).

August 1947 saw 1064 ATC squadron off to another week's camp, this time to 20 MU, Aston Down, which held hundreds of aircraft in storage for further use — or, sadly, for the breaker's yard as many Oxfords were already in the process of being destroyed. In total I counted approximately 90 Lancasters, 8 Mustangs, a hangar full of Austers (reputed to be for sale on the civilian market), and 63 Tempests in the EJ, MW & SN serial ranges; among them was MW763/'HF-L', later exported to India as HA586, but this is currently back in the UK under restoration as G-TEMT! Fortress 2 HB778 was noted visiting from Holland on one occasion. Flying experience was available in abundance and I managed to get airborne in Oxfords HM978, RR327 and Harvard KF974, although the real 'jewel in the crown' was a 75-minute flight in Lancaster NX785 (code '9X') on an air test. After take-off I was invited to visit the bomb-aimer's position in the nose where, while lying prone, you can imagine my delight when a Spitfire joined us underneath in formation for several minutes over the Bristol Channel! I can still visualise that scene after all these years. Port and starboard engines were then feathered in turn, after which a touch-and-go landing was made at Kemble between rows of Lancasters awaiting their fate and lining each side of the runway; we finally returned to Aston Down feeling very elated after such a rare experience. Before we left, Mosquito KB436 made a crash landing reputed to be for a film of some nature.

Apart from the discovery of the Bertram Arden collection of vintage aircraft near Exeter earlier in the year (well tabulated by me in *Tail Ends of The Fifties*), an example of the prognosis for many trainee pilots arrived at Exeter airport on 19th October 1947; this was in the form of Chipmunk G-AKCS of Loxham's Flying Services from Squires Gate (Blackpool), which was on a demonstration tour of the UK and caused much interest and excitement at the time, being one of the first to be seen in the UK.

I cannot conclude my recollections of 1947 without mentioning the surprising sight of no less than eight Blackburn Firebrands on 15th December, in two flights of four tracking south-west around the south Devon coastline, all with EK7?? serials. Possibly they had disembarked for a spot of Christmas leave from one of HM carriers in the Channel? Finally Tudor 2 G-AGRX was logged on 28th December.

I can best open January 1948 with the following log extracts:

5th January: Brigand RH754 armed with rocket projectiles over the Lyme Bay Ranges.

16th January: Firefly PP657 and PP617 on delivery to Culdrose for 792 Sqdn.

22nd January: Tudor 1 G-AGRI, on test out of Boscombe Down, also Sea Otter RD894 circling Sidmouth.

27th January: Hoverfly KL104/'P9-T'.

28th January: Wellington RP646, and Dominie ambulance with red cross aft of roundel.

9th February: Seafire coded '101VL' with outsize code letters, circling the area.

On 15th February I was at Exeter airport to witness the first flight of Super Ace G-AKFD at the hands of Rex Stedman, Chrislea Aircraft test pilot; we had already seen the first Ace G-AHLG powered by a Lycoming engine on test in the local sky, but with the new Gipsy Major engine G-AKFD took on a very much smarter profile. In those days at Exeter one could walk across to the active runway for a close up photograph!

17th February: Halifax B.VI PP214/'TC-AB'.

18th February: Firefly Z1899.

26th February: Theseus Lincoln RA716/'G' on test from Filton — where it had been flown for the first time by Bill Pegg on the 17th.

29th February: Martinet NR300 was seen in the hangar at Exeter where it later became a 'hangar queen'.

8th March: Sea Otter JN201 circling coded '701/VL'.

10th February: Hoverfly KK987 — flew sideways down the Sid Valley!

12th February: Halifax A.XI RT924 and Brigand RH742.

Another family holiday in Reading found me at Woodley aerodrome on 25th March and what a transformation at Miles Aircraft since my last visit! Gemini production was in full swing, and among the two dozen completed specimens logged were EI-ACW, EI-ADM, OO-NAV and F-BDAF, F-BDAG, F-BDAH and F-BDAI, the latter awaiting delivery to Air Madagascar. These were to have been G-AKHL to 'KHO, but the British registrations were not used and the aircraft were never to be seen again in the UK. One hangar contained Hawk Majors G-ADMW and G-ADWT with, in the corner, the one-off M.68 G-AJJM which was in the process of being dismantled. Outside, the Merchantman U-21 was awaiting a similar fate. Martinets DL429, MS796 and RG906 also looked the worse for wear and were for eventual disposal, I was told. A sorry-looking fuselage outside of Junkers Ju.52/3M D-AUAV was the headquarters of the Reading Sky Observers' Association club run by one John S. Webb and used for local meetings. I did not have the privilege to come across John or any of his members, but the Ju.52 was open for inspection and surrounded by some amazing abandoned aircraft which would certainly do proud in a museum today; they were Miles M.20 AX834, Miles M.18 U-6, Miles M.64 U-11, Miles Libellula U-4, the remains of Britain's hope for supersonic flight, the M.52, a V-1 flying bomb and various other bits and pieces! Also seen near the factory were Sparrowhawk G-AGDL, M.18 G-AHOA, Falcon G-AECC, M.28 HB-EED, Messenger HB-EEC, and Ryan Navion NC 91607, the latter looking very smart and representing future aircraft design.

A return visit on the 28th found the remains of three discarded Aerovans, G-AISG, G-AISJ and G-AJOB, all written off in earlier crashes, but fortunately this had not been the fate of a beautiful cream and red Master, G-AHOB. A Messenger, G-AILI (fitted with a Praga 'E' engine) was noted, Miles M.18 U-0222 had been broken up, but best of all, the Miles Gillette Falcon L7905 was present, albeit with the engine removed. It was good to see both Marathon prototypes G-AGPD and G-AILH; the former survived only two months more as it crashed not far from Thruxton on 28th May while *en route* to Boscombe Down for evaluation; the tailplane separated, with tragic results for the two on board.

A visit to nearby White Waltham the following day produced a beautifully-coloured Cierva C.30A, G-AIOC, no less than seven Fairchild Arguses, G-AJAT, G-AJDO, G-AJPI, G-AJSO, G-AJSR, G-AJSM, and G-AJXA, Moth Minors G-AFOB, G-AFPD and G-AFPR, US Embassy Flying Club Piper Cub NC79800, Consul G-AIOY of Solar Air Services and J/4A Cub G-AFWS: those sure were the days for unrestricted spotting!

The year 1948 saw tensions rising between East and West, followed by the commencement of the Iron Curtain regime followed by the blockade of Berlin. This, in turn, found the Royal Observer Corps re-activated in a postwar role, which seemed an ideal opportunity for me to join my local Post W/4 in Sidmouth, affiliated to No.10 Group Headquarters in Exeter. Weekly meetings were held, incorporating aircraft recognition, of course, and also the art of height estimation of overflying aircraft with the aid of a Mickelswaite height projector mounted on a plotting table. This was often used in conjunction with the RAF for live exercises at the Post, which was situated to the west side of the valley atop Peak Hill and affording (on clear days) resplendent views to Portland Bill in the east and Start Point to the west. On 26th April four Sea Hornets and no less than 16 Seafires passed over in close formation, a sight we can only dream about in this day and age!

Meanwhile the first week of September saw 1064 ATC Squadron back at 20 MU Aston Down for another week's camp. This time 15 Lincolns had moved in to join the 34 Lancasters previously noted, and Tempests were in abundance — including the Mk.6 in the NX and SN serial ranges — all in superb order. More heavy metal was in the shape of three Lancastrian C.Mk.2s, VL970, VM730, and VM731; they were reputed to be converted for civilian use, but this does not seem to have ever happened. At the other end of the scale Auster AOP.7 VW999 flew in from Rearsby for the Holding Unit, whilst another hangar contained five less fortunate brothers lying positively sick after previous accidents: these were MT144, TJ707, TW562/'PF-L', TW563 and TW573/'PF-K'. Recent arrivals from the jet age were Vampires TG330, VF278 and VV187.

The Ferry Pool was kept busy each day with its five Ansons delivering their cargo of ferry pilots to various locations around the UK. Most of the cadets hitched rides if a seat was available and my most memorable trip was to Luton, Waterbeach, Biggin Hill and Wroughton. At Luton during the lunch stopover there was even a twin-tailed Prentice VN864 in evidence — experimental, thank heaven! Back at base Oxfords V3631, X7241, AB658, BG543, BG843 and PH183 were awaiting an uncertain future in the scrap compound.

The next venue on the 1948 agenda was the SBAC display at Farnborough, my first of many visits. This has been well tabulated in the popular aviation press, so I will only say that the portrayal of what British industry could produce in those days left a vivid impression on one's mind of the likely future developments in aviation. This also gave the opportunity to visit London Airport (as it was known in those days), which at the time of our visit was dominated by Constellations, Yorks, Lancastrians of BSAA, Tudors G-AGRG, G-AGRH, G-AGRJ and a Mk.4 G-AHNN, and a couple of Languedocs of Air France (F-BATZ and F-BCUI); while just as we were leaving, York LV-AFZ of FAMA landed.

Close on the heels of these activities came an invitation to RAF Thorney Island for a week's camp with the Royal Observer Corps. It was a glorious summer that year, which made sleeping under canvas that much more enjoyable, plus the fact that civilian cooks dominated the mess hall, to our utmost delight! Apart from the usual lectures, no air experience was given, but by contrast, we were taken to sea by the resident Air Sea Rescue unit and given the chance to observe the part they played in survival at sea. The resident Squadrons at this time operated a mixture of Meteor Mk.3s and 4s, while Anson TX239 made a wheels-up landing in front of us! Visitors included Barracuda RJ948, Sea Hornet TT198, Hoverfly KK985, Firebrand EK744, Spitfire TE328/'6D-Z' and Lincoln RF447/'WP-P', to name a few. As it was Battle of Britain week there was a flying display, with a promised highlight to be the very first public appearance in Europe of a flypast by USAF Lockheed Shooting Stars. At the prescribed time all eyes turned skyward, only to see after what seemed an eternity six silver shapes to the east heading north which would have been more benefit to the residents of Bognor Regis than ourselves; 'nuff said!

Back at Exeter airport, Chrislea Super Aces were coming off the production line slowly but surely; I was fortunate to log VP-YGI, VP-YGM and VH-BRO before they were dispatched overseas, and also to see the elusive G-AKUZ.

The final highlight for 1948 was a private visit with the ROC to A&EE at Boscombe Down, normally out of bounds to the general public. Here we saw early Sea Hornets and Vampires on test, Fairey Primer G-6-5 competing against Chipmunks G-AJVG and G-AKDN for the lucrative RAF training order, Tudor G-AGRI, Yorks MW304 & MW313, Brigands RH753 & RH763, Firebrands EK732 & EK742, Lincolns RE232 & RF354, Hastings TE580, all-silver Tempest PR550, Sea Furies TF902 & TF958, Harvard FX402, Seafires PS952 & PS954, Prentices VR190 & VR 191, Viking VL226 (ex-G-AIJE), Valettas VL249 & VW214, Firefly PP604 (with 'JB' on fin), PP605, PP482, TW722 & VT393, Oxfords HN379 & NM331, Avro XIX G-AKUD (the former VM373), Mosquito NF.38 VT854 and TT.39s PF489 & PF606, plus several Meteor 4s also under evaluation: a great day out on a bleak November day!

Spotting activities over Sidmouth continued unabated into the New Year of 1949. The log of the first quarter has recorded sightings of:

17th January: Anson NK614/'605' Royal Navy.

27th January: Hoverfly KL100.

31st January: Solent G-AHIO, circling the area very majestically. February 16th saw Dakota LN-PAS en route to Culdrose with urgent spares for a Norwegian vessel stranded in Falmouth harbour, and again on the 21st.

Come 3rd March Constellation F-BAZL was a welcome sighting, whilst Expeditor KP127 on the 11th, and Sea Fury FB.11 VW 701 (in primer, presumably on maker's test), was interesting.

In late May another ROC visit to Boscombe Down was arranged, to the delight of every member! This time we were rewarded with the sight of one of the very few Lincolnian conversions, RF561. This drew much comment from members as very little had been published about these, with only a handful having been converted for the Argentine Air Force and as meat freighters for Paraguay, I believe. Ercoupe VX147 was resplendent in natural metal finish and, although no longer in existence, is emulated to this very day by G-AVIL. Wyvern TS387 was a pre-production prototype used as a handling trials aircraft, the first time many of us had seen one at close quarters, and consequently we were surprised at the sheer size of the machine. Others of note were the Sturgeon 2 VR363, Auster A/245 VL522, the all-black Brigand VS818, Sea Meteor EE387 with arrester hook, Sea Fury Trainer prototype VX818 and Prestwick Pioneer G-31-1, to name just a few.

Days later a plain brown envelope dropped through the letterbox marked OHMS (On His Majesty's Service) duly informing yours truly that I was due for 18 months' National Service and that I should proceed for a medical and fitness test in Exeter, to be followed by a selection process. Having come through the medical as 'Fit A1', I was then back in Exeter a few days later in some obscure room in the Museum for the briefing and selection process. This, to my surprise, was conducted by an Army reserve officer, who, after the customary pep talk regarding our forthcoming contribution to the nation's well-being, promptly declared that those persons sitting on his right-hand side of the class would automatically be selected for the RAF, while those of us on the left side would be drafted into the Army! I immediately stood up and suggested out loud that I had not served in the ATC to be press-ganged into the Army of all things. This outburst naturally caused a great deal of discord amongst ourselves and in the end it was decided that, if I could pass the regular RAF recruiting test at the RAF enrolment centre just across the street, then it would count as a pass to join the RAF for the duration of my National Service! So there I proceeded post haste, took an aptitude test involving shapes and patterns, was tested for colour-blindness, and then it gave me the greatest pleasure to report back to this disgruntled officer to say that I had passed!

During the closing days of April 1949 came the inevitable official call-up papers, together with railway warrant, to report to RAF Padgate in Lancashire, the RAF reception centre for National Service recruits. After a formal and friendly welcome by the Duty Officer of the day my fellow recruits and I were issued with a 1250 identity card, service number (which I still remember today — 3120503) and an ATC intake number; we were then given a service haircut, uniform, and numerous cleaning accessories including a 'housewife' kit — which, after much speculation, turned out to be just a needle & cotton set for running repairs! Then everyone had to stand in line for a vaccination jab against smallpox, with dire warnings from the Flight Sergeant in charge if anyone should faint! We were then confined to camp for seven days, in which time all kit had to be marked with our service number and our boots polished to perfection, especially toecaps to eradicate the 'orange peel' effect; the trick here was to use a hot iron, according to the 'know-alls' in the billet, but it seemed to work . . .

My notes at this time record a solitary Lancaster III PB480 (later 6710M) parked on the parade ground, and Spitfires 5378M and 6062M (coded 'FJ-Y') at the main gate. After a week's confinement we were allocated to recruit training centres, either at Bridgnorth, Wilmslow, Hednesford, or West Kirby on the Wirral (my allocation), whilst others stayed on in Padgate.

As we were gathered together on Lime Street Station in Liverpool, the Tannoy system announced: "Will all passengers for West Kirby board the train now arriving at platform two."

"You're not passengers, you're sheep!" proclaimed out loud our escorting discipline corporal, much to the amusement of the locals present; just how small can one feel in such a situation?

The long march from West Kirby was just as demoralising in the rain, especially when the parade ground came into view with bods marching to perfection like Guardsmen at the Palace; would we ever make out like those intakes, we wondered? Eventually we reached our billets, which were devoid of beds, the metal frames being outside in the rain waiting to be cleaned up by the new temporary inmates.

So much has been written over the years regarding the experiences of National Servicemen at these training camps that I intend to be fairly brief on the subject, as the emphasis of this chapter is of course about interesting aircraft of the period. There can be no doubt that the discipline was tough, but we all came through much fitter and better for the experience.

Many of us had occasional food parcels sent from home, as the food at times left much to be desired. One day it came to my notice that one such parcel was awaiting my collection at the station Post Office situated opposite the Guard Room. Coming straight off the parade ground to collect my goodies, a voice bellowed: "Airman!" I hesitated and then looked in the direction of the Guard Room.

"Yes, you airman, come into the Guard Room".

What could be wrong?

"Fancy walking about the camp dressed like a nudist!" retorted the Sergeant-in-Charge! It appears that the top button on my denims was undone on this sweltering hot day, so I was duly told to get a haircut and bring the hair back in a paper bag. Then second thoughts prevailed: "never mind the paper bag, just report back!" Oh dear!

I did manage to travel over to Speke, now John Lennon Airport, at Liverpool one Saturday afternoon. Here Dakotas of BEA and Aer Lingus were very prevalent, including G-AGHL, G-AGIW, G-AJIA & G-AJIB of the former and, from across the Irish sea, EI-ACK, EI-AFC, EI-ACD and EI-ACI. Other visiting aircraft included Anson G-AIRN of Starways and VV297 (RAF), Proctors G-AHES and G-ALFB, Tiger Moth G-AHNC and a couple of RN Harvards, EZ316 and EZ402, both coded 'JB'.

Squires Gate Airport at Blackpool was also on my list, and this I was able to visit a fortnight later. Inmates included a rare Argus 3 HB722 with Ranger engine (later G-AKPX and OH-FCA), Cessna Airmaster G-AEAI, Short Scion G-AEZF, Tipsy Trainer 1 G-AFRV, DH.60G-III Moth Major G-ADHE and Viking VL246 of the King's Flight. There were also 12 Proctors in various stages of conversion for use on the civilian market, although these included one unfortunate specimen, NP357, being reduced to spares. To complete the picture there were 14 Autocrats, eight Rapides (plus Dominies HG721/'TWY-D' and RL949), Hawk Major G-ADCF and Dakota G-AGZF of Scottish Airways.

Back at West Kirby our passing-out parade was a hectic rushed affair as far as I can remember, because our entire intake was urgently required down south to be based under canvas at RAF Hornchurch. We were to be employed at London Docks to unload various vessels because of an unofficial dock strike which had been unresolved for some time, so once there we set about our new mission as a matter of urgency. One afternoon it was my turn (with another bod) to collect the slops from outside each tent and load them on to an open-sided truck, which when full was driven to the sewage farm on the field. Sitting atop the cab I was horrified to note that our driver had not given way to an approaching Slingsby T.21 (WB919) at the active runway. Ever closer, and feeling for our lives in no uncertain manner, my colleague and I abandoned the truck in haste, taking a few buckets of swill to the ground in the bargain. It was horrific, and nothing short of a miracle that we were not hit! The subsequent court of enquiry found the driver negligent in the extreme, and I think that he was sent to Colchester military prison for his actions.

My choice of trade for my 18 months was fabric worker, as I had learnt the trade in the upholstery business. It was just my luck that the RAF was in the process just then of phasing out fabric-covered aircraft, and so my services in this field were no longer required: to cut a long story short I was posted to No.2 MRU at Colaton Cross near Plymouth, which the local bus driver always referred to as "Butlins" at the camp bus stop; in reality it was a Medical Rehabilitation Unit, where aircrew who had been involved in a crash came to recover, along with numerous other sick personnel.

In contrast to the training camps the atmosphere could not have been more relaxed: boat trips were arranged on the nearby River Yealm for patients on the road to recovery and golf at nearby Bigbury-on-Sea for the fittest! Even the corporal in charge of my billet was an aircraft enthusiast, one Donald Gilpin, who later became a founder member of Air-Britain in 1948. We enjoyed many good times together spotting at Plymouth (Roborough) and the surrounding area. I secured a job at station HQ with my own little office, printing out the Station Orders on a Gestetner printing machine (oh, that messy ink!): computers were but a pipe dream in those far off days! I then had to distribute the Orders to each section of the camp. Weekend passes were valid from 1200 hrs Fridays until 0800 hrs on Mondays, and one could hitchhike in uniform up the A38 to Exeter and thence on to Sidmouth with no problems whatsoever. Oh Happy Days!

The Miles Sparrowhawk G-AGDL seen at Woodley on 25th March 1948.
Gemini G-AKHA is in the background. Photo: Noel Collier.

A line-up of Geminis for export to France seen at Woodley on 25th March
1948. Photo: Noel Collier.

Consul G-AJXE of the MCAFU at Croydon. Photo: John Havers.

Anson G-AGPB of theMCAFU at Croydon. Photo: Reg Havers.

CHAPTER 15

SOME SPOTTING MEMORIES OF THE LATE 1940S

by

JOHN HAVERS

With advancing years memories seem to play an increasing part in one's life, with some things being completely beyond recall while others seem to become embellished. Fortunately, where aviation is concerned, I do have my logs, notes and diary entries to remind me so that I can give an account of those far-off days when civil aviation was emerging from the dark days of war.

A diet of wartime military aircraft, and particularly the collection of code markings (because serial numbers were so hard to read), gave way in late 1945 to recording civil registrations, which in those days spread full-size across both lower mainplanes. One of the earliest I recorded was DDL FW.200 Condor OY-DEM on the 4th September over Essex *en route* for Northolt. My call up for military service in the same month resulted in my having very little opportunity for continuing the hobby, but by the spring of 1946 I was on the staff of a German POW camp at Staines in Middlesex, involved with the building of the King George VI reservoir. This was right on the fringes of London Airport at Heathrow and very soon I was enjoying the sight of Lancasters, Lancastrians and Yorks of British South American Airways (BSAA) and similar ones of BOAC. The ubiquitous Dakota was regularly seen, principally of Aer Lingus, BOAC and Railway Air Services, the latter from Northolt. Lighter aircraft included Auster variants, Aerovan G-AGOZ, Rapides and Proctors, which seemed to follow the A30 to and from the London area.

One of my first duties entailed escorting POWs to Millbank Hospital in London, and the 6th of June proved to be a particularly lucky day for, while we were walking (marching!) along the Thames embankment, 286 military aircraft passed over us in 20 minutes. This was the final dress rehearsal for the Victory Day flypast, led by Hurricane LF363 flown by Douglas Bader. Following came 3 Sunderlands from Calshot, 3 Halifax C.VIIIs, 12 Lancaster VIIs from Graveley, and then came a massed formation of 72 Mosquitos in eight squadrons. Beaufighter TF.Xs from Thorney Island were next, followed by Firebrand TF.IVs from Ford, theN Firefly 1s from Lee-on-Solent, Seafires, Spitfires & Hornets from Horsham St. Faith, Tempest IIs from Chilbolton and Tempest Vs from Manston. The beginnings of the jet era were represented by six squadrons of Meteors from Bentwaters and Boxted with one squadron of Vampires bringing up the rear, a sight unlikely to be repeated.

The *Aeroplane Spotter* (of fond memory) for 29th June 1946 mentioned an open day at RAE, Farnborough on the following Sunday and so it was out on the road to hitch-hike my way there. This was to be my first major airshow apart from prewar Empire Air Days at Debden, which in no way prepared me for what was to be a most interesting day. Here were displayed some 48 of the latest products of the UK industry which I was able to inspect at very close quarters — along with an estimated 25,000 other visitors. At the time, I recorded arriving to see the Avro XIX G-AGNI taking off and making a number of low passes, which was the pattern for most of those that followed. After walking around the static aircraft it was noticed that Tudor II G-AGSU was moving to the end of the runway, and it eventually took off after the crowd were moved away with some difficulty — no Health and Safety then!

Tudor I G-AGRC soon joined it for a spirited display at low level. By contrast the tiny BA Swallow G-AFGC landed and parked, but soon there was a call over the Tannoy for the pilot, as his aircraft was in danger of being broken up by the crowd! Next came other Avro products in the shape of BOAC York G-AGNL and Lincoln RE415.

Vickers-Armstrongs' blue Dragon Rapide G-AHKB was noted taking off from the far end of the runway and, once the larger aircraft had cleared the area, the Reid & Sigrist Desford Trainer G-AGOS showed what it could do. A RATOG-fitted Seafire XV SW813 demonstrated that, because of quite a strong wind, the aircraft required a run of only a few yards to get airborne; it seemed to shoot into the air like a shot from a gun! While this was happening the prototype Slingsby Kirby Kite II sailplane got airborne after being towed into the air by a Jeep, but when making a final turn before landing the port wingtip struck the ground and it collapsed in a heap, although the pilot, W/C Coton, Chief Test Pilot of the RAE, stepped out unhurt.

My first sight of a helicopter was of the Sikorsky Hoverfly Mk. 1, which spent much of the show in the air.

Jet fighters now appeared in the shape of Meteor IV EE522 and Vampire F.1 TG285, which were demonstrated as only they can be. Words could not properly convey the effect of hearing at close proximity the hollow sort of noise of the Meteor and the swishing scream of the Vampire, the latter so ably flown by Geoffrey de Havilland. His demonstration started as he opened the throttle; he became airborne just about where the runway began and almost at once started a steep turn, then proceeding to work up speed at 50 feet around the perimeter of the aerodrome. After two circuits he had sufficient speed to swing up into a couple of upward rolls, and then he turned downwind, passing over the crowd at a very low level.

Maurice Hartford then flew the Hastings C.1 TE580, providing a respite from the terrific speed of the jets before Jan Zurakowski gave an outstanding display in the Martin-Baker MB.5 R2496. Viking G-AGOM then demonstrated flying on one engine. To bring the flying display to an end, along came Seafang FR.32 VB895 and Firefly F.IV TW687 followed by the slower-speed Proctor 5 G-AGTC.

In the static display were noted some civil aircraft, Autocrat G-AHHD, Consul G-AHJZ, Dove G-AGPJ & Miles M18 G-AHKY. Military hardware consisted of: Auster AOP.VI TW562, Beaufighter TF.X NT913, Firebrand TF.IV EK746, Fury F.I LA610, Hamilcar I RR944, Horsa II RZ246, Lancasters B.II RE415 & III LL780/G, Martinet TT.I NR598, the Meteor F.IV EE444 *"Britannia,"* Mosquitos FB.VI NT720 & NF.36 RL263, Prentice T.I TV163, Queen Martinet I PW979, Sea Otter ASR.2 RD922, Spearfish TD.I RA356, Spitfire F.24 VN318, Seafire XVII SX314, Sea Fury FX SR666, Sturgeon I RK787, Tempest F.I NX147 and York C.I MW313. A truly memorable day!

Back at Staines overflights continued with the occasional new sighting, but it was not until my trusty bicycle arrived from home that a visit was made to London Airport on the 3rd August, the first of many. By the standards of today the number of aircraft seen was quite insignificant, but I was in time to see the BSSA Lancastrian G-AGLW arrived from Lisbon on 3 engines carrying Lt. Col. G.O. Simson, the British Military Attaché, who was seriously ill. After take-off from Lisbon the port outer was losing oil and so Capt. J.B. Linton shut down the engine; normally he would have turned back but due to the sick passenger he decided to continue. Among other Lancastrians, Yorks and Dakotas were DC-4s NC90426 and NC90905 *Flagship Boston* of American Overseas Airlines.

Visits to Heathrow on the 17th & 18th August revealed, among others, Lancasters G-AHJT & 'HJU, CF-CAN of TCA, York ZS-ATP *Springbok* and 'ATR *Impala* of SAA, MW175 leased to BSAA for crew training and Halifax G-AHZN *Port of London* of London Aero & Motor Service (LAMS).

A cycle tour on the 24th August took in the West London airfields of Hanworth, Heston (both no longer with us), Northolt and Heathrow. At Hanworth were noted Sidney Cotton's Lockheed 12A G-AGTL *Caprice*, BA Swallow G-AELG, Bond Air Service's Autocrat G-AGYG and Proctor G-AHMS. Seen in poor condition was the VEFJ.12 YL-ABS, while in the General Aircraft works area were a Hamilcar II glider and the powered version designated Mk.X.

Heston also produced a BA Swallow, this time G-AEOW, and Prince Bernhard of Netherlands' Siebel 204 PH-NAV, while away in the distance was a Black Widow, a Firefly and a Meteor. Northolt, being the main base of BEA, had a good crop of Dakotas and Vikings plus ABA DC-4 SE-BBF *Vastan*, as well as Railway Air Services' Avro 19s G-AHIC and G-AHII.

The last call, at Heathrow, produced the usual Dakotas, Lancasters, Yorks and Liberator AM920 (later G-AHYB) used by BOAC on the London/Prestwick/Montreal mail service.

The autumn of 1946 brought my first sightings of Bristol 170 G-AHJF of British-American Air Services, DC-4 EC-DAP of Iberia, Constellations G-AHEN of BOAC and NC88857 *Clipper Flying Mist* of PanAm. Aerovan OO-HOM overflew on 30th September, the day after its C. of A. was issued at Woodley and likely on delivery, for it was lost on 6th October in a forced landing in Denmark while *en route* Hamburg-Oslo with a cargo of grapes. On the 15th October I saw York LV-XGP of FAMA on delivery, and similarly at the end of the month Viking VT-AZB of Indian National Airways. Skyways Lancastrians G-AHBZ *Sky Ambassador* and G-AHCA were a feature of November, along with Ju.52/3M G-AHOG of BEA and Constellation PP-PCG of Panair do Brazil. With December and its shorter days came first sightings of a number of Air France Dakotas.

A move in January 1947 to the unit HQ at Woodmansterne in Surrey brought me into one of the coldest and longest periods of snow in living memory; a grave shortage of coal meant that living in a Nissen hut was not the most comfortable thing to do. In turn I was now within the orbit of Croydon but, with three months of very poor weather, sightings were few apart from the fact that most of my days were spent office-bound. The aircraft to be seen were mostly Ansons, Austers and Dragon Rapides, with an occasional Dakota and Ju.52/3M.

On returning to Staines in April to take charge of the nearby Laleham camp, I was in time to see Mosquito PR.34 RG238 leave Heathrow at 2005 hrs on the 30th; this was attempting to beat the multi-seat flight time to the Cape, the record having previously been gained by F/O. A.E Clouston and Mrs. Kirby Green in a DH.88 Comet during November 1937. This time it was the turn of S/Ldr H.B. Martin DSO, DFC and navigator S/Ldr. E.B. Sismore DSO, DFC, who completed the 6,717 miles in 21 hrs and 31 mins at an average speed of 312 mph, landing at Brooklyn Airport, Capetown after stops at El Adem and Kisumu. Much of the usual activity from London Airport continued with Dragon Rapide VP-UAW of the Uganda Company and F-BBYP, an AAC.1 of Aerocargo, on 3rd May.

Later in May meant a further move, this time to Chessington, Surrey with the opportunity to view both London Airport and Croydon traffic. The highlight was on 11th June when nine B-29 Superfortresses of 340th BS, USAF, based at Marham on a good will visit, flew towards Thames Ditton, their turning point for a flypast over London. A BBC commentator was on board one of the aircraft and so it was possible to listen to a broadcast as they passed overhead.

By late July I was back again at HQ behind a desk, which once again severely limited my spotting activities, but August was notable for two things, a first visit to Croydon Airport on 17 August and my first flight. Accompanied by my brother Reg and Army colleague Bert Gutmann we took a flight in Proctor 4 G-AJTP of Newman Airways (operated by Island Air Services) for a classic 10/- (50p) trip around the circuit. These were the days of numerous charter companies with Ansons, Consuls, Proctors and Rapides, when KLM were still flying into the airport with Dakotas, plus such highlights as John Mahieu's Lockheed 14 OO-API, BOAC Lancastrian G-AGLT and CIE Air Transport's Goeland F-BCCB.

The move of HQ to Addington in October 1947 took me to the east of Croydon, but the airport was still a regular call where one was always sure of seeing something new. Came March 1948 and it was time for demobilisation; this took me back home to Essex and the opportunity to observe activities at the embryo Stansted Airport. Following use by the USAAF it had been taken over by London Aero & Motor Services (LAMS) in December 1946 as a base for their fleet of royal-blue-painted Halifax C.8 freighters, and as the cargo airport for London. Flights were made worldwide, but by the end of 1947 the company was in difficulties and so the spring 1948 saw little happening at Stansted. Some aircraft later operated using the name Stansted Airport Ltd. before taking up the name Skyflight Ltd. for a brief appearance on the Berlin Airlift. One Halifax C.8 seen on overhaul and later flying during April was ZS-BTA of Alpha Airways (the former G-AGZP), one-time personal aircraft of the Maharajah Gaekwar of Baroda: its usual feature was having the entrance door on the *starboard* side. Stansted was also home to Kearsley Airways, with their Dakotas G-AKAR, G-AKCZ, G-AKDT and Lockheed 14 G-AKPD.

The 3rd July saw me on a visit to Broxbourne, then the home of the Herts & Essex Aero Club, where the aircraft to be seen included their well-known fleet of Tiger Moths G-AIDR, 'IDS, 'IDT & 'IDV, Rapides G-AGZU & G-AKTY and W.T Franklin's Gemini G-AKHV. Tucked away in a hangar was the smart silver and green Hawk Trainer Mk.II G-AKNA, fitted with a Cirrus Major 3 engine which unfortunately made it ineligible for a C. of A.

A week later found me at Gatwick for the first postwar *Daily Express* Air Pageant; this featured such events as the Goodyear Duck NC5506M, Stinson Reliant NC2311 (demonstrating towline pick-up), Ranald Porteous' outstanding aerobatics in the Miles M.18 G-AHOA, Fulton Airphibian NC74104 (designed to be converted into a car in seven minutes), plus airliners (including Solent G-AHIU) and much military hardware.

It was around this time that we heard with regret that the *Aeroplane Spotter* was to cease publication, but the good news — as it subsequently turned out — was the formation of an organisation called Air-Britain. Without this I am sure many of us would not have got involved with recording aviation history as it was made over subsequent years.

For me it was time to move on; I decided that a career in civil aviation had an attraction, and so late September 1948 found me employed as an administration officer with the Ministry of Civil Aviation at Croydon. This was to run the office for Stanley Heath and his team of radio surveyors who were responsible for the annual inspection of radio equipment installed in UK-registered aircraft used for public transport purposes and based in southern England. My job was to locate were the aircraft was based and to arrange for a survey, which in turn brought me into contact with many of the colourful characters to be found, particularly in the charter companies of the day.

Apart from my day-to-day work it gave me the opportunity to observe at close quarters the interesting movements at Croydon. Field Aircraft Service completed engine overhauls at the airport, which brought in Dakotas for an engine change, while others routed through Croydon on their way for overhaul at Field's base at Tollerton. These were mainly from overseas operators, and among those to be seen were G-ALCA, G-ALCB and AP-ACF of Pak-Air (Karachi), SX-BAC, 'BAH and 'BAI of TAE, ZS-BTN of Mercury Aviation, ZS-AVD, 'AVL, 'AYB and 'BRX of Pan African Air Charter and ZS-BYH of Sudair International; each day brought something of interest.

A regular visitor was Lockheed 12A ZS-BAJ *St. George* of Mitchell Cotts, and during my time at Croydon I met Bill Mellor, the pilot who regularly flew the aircraft between the UK and South Africa; one day I was privileged to hear at first hand his story of how he delivered the DH.86B G-ADYH to Australia which, much later, he related in his book *Three Decades a Pilot*.

Just before Christmas 1948 I was taken by Stanley Heath on a familiarisation visit to Vickers at Brooklands and Wisley for my first opportunity to visit an aircraft factory. Here I was to see Vikings G-AJCD, 'JDK and 'JDL partly completed on the production line, as well as Valettas VW180, 181 & 182. Viking VP-TAV *Jamaica* (formally G-AGRS) was being prepared for BWIA and Warwick RP589 and Wellington RP488 were also noted. Moving on to Wisley, we found on the flight line Vikings G-AHOP, VP-YHT of Central African Airways and VL228, Viscount VX211 (G-AHRF) and Nene-Viking VX858 (G-AJPH), while a lone Tempest, NX151, was seen receiving an engine change following a force landing.

A final memory from my working days at Croydon: on the 8th March 1949, among the ex-RAF Ansons awaiting conversion, was G-ALFJ, which had arrived the previous November from RAF Kemble. On this typical March day, cloudy with some haze, preparation of the Anson for a flight to Blackpool Squires Gate (where it was to be overhauled for the issue of a C. of A.), began early in the afternoon, but some difficulty was experienced with starting the starboard engine.

A little before 1600 hours S/Ldr George Hinckley took the Anson off runway 122, but when at a height of only about 30 feet the port engine stopped, causing a swing to port. Knowing the aircraft was to leave I had been keeping an eye on progress, but then I saw it leave the ground and immediately disappear from sight to the left away from the runway centre-line. By the time I reached the front of the Terminal building the Anson was well and truly embedded in the roof of 'D' hangar, the tail falling back on to the roof of the workshops of both Standard Radio and the Dunlop Aviation Service. Wreckage penetrated the hangar roof and damaged Consul G-AIUS of Stewart Smith & Co. Ltd. and the Gemini G-AJWE of Scaffolding (GB) Ltd. which were parked below. Fortunately Hinckley survived the accident, although he suffered two broken legs.

By now my working days were swiftly coming to an end at Croydon, as the Radio Surveyors were being transferred from the Ministry of Civil Aviation to the Air Registration Board (ARB). Fortunately I too was able to secure a job with the ARB, but this meant working in London, where I began on 21st April 1949, a most rewarding career which was to last with them — and following their absorption into the CAA — until 1978. Very soon I was part of the approval process for maintenance schedules, which each UK operator of aircraft for public transport was required to have; this was later to bring me into contact with most of the independent operators of the day, and a very colourful lot they were too in every sense of the word!

July 1949 saw the staging of another *Daily Express* Air Pageant at Gatwick, which followed a similar pattern to that of the previous year. Highlights among the lighter aircraft included the diminutive Wee Bee NX90840 flown by Karl Montijo, which managed two circuits of the perimeter track. The scarlet and white Pitts Special *Little Stinker* NX86401 gave a display of aerobatics, as did the Patrouille L'Étampes flying four Stampe SV.4Cs. Capt G. Sonderman brilliantly demonstrated the Fokker S.2 Instructor PH-NBX and we also saw one of the early demonstrations by Ranald Porteous of Auster G-AJIZ with the Goodyear self-aligning undercarriage.

My first SBAC Show at Farnborough followed in September and on a Trade Day too, the first of many over successive years. These early years could be guaranteed to produce a host of new prototypes for each show, some having only flown for the first time in the preceding week. Looking at the list of participants for this 1949 show it is interesting to see that among them Avro 19 G-AHKX is still flying today, while examples of most still exist, albeit largely in museum collections.

The remainder of 1949 apart from my working day was quiet from the spotting point of view because I was due to be married to Betty in the November. But fortunately the quiet spell didn't last too long, and the trick there was to marry someone who had spent some of her working life in aviation! Since then we have had a tremendous life together following the many facets of the aviation scene.

CHAPTER 16

FROM SCHOOLBOY TO PILOT

by

REX NICHOLLS

My interest in aeroplanes dates from my earliest recollections, and by the beginning of WW2 I was well hooked. As early as the 4th September 1939 I was evacuated from Croydon (my home town) to Shoreham-by-Sea, Sussex; there could have been no finer 'posting' for me, for from living about two miles north of Croydon Airport, with all its commercial flying, I came to live just half a mile from Shoreham Airport — across just the width of the River Adur which formed the eastern boundary.

Whereas Croydon airport reverted to RAF use during the war and became a fighter station, Shoreham took over what was left — and was allowed — of civil aviation from Croydon, so I regularly saw the silver Ensigns, Albatrosses, HP.42s and DH.86s still flying in their civil marks. The airport buildings at Shoreham had been camouflaged, however, and a few dark streaks were to be seen on the grass manoeuvring areas, meant to represent hedgerows in an attempt to break up the appearance of an unusually large area.

There was much coming and going of small fry, notably DH Dragons, Dragon Rapides and Dragonflies, mostly crudely camouflaged but retaining a silver rectangle with the civil registration still visible. Three accidents occurred during the time I was at Shoreham. A British Airways Lockheed 14 landed wheels-up, Dragonfly G-AFTF failed to clear the western boundary on take-off, and an Airspeed Courier collapsed its undercarriage and slid into the embankment on the eastern boundary, bending its starboard wingtip. The Lockheed was dismantled and placed as deck cargo on a coaster sailing from Shoreham to Bristol, the Dragonfly was duly repaired, and I suspect the Courier also flew again.

Of the regular foreign visitors to Croydon, Air France, Sabena, KLM, DDL and ABA had to transfer their services to Shoreham, so I would regularly see Dewoitine 338s, SM.73s, DC-2s and 3s. One day, seated on the beach, I was momentarily alarmed to see a large four-engined monoplane not more than 300 feet above the sea coming straight for me. I soon recognised it as a Focke-Wulf FW.200, having seen one at Croydon in August 1939, but whether this was a Condor or the military version, the Kurier, was not immediately apparent. So I crouched close to one of the groynes in case it became aggressive, but all was well; it turned out to be one of DDL's two Condors, painted orange overall to denote its neutral status.

One day I saw one of Imperials Airways' Ensigns take off. It chose the rather short runway 33 for this and laboriously climbed out close to Lancing College and on over the downs with not much height to spare. I was able to watch it for quite some time and when I last saw it the huge wheels of the undercarriage had risen only about a third of the way into the inboard engine nacelles.

RAF presence at Shoreham was limited but I saw a Whitley there one day. Of greater interest were the four occasions I saw formations of Fairey Battles, each of about 12 aircraft. These would arrive about mid-morning, presumably refuel crews and aircraft and then set off southbound over the sea. I believe them to have been reinforcements for Battle squadrons already operating in France. More exciting was the similar activity of a dozen Lysanders. When they took off they climbed in a turn to the left and formed into a line astern formation stepped down to the rear — a magnificent sight.

Early in September 1939 three Blenheim IVs were parked to the east of the terminal building. They were in standard RAF green and brown camouflage but wore no roundels; instead they had civil registration letters in the batch G-AFXD to G-AFXO and were bound for the Greek Air Force. These were the first Blenheims I ever saw, but soon after a Mark 1F overflew displaying the half white, half black undersides that were soon to be superseded on fighter types.

I also had my first sighting of four RAF types all in one go. This comprised a line-astern formation with, in the lead, a Bristol Bombay in silver overall finish, followed by a Wellington I (i.e. no nose or tail turrets); then came a Defiant in prototype silver finish and black anti-glare panel on the engine cowling, and last was a Hawker Henley in silver finish with broad black diagonal stripes overall. The formation approached from the north at about 3,000 feet and turned left to fly away to the north-east. This was intriguing enough, but when I saw the same formation about two weeks later following the same route my interest was greatly aroused. I have not learned anything further since then, but it may be that they were test specimens, flying from RAE Farnborough and then to Martlesham Heath, perhaps put up to give the Royal Observer Corps some recognition practice.

On two occasions foreign air forces put in an appearance. A very neat vic of nine Morane-Saulnier MS.406s flew up from the south and, expecting the chance to view more closely our French ally's equipment, I was disappointed when they turned and flew back the way they had come. Some Armee de l'Air Caudron Goelands also appeared from time to time, mixed in with civil specimens.

It was the 10th May 1940 when I learned that there was an aeroplane in Shoreham Docks. We used to visit the docks from time to time to look over the coasters there, so a quick run through the town brought us to the entrance where inside, in all its glory, a Fokker T.8W stood on its floats. Somehow the cranes, fitted with grab buckets normally, had got the T.8W ashore. There was only a short time to study the aeroplane before an Army contingent arrived and shooed everyone away. However, two days later I was seated on the beach when a tug emerged from the harbour entrance towing the T.8W; this cast off, started its engines, and took off heading west, almost certainly bound for Calshot where it probably joined seven others which had fled Holland to escape the invading German forces.

Another marine aircraft to put in an appearance was the last — or next to last — Short Empire flying boat, either G-AFPZ or G-AFRA probably on a test flight from Rochester. Of particular note was the Union flag painted on each side of the keel, easily seen as it passed directly overhead.

Then it all ended and my aeronautical paradise came to a close as the threat of a German invasion exercised the minds in authority: we were to move to Woking. The RAF took over Shoreham Airport; we could no longer occupy our favourite viewing points, and the civil aircraft had to go elsewhere.

The train journey to Woking involved a change at Farnham, which gave an opportunity to see a Hampden flying by. I spent a boring week in Woking, where there was no school organised and the bad weather didn't help. I recall what I took to be the Fairey P4/34 beating up the locality with a series of dives, but it may have been the similar-looking Fulmar, of which I had heard nothing up to that time. The journey home to Croydon by train produced one interesting item — the Monospar ST.25, no doubt operating from Farnborough, with a clumsy collection of struts ahead of the nose supporting a nosewheel for tricycle undercarriage tests.

I returned to school in Croydon to find all the usual pupils there, as the evacuation scheme had collapsed. There was some flying to be seen, mostly by Lysanders based at the airport including those operated by No. 11 AACU. When German activity increased at the beginning of what was to be called the Battle of Britain, the Lysanders could be seen scuttling home at the time the public air raid sirens gave warning of attack.

Of the Battle itself I saw very little. This was due in part to the hazy weather conditions or at times complete cloud cover. On the clear days I recall seeing a group of about 50 Heinkel He.111s flying south-east on their way back to their bases in Northern France, their pale blue undersides almost blending into the clear sky above them. Another day, six Messerschmitt Me.109s passed over towards London, seemingly not part of any escort to bombers; they flew a very tight formation, contrary to later reports that the Luftwaffe fighters favoured a loose 'finger four' grouping.

One morning our school lessons were interrupted by the air raid sirens, the signal to take to the shelters. As we walked across the playground to the brick-built shelters a large German formation could be seen approaching from the south-east. They were still too far away to identify types but there was a mix of small and large bombers with their fighter escort; recognition would have been easy against a cirro-stratus background. Also visible at close hand were four separate squadrons of Hurricanes climbing furiously towards them. One was almost certainly from Croydon, another from Kenley, so I surmise the other two were from Northolt and Hornchurch. The scene seemed set for a mammoth air battle, but we children were banished to the interior of the air raid shelter while the teachers stood in the entrance and thus denied us any view of this action. We could only sit and listen to the considerable noise overhead.

At odd times during the Battle a low cloud-base dominated the weather situation. Thus individual Heinkels — and once a Junkers Ju.88 — would cruise around just below the cloud cover, into which they could dart if menaced by defending fighters. It seemed as if they were simply on reconnaissance, but none of our anti-aircraft guns ever fired at the ones I saw, even after one did drop a few bombs.

As the Battle of Britain waned, aerial activity was very much reduced by day, but then the so-called 'Blitz' began, which lasted through the autumn of 1940 and into the following spring. There were no sightings of enemy aircraft or our night fighters, of course — but quite a lot of noise overhead on most nights.

I left school in the summer of 1942 and, soon after, joined the Croydon Spotters' Club, Number 404. We met on Friday evenings in one room in a large house in the centre of Croydon and studied pictures and silhouettes of aircraft types most likely to be seen in UK airspace. A cumbersome projector called an epidiascope was used to display the images of aircraft on a screen. As skills in aircraft recognition improved, parts of aircraft were shown and in quite a few cases, the precise mark number of the type had to be stated. This detail was necessary when we entered aircraft recognition contests against other spotters' clubs and teams from Air Training Corps squadrons. With two other SC404 members, Peter Wood and Ralph Spackman, a team was formed and the three of us entered several contests around the Croydon area. As our skills increased, we managed to win a sizeable number of them, and it was a spin-off from this activity that led me to accumulate, some 55 years later, some 16,000 hours flying on 102 different types!

From October 1942 I recorded, in small pocket diaries, the aircraft seen each day by type, and these I maintained until June 1945, when I was called up. The period in 1944 leading up to D-Day and beyond saw such a plethora of types that there was barely enough room on each page to record them. A most remarkable sighting at that time was one summer evening when an estimated 400-500 Lancasters passed overhead Croydon southbound. Bomber Command types were seen rarely as their bases were in the east and north but these Lancasters could possibly have been flying to attack Caen in France. Only once or twice did I see large formations of USAAF B-17s and B-24s. Croydon received a fascinating collection of types over the months, mostly just visiting, it would seem.

As the war drew to a close the RAF and the Royal Navy began ditching their surplus trained personnel, using the Army as their dumping ground, so despite my volunteering for the RAF I was obliged to join the Army. I was trained as a wireless operator and, when qualified, was posted to a so-called reinforcement battalion to await a permanent posting. While there I noted a handful of men, slightly older than most of us, wearing RAF wings on Army uniform. These were some of the RAF's throw-outs, the wearing of wings a sop to their no doubt embittered feelings.

After initial training at Canterbury, where I saw a Junkers Ju.352 overflying, it was up to Yorkshire, where aircraft sightings were rare. Then to Germany, again with little luck at spotting anything, although I did note a Northrop Black Widow flying over Bonn. The next and final posting was to Berlin, and here the aviation side of things looked up a bit; I soon found my way to RAF Gatow and the American-operated Tempelhof. Gatow would host a garrison flight such as half a dozen Tempests or Mosquitos. British European Airways flew a daily service from Northolt with Vikings and there were frequent visits from RAF Transport Command Dakotas. Tempelhof was fairly busy with Douglas C-47 traffic and was home, it seemed, to half-a-dozen or so Boeing C-108s (former B-17s with gun positions removed and a large picture window where the waist gunners used to sit). American Overseas Airlines regularly flew in a DC-4, which fitted easily under the cantilever roof and protected crew and passengers from the elements. The company also had a C-47 which shuttled to and from Frankfurt.

Both airfields had their aircraft dumps, but at Tempelhof the Americans had cut up large numbers of aircraft into pieces too small to be recognised; this treatment had not been suffered by a Lockheed P-38 Lightning and a Stinson L-5, but both were well wrecked. In marginally better shape was the Lufthansa Ju.52/3M D-AMFR *Ludwig Hautzmeyer*; it was in a drab dark green overall finish and the cabin seating comprised a long bench down each side. At the time I had no idea who Ludwig Hautzmeyer was, but many years later I learned he was a fighter pilot in the German Air Force in World War 1 and lost his life in the crash of a KLM DC-2 at Croydon in 1936.

The Russians provided glimpses of their equipment from time to time; these included a bunch of about 50 Lavochkin fighters in no particular formation, a trio of Petlyakov PE-2s, occasional Li-2s (Russian built C-47s) and Polikarpov PO-2s. A two-seat Lavochkin variant was flying circuits and bumps one day at Spandau airfield, just outside the British sector of Berlin. The Polish airline LOT flew Languedocs overhead, *en route* Warsaw to Paris, I believe.

I left Berlin to return home at the end of March 1948, and soon set about making good use of the camera and films I had acquired in the city. Croydon Airport, just a 15-minute cycle ride from home, was the prime site to visit and I began to find my way inside to some extent. I had kept in touch with Peter Wood while abroad, and soon after meeting me again he informed me of an International Rally organised by the Royal Aero Club at Gatwick airport on 19th June 1948. We decided to go and to meet Ralph Spackman there; I had not kept in touch with Ralph for three years, so it was a surprise to learn that he had acquired a private pilot's licence in that time. Subsequently he would take us up one at a time in a Piper J-4 Cub Coupé, which was a side-by-side two-seater as distinct from the more prolific tandem-seated J-3 Cubs. Thus the 25-minute flight in G-AFVF was the first entry of many thousands in my logbooks over the ensuing years. The type was a rarity compared with the J-3 and ex-military L-4 variants. A week later G-AFVF was involved in a taxying accident at Gatwick and was written off; thereafter all flying in a Cub was performed in the L-4H G-AJDS. I made a total of 28 flights with Ralph in the Cub, visiting 15 different aerodromes up to Christmas of 1948 including Pebsham and Dunsfold.

The former was just an area of grass between Hastings and Bexhill, and did duty as a rubbish tip for the dustcarts from the local authority. A man in a diminutive hut, the only edifice, recorded the arrival and departure of the dustcarts — and added the Cub for good measure. There might have been a windsock as a sole indication that it was also an aerodrome. I recall the return flight to Gatwick as we were flying into a brisk westerly breeze and a westbound train easily overtook us. The Cub's engine was rated at 65 hp and gave a cruising speed of one mph for each horsepower! On our arrival at Gatwick the Cub's owner, one A. J. Walter, the UK agent for Piper Aircraft Corporation, wanted a piece of equipment delivered to Skyways Ltd. at Dunsfold and so off we went again to land at that 'holy of holies', banned to casual visitors at that time.

It was mid-1949 before I flew with Ralph again. This was to be something much more ambitious, a trip to Holland, and Ralph had arranged to hire from Elstree a Taylorcraft Plus C-2 G-AHBO (which had been registered G-AFUD prewar). We collected the aeroplane and flew across London to position it to Croydon ready to set off the next morning for Holland; however, while discussing the proposed flight that evening Ralph declared himself dissatisfied with the Taylorcraft so, instead of going over to Holland as planned, we flew it back to Elstree the next day.

I couldn't see much wrong with it, although it did have odd wheels! (One, I suspect, was its prewar wheel and tyre, the other a postwar specimen as fitted to production Austers.) Ralph then had to spend the next two days attempting to find another mount, and finally announced he had found a 'new' Tiger Moth at Gatwick, hired out by Sqdn. Ldr. Hughes of a company called Aerocontacts. The aeroplane in question had had its RAF markings oversprayed in a shade of red described as 'flame' in the obligatory document for overseas flights, the *carnet des passages,* while the wings and tailplane were silver. It certainly looked brand-new and it was claimed to have one big advantage, a long-range tank, which had been achieved by swapping the standard 18-gallon tank for a 25-gallon one from a Queen Bee, the radio-controlled target drone version of the Tiger Moth. So G-AKTY was to be our conveyance for the next few days. We made a brief acceptance flight in *Katy* — as she was always called — and set off from Gatwick to Le Touquet the following day. I soon overcame the brief sensation that I might fall out of the open cockpit and settled down to enjoy the journey. From Le Touquet we headed for Amsterdam Schiphol, a journey of 2 hours 40 minutes, which the Queen Bee tank made comfortably possible.

Schiphol was a busy airport but they fitted us in on one of the long runways and *Katy* was parked almost under the port wingtip of a KLM Constellation. There was no radio work in all this as, in common with the majority of light aircraft at the time, *Katy* had no radio; her navaids comprised a compass in each cockpit (I didn't know how to read mine!), one map — which Ralph used and I never saw — and two sets of eyeballs! Clearing Customs found us in the confines of the terminal building, and it was with some difficulty that we managed to get back to the Tiger Moth to get it refuelled and prepare for the next flight. When all was finally ready Ralph and I climbed aboard, strapped in and waited for someone to swing the propeller. There were several overall-clad personnel moving about the apron, but the person who offered to do the honours was attired in a uniform which would have made any admiral proud! He fussed around *Katy's* engine cowling, peering in each side as he opened the hinged side-panels in turn, interspersing these actions with bursts of ineffectual propeller swinging. Ralph, seated in the rear cockpit and thus further away from the propeller, attempted to make helpful suggestions, but to no avail. I knew nothing of the prop-swinging ritual and could offer no help. Something that *was* obvious to me was that Ralph had no intention of getting out to show what was needed.

A semi-circle of technicians ('greasy rags') gathered around *Katy's* nose but at a distance calculated to avoid them getting involved. Then another 'admiral' appeared and joined in, as did a few other bodies. While they were all fiddling around, a very tall lugubrious-looking individual came up, peered over the heads of the assembled helpers, reached over with his long arm and outstretched forefinger and depressed the small brass plunger on the carburettor. I later learned what this was all about, and that the procedure was necessary to get a Gipsy Major engine in a Tiger Moth to start. The two 'admirals', and the others around them, seemed not to notice the action of the tall one, who promptly wandered off. They more or less began congratulating one another when they saw the thin stream of fuel dripping from the carburettor over the apron, the standard indication that the engine priming action was complete. In grandiose style the first 'admiral' got everyone to move well clear and, after a swing or two, managed to get the engine running. We were now in business for our last flight of the day, to a small aerodrome called Teuge, near Apeldoorn.

When we arrived in the area where Ralph estimated Teuge to be we could see no sign of it. As I had no map, it was down to Ralph to identify the strip, but the landscape comprised scores of hedgeless fields, none of them looking like an aerodrome. Ralph said something about having to return to Schiphol, and that the flight time involved would leave little daylight thanks to the engine-starting fiasco; then we spotted a good clue — a glider parked beside a barn! There was nothing else in the way of an aerodrome indication, but Ralph wasted no more time and set *Katy* down nearby. The landing run was short, as the grass came up to the leading edges of the Tiger's lower wing. However, the intended flight had been achieved in a flight time from Gatwick of five hours.

We could stay only one night due to the many delays, so the following day we planned the return route so that we could take in visits to two other Dutch airfields. Our first target was Gilze-Rijen, a former Luftwaffe nightfighter base which by 1949 had become a Dutch Air Force base and home to the Rijkslucht-vaartdienst — National Government Aviation School (RLvS). There were considerable numbers of Dutch Air Force Harvards, all in green and brown camouflage, while those of the RLvS were yellow overall and looking very smart. An Oxford, a Meteor, a Proctor 4 and an Auster made up the rest of the military hardware. The RLvS also had about a dozen Beech D-18s in shiny metal finish and a trio of Junkers Ju.52/3Ms. While looking around and taking a few photographs we were approached by a member of the staff who was English, who hinted that we were not entirely welcome there, so we agreed to leave right away, having seen all we wanted.

We received more skilful help from the several mechanics working on the Air Force Harvards, who soon had *Katy* running, and Ralph set off along the taxiway with a view to gaining the take-off point on the single runway. We passed several Harvards, all draped with servicing personnel who stared dumbly at us, and then we suddenly found that the track ended in an area of bushes. We couldn't turn in the confined width of the taxiway, so Ralph had to throttle the engine right back, climb out and lift

Katy's tail round, and then climb aboard again. Then one man had a good idea, pedalled up on a bicycle and beckoned us to follow him. He then guided us round about 75% of Gilze-Rijen's perimeter, no mean distance with such a large base. At long last we were at the runway and were very soon airborne, destination Ypenburg, a 50-minute flight away; this was the base of a section of the RLvS and operated a version of the Tiger Moth not seen outside Holland. Their yellow-painted specimens had a glaringly obvious modification. It seemed that the Dutch were distrustful of the standard anti-spin fairings, or strakes, which were about 2 ft 6 in long and attached at the top of the rear fuselage immediately in front of the tailplane. These they had discarded, then they had removed the standard horn balance from the rudder to give it a straight leading edge over its full height before fitting a large triangular fin extending forward to a point just behind the rear cockpit; needless to say, this modification did nothing for the aeroplane's appearance. As Ralph now mentioned having had difficulty with taxying *Katy* at Gilze-Rijen, we went to the tail unit to look at the tail skid, but there wasn't one! It had completely worn away on the taxiway surface, which was made of rough bricks instead of smooth tarmac as in the UK. In fact, not only was the shoe worn away but also several inches of the steel rod to which it had been attached were missing!

Fortunately Ypenburg, having quite a few Tiger Moths, held plenty of spares and Ralph was able to track down a compete tailskid assembly, which we were obliged to take although really we only wanted a shoe and rod; he regarded the whole deal as exorbitant but there was no option. So *Katy* competed her continental tour with a bright yellow tail end in contrast to her flame fuselage. From Ypenburg we flew to Le Touquet in just over two hours and then it was home to Gatwick. The total flight time was 11 hours and I found this example of air touring 1940s-style most enjoyable.

A few days after the Dutch trip Ralph received a request from Sqdn. Ldr. Hughes to take *Katy* to Wolverhampton. Hughes had entered the Tiger in an air race there, but chose to drive up the preceding day in order to have his car handy. Ralph invited me to join him, then we would watch the flying events before flying *Katy* back to Gatwick. All went well until the time to depart Wolverhampton for Gatwick, when the weather intervened, and as any flight southward was out of the question Ralph and I accompanied Hughes in his sumptuous American limousine back home to Croydon.

About six weeks later we abandoned *Katy*, fickle swains that we were, and became involved with *Lucy*; this was another Tiger Moth (G-ALUC), which had been civilanised by Bill Webb at Croydon. Not as colourful as Katy, she nevertheless looked smart in her new silver overall paint scheme with navy blue letters and struts. But it wasn't her looks that were attractive, more her Croydon hangar, a mere 15-minute cycle ride from our homes compared to an hour-long bus journey to Gatwick. It was at this point that I asked Ralph if he would let me fly the aeroplane to a small extent, as up until then I had not touched the controls at all. So I began handling *Lucy* for short spells of straight and level flight which by this time had been preceded by three dozen hours of passenger flying. G-ALUC still flies to this day, based on an airstrip in Kent.

On a later occasion, and for a reason I cannot recall, Ralph hired Auster Autocrat G-AJEH from the Redhill Flying Club, and we flew from Redhill to Weston-super-Mare and back; I believe we had someone occupying the rear seat. The outbound flight took us over a yard with parked in it, a Royal Navy yard with about half a dozen aircraft and no adjoining aerodrome, and I was surprised to see that the small collection included a rare Westland Welkin, a twin-engined, high-altitude, single-seat fighter with a wingspan almost double that of a Spitfire.

Two short trips in *Lucy* completed my flying to the end of 1949. In the eighteen months I had been flying with Ralph I had learned a lot about flying around southern England, come to know several aerodromes, seen a little of what went on across the Channel, and seen how the weather affected flying at private pilot level.

Forward into 1950, when I did more hands-on time, but Ralph said he could not teach me to fly as he didn't hold the necessary flying instructor's rating on his licence. He suggested I join a flying club, either the one at Gatwick with the Piper Cub (at £3 per hour) or the Experimental Flying Group of the Ultra Light Aircraft Association with a de Havilland Moth Minor, G-AFOZ, at Redhill at £1.75 per hour. Apart from the price, Redhill was closer to home than Gatwick and this mattered because I cycled everywhere, so under the guidance of Miss Jean Bird I began a proper course of training for the PPL and flew my first solo in November 1950.

The prewar Luton Minor G-AFIR sits in Arthur Ord-Hume's back garden at Hatch End. Beyond the hedge is 'Hatch End' aerodrome.
Photo: Arthur Ord-Hume.

Luton Minor G-AFIR was eventually towed to Elstree Aerodrome behind the family car, Standard ASR269. The MCA was to be told that it was going to fly, and then challenged to arrest the pilot for not having a Permit!
Photo: Arthur Ord-Hume.

Arthur's pride and joy shows its unintended new shape following engine failure. Photo: Arthur Ord-Hume.

Thanks to newspaper publicity, Arthur's plight became an embarrassment to the MCA, and the myrmidons of power relented enough to give him a Restricted Test Permit. Here the great photographer Charles E. Brown captures his moment of triumphal bliss from the Elstree-based Autocrat G-AGXT. Photo: Charles E. Brown.

CHAPTER 17

A POSTWAR HISTORY OF LUTON MINOR G-AFIR

by

ARTHUR W.J.G. ORD-HUME

(This is a much-shortened version of a chapter from the book On Home-Made Wings, *first published by GMS Enterprises in 1997, and is reproduced here after adaptations by the author. If you haven't yet read this book in full — or its sequel,* Flight on Frail Wings, *then it is recommended that you do so without delay, as otherwise you will miss learning a lot about both building and flying light aircraft in the immediate postwar period — and, indeed, what life in general was like in those days — as Arthur, one of that period's surviving and most stalwart aviation supporters, recalls in detail.— Ed.)*

The Luton Minor is an aeroplane with several quite pronounced and readily-distinguished features — and that happens to be as well as its v-e-r-y slow flying speed. It is long, thin, with a short, wide, fat wing, the sort of rudder which inspires recollections of a kebab, a tail skid which looks like it originally saw service as a small medicine spoon, and an engine which makes a very funny noise. This noise is interesting because the faster the engine goes the louder the noise gets, but it doesn't actually *sound* any faster! And when you switch the engine off (a process best adopted after landing), it wheezes like an old man on his last puff . . .

* * * * * * * * * *

It all started on Wednesday 13th April 1948, when my colleague, college student Paul Simpson, and I set off in ASR 269, the 1937-vintage Standard, to collect G-AFIR from Leicester. We left Evelyn Drive, Pinner, at 08.15 hrs with Austen Chamberlain's peculiar little four-wheeled trailer stuffed into the back of the car. Obtaining sufficient petrol for the journey had presented a major problem, particularly since fuel restrictions meant that we had to carry enough for the complete there-and-back trip; you were not permitted to visit fuel pumps outside your own area.

Our journey was long and slow. The characteristics of the old Standard were never sullied by such indelicacies as an aspiration to speed and at 50 mph everything tended to shake rather. It was also that pre-motorway, bypassless period when you had to navigate your way through every village and town, and fight every slow-travelling commercial vehicle (these were limited to 40 mph and carried the old white 'C' licence disc stuck in the windscreen) in an attempt to overtake.

We completed the 113 miles in exactly five hours — that's 22.6 mph — and the only serious problem we encountered was that it happened to be market day in Leicester. At last we were at Squires' old garage at 4 Warner Street, Barrow-on-Soar and looking at G-AFIR, now taken down from its roosting place in the rafters. The aircraft looked what is best described as 'rough'. It was painted a very dark green with rather crude registration letters daubed on in white. The one-piece wing was silver and the huge registration letters were painted across the span in maroon. The rudder bore the once-familiar trademark of an already long-forgotten prewar motor oil, a red diamond with the word VIGZOL in the middle. The cockpit was painted out in grey and the seat and seat-back were upholstered in blue leathercloth.

Somehow the Minor looked bigger when we pushed it out and stood it next to the car; in fact, small though it was as an aeroplane, it succeeded in dwarfing the car. Paul had decided to tow the fuselage by the engine mounting on its own wheels, with Chamberlain's builder's trolley tied under the tail to support the rear. With hindsight this was a silly thing to do for it meant that we had a rigid and unsteerable six-wheel trailer, but we had to find that out the hard way. A bicycle rear light was tied on to the stern post, a cheque for £25 changed hands and, 2½ hours after our arrival, we were loaded up and ready to leave.

We knew that driving was going to be hazardous because, while right turns would be fine, those to the left would have to be made very wide (or the fuselage lifted round), otherwise the wingtip would touch the fuselage side. As we prepared to pull out of the garage yard, a local policeman who was cycling past stopped, got off his bike, and took a closer look. This was some years before the once-popular Northern-born comic, the late Al Read, came on the scene, but this policeman was a true 'Al Read' character.

"Where're you going with that lot, then?"

"London."

"London? I say you'll never get there with that, I say you'll never get that far."

Anyway, he didn't attempt to stop us, so off we went. The return journey was somewhat eventful, but we finally reached Pinner at ten minutes past one the next morning; our average speed worked out to have been less than 9.5 mph! The next morning, after curious looks from the postman, the milkman and passers-by, we tackled the job of tidying up the front garden. Once the undercarriage had been removed, the fuselage was only 2 ft wide and Paul and I were able to carry the Minor down the side passage and into the back garden, set it out on the lawn and assemble it for the first time since before the war. Years of grime and birds' droppings covered it, so the first task was to wash it down using warm water and 'Oxydol' washing powder.

It was the hottest Easter weekend for 100 years and it was also the Elstree Easter Monday air display. New legislation had just been introduced which said that all gliders and sailplanes had to be registered as ordinary aeroplanes. For the owner of a high-performance sailplane, painting letters onto a highly-polished varnished wood body was anathema, but everybody had to do it. My friend Dudley Hiscox was bemoaning the fact as we painted G-ALJN on his Olympia's highly polished fuselage, and Ladislav Marmol (who had recently attempted the world endurance record for a single-seat glider, but had to abandon it after 33 hours 5 minutes — 11 hours and 12 minutes short of the record) was equally upset about having to paint G-ALMP on his sleek Zlin 24.

A quick inspection of the Minor airframe showed that there was a lot to do. As the result of being stored throughout the war under a hot tin roof, all the plywood skinning was dried out and brittle; it would probably all have to be replaced. Furthermore, all the metal fittings were corroded and needed replacing, and all the fabric would need careful rubbing down to remove dope cracks. The ailerons, for some reason quite contrary to the original constructional drawings, were fully covered in plywood and were badly warped: one trailing edge was, in fact, twisted like a switchback. All in all, virtually all the aircraft would need extensive restoration.

The ARB sent down two surveyors to look at the aeroplane, and they confirmed all that I had already discovered — namely, that the aircraft would be a 95% rebuild. They then raised the point as to whether it would come into the category of a restoration or a new aeroplane. Technically, they said, a 'rebuild' was considered to be less than half the airframe. On the other hand, if it were to be considered a 'new' aeroplane, then I would not be allowed to get a Permit to Fly for it, even though I now possessed the prewar Permit. Again it would be impossible to get a C. of A. for the machine.

Then all at once the task ahead became blindingly clear! The entire inspection procedure which I had undertaken could be reduced to one very simple operation. All I had to do was to jack up the registration letters, fit a new airframe, and then complete the job by replacing the registration letters with some newly-painted ones . . .

As the summer of 1949 progressed, I had to plan a course of action. Firstly, materials had to be sourced and collected, and then there was the question of which motor to use. It was at about this time that I first met Harold Best-Devereux, who was then working as an assistant under my ARB inspector. Best-Devereux had worked at Luton Aircraft when he was a boy before the war and had had a hand in building parts for the Minor and its larger sister, the Major. He came and spent an afternoon with me, as the result of which we enjoyed a working relationship for many years to come.

The original Anzani engine had been discarded before the war, and with the aircraft was now a curious flat-twin French motor called a Mengin which had formerly been fitted to the ill-fated Avions SCAL Bassou. I had been proposing to install this but it remained a source of worry: for a start it was fitted with single ignition, whereas progress rightly dictated that it was imperative to equip all engines with dual ignition. But in the Micawber-like hope that 'something would turn up' I decided to forget about the engine problem for a while and get on with the airframe; this work I knew and was proficient at.

That summer we went on holiday to Bognor, where one of my mother's professional friends, B.C. Hilliam (one half of the old Flotsam & Jetsam radio duo) was performing locally that season. I had known Hilliam since I was a wee schoolboy, and so our holiday was spent in close involvement with the show and with his singer, Arthur Richards. Arthur had some contact with the company LEC Refrigeration, which had a factory on the outskirts of Bognor and operated their own private landing strip for its company aircraft. We went over to look at this, accessible only by walking through the factory and crossing a stile and the railway line to a small blister hangar rather like the Experimental Group's one at Elstree.

But this visit to Bognor was notable for the start of another friendship. Also staying at our hotel was a nervous young man making his first steps as a stand-up comedian; he, too, was in the pier show, and it was he who described Bognor as being "bright black with here and there a vivid streak of grey." His humour was strange, outrageous, very, very funny — and yet he was privately a quiet, introspective person. His name was Tony Hancock and he became a family friend.

The work on G-AFIR proceeded, and after some while I managed to complete the fuselage structure. Finally, after several days of hard work at Pinner Hill, a lot if it spent waiting for the damned paint to dry and keeping the flies off it until it had, my friend Derek Mathie and I walked the fuselage downhill to Evelyn Drive. Then we learned that the Colne Valley Catchment Water Board had bought a huge parcel of land, including part of Elstree aerodrome, for the creation of a new reservoir, and that as a result we would have to vacate our Experimental Group's hangar within a month.

A fellow called Walters contacted me around this time asking if I would like to buy a Dart Kitten, the attraction being that it had a JAP engine attached to its front end. He wanted £50 for it but with no Permit to Fly. This was G-AEXT, but knowing that somewhere down the line I had to learn to say "no" to offers, I declined. With only a fortnight left at Elstree we had the engine running in the Ding Bat (G-AFJA), and we also possessed the Zaunköenig G-ALUA (unserviceable) as well as the Auster G-AIGT and the Bibi G-AGSR; then Jean Bird, our Group flying instructor, tipped the Bibi on its nose and broke the prop — a major setback as the aircraft was newly fabric-covered and painted. It would now be physically impossible for the Group to move out, and in fact we stayed till the end of the year before the Ministry of Supply intervened. Even so, it was to be February 1950 before we actually moved the Group to Redhill.

* * * * * * * * *

Over a year then passed, during which Paul Simpson sucessfully flew the Aeronca G-AEVT (which we had recently restored together) before one day he finally put himself in hospital in Loughborough (where he was attending College) after crashing it on his way to our local strip at Pinner on 11th June 1950. *(This account is recalled in detail elsewhere in* Flight on Frail Wings *— Ed.)*

In the meantime I had come to the conclusion that I was going to have to purchase a new engine for the Minor; the ULAA (Ultra Light Aircraft Association, forerunner of the PFA) had just bought all the remaining Aeronca J.99 JAP engines and spares. My chief drawback was how I could raise the price of a brand-new engine and mount (about £75); with all cash tied up in the Minor and the Aeronca, a church mouse might justifiably have been judged better off than I was at that time.

However, salvation was close at hand. Lord Kemsley had formed the Kemsley Flying Trust to help those with limited resources but with some measure of talent to get airborne. However, money could not be given to individuals, only to recognised Groups: the answer was for me to form myself into a Group, so my father, mother and I co-opted Paul —who was still recovering from his crash — onto the committee of HEULACC (the Hatch End Ultra Light Aeroplane Constructors' Club), paid our 25 shillings ULAA affiliation fee and sat back to wait. In November I got a letter saying that the Club's Kemsley loan had been approved and that I now had £95 to play with.

Despite all sorts of essential expenses on a propeller, instruments, insurance and so on, the Minor was finally ready to fly by mid-April 1951. One evening, when most of the flying had ceased at Elstree for the day, I started up the JAP (which eagerly clattered into life), taxied out to the runway and smoothly opened the throttle. The tail came up very quickly, and before I could believe it we were flying steadily at a height of 10 feet!

Next was the simple matter of paperwork, for it was noticed by the Ministry wallahs that (a) I had a brand-new aeroplane, and (b) it was fitted with a new type of engine with which the aircraft had not flown before the war. The ensuing battle was long and arduous, culminating in my request that I should be arrested for breaking the law by not having a piece of paper. Finally, the absurdity of the situation triumphed and, thanks to very helpful national press coverage of the problem, the Ministry relented and eventually, my Permit to Fly arrived from the MCA; this I stored in the luggage space behind the seat as the Law required that it be carried in the aircraft at all times; however, I did not notice any improvement in the performance of the machine as a result.

Then came the day I was flying along merrily on the way to the strip at Hatch End when the engine cut with an air of finality. Difficult wind conditions brought me to the only attainable large field, in the middle of which was a predatory oak tree. I was trying to avoid it but it was too quick for me and I clipped its top with the tail. This procedure tended to retard my forward motion somewhat, because the next thing I knew was that I was falling out of the sky and performing a singularly heavy and unconventional downwind landing on the port wingtip and the nose. In the words of my late-lamented friend Gerard Hoffnung, at this point I think I must have lost my presence of mind. However, I wasn't badly hurt, although without any shoulder straps I had been flung forward into the instrument panel and my nose, never knowingly small at the best of times, began to swell. The most blood came from my lower lip, which was split halfway down my chin. The effect of this was interesting because I could now close half my mouth tightly (the east side) while leaving the other half wide open: it was, one had to admit, novel.

Some days later, while I was wondering how to go about another rebuild of 'FIR (I had just £12 in my pocket), a letter came asking me if Rayant Pictures of Wembley (an offshoot of 20th Century Fox) could come and film the aeroplane and the house. This they did, although I never made a brass farthing from it — despite what many people who ought to have known better thought.

It was a long year later that I had a new pair of wings, fresh tail, new fuselage, struts, undercarriage and propeller. Once more I was able to run the engine in G-AFIR, and it was later in 1956, after an extremely cold winter (on May 20th in fact) that G-AFIR took to the skies at Elstree once again.

After a look around at grass and sky to ensure that all was clear, I opened the throttle, quickly passing through that notorious carburettor flat spot. The JAP popped, banged and farted up to full revs, all 2,235 of them and, without any conscious effort on my part, I knew that the tail was up and we were rolling fast(ish) on the tarmac. Holding the stick delicately between forefinger and thumb, I gently eased it back a fraction, and in a trice came that fantastic smoothness when the wheels stop picking up all the vibrations from the elderly cracked ashphalt and concrete.

Later, when G-AFIR was back in the hangar, I asked myself if it had been worth it. That night, back at home, I looked into the empty shed, still bearing the obvious traces of an organised departure. There was my old fuselage trestle made out of a fish box stood on one side with a pair of planks screwed on to the lower edge to give it stability. That fish box had come up by rail from Portsmouth when Ted Hawes of Hants & Sussex Aviation had made my first undercarriage. The old tarpaulins, tatty and torn, lay heaped at one end of the shed. Odd bits of thick string and rope littered the floor. I inspected the worn spots on the back lawn, removed the abandoned protective sacking from the top of the garden fence, had a large whisky, and went to bed like a babe.

The dream — my personal dream — was reality once more.

(Editor's note: G-AFIR has been rebuilt once again in recent years by its current owner, Arthur Mason [who has also built and flies Pietenpol G-ADRA], and it is hoped that it will be airworthy within a year or so — as time permits.)

CHAPTER 18

AN ENTHUSIAST DURING THE FORTIES – MAINLY ON A BIKE

by

REG HAVERS

When the year of 1940 opened I was 10½ and living at Great Dunmow, a small market town in north-west Essex. I had a passing interest in aviation at that time but it was undoubtedly my brother John who helped to make it into an absorbing hobby. I do have some memories of my early years, the first being the forced landing of Bristol Bulldog K2210 on 16th October 1935 at Folly Farm, just west of the town. In the next year, during a family visit on 29th June to the Campbell Black Circus at the nearby village of Great Easton, I recall a Pou du Ciel and a DH.83 Fox Moth. Other prewar memories are of a Fairey Battle K7652 of 218 Sqdn., Upper Heyford, which I went to see with my brother on 29th March 1938 when it force-landed near to Throes Corner, alongside the A120 road east of Dunmow. That was followed on 18th October by the nighttime collision over the town of two Vickers Wellesleys of 148 Sqdn, Stradishall. The aircraft, K7714 and K7716, were both destroyed in the subsequent crashes and all crew killed, but fortunately they missed the town, although one was only yards away from a row of houses. My father, Charles Havers, who was the local Police Inspector, was heavily involved in investigating those crashes, together with several of his colleagues.

Mention of my father reminds me that he took John and myself to the Debden Empire Air Day on 20th May 1939, where we were entertained by Spitfire, Hurricane, Wellington, Whitley and Harvard among the dozen or so types present. Although Dad never expressed a great interest in aircraft, it seems that he must have been amongst the early band of enthusiasts; on 26th June 1912, at the age of 19, he cycled (accompanied by his sister) to an aerial display at Hylands Park near Chelmsford, where the pioneer airman Claude Grahame-White was celebrating his marriage, due the next day. Maybe this is where we caught the aviation bug!

It was not until early July in 1940 that much enemy air activity was apparent; we were always well aware when there was a 'red' warning as the air raid siren was situated immediately above the bedroom which I shared with brother John. At about that time I was on holiday awaiting entry into Braintree County High School, and often accompanied my father on his visits to his constables in the outlying villages and to various 'incidents'; those included such seemingly futile tasks as searching for bomb craters somewhere near Cornish Hall End at the extreme north-eastern edge of my Dad's area to find bomb fragments for identification purposes. Another futile 'incident' occurred during the period when we expected German paratroops to descend upon us almost any day and there was a need to investigate a report of a parachute seen in the Throes Corner area of Little Dunmow; that led to a long slog across acres of land and all we found were some sheets of newspaper, which somebody must have seen billowing in the wind.

To my mind a far more interesting 'incident' occurred on 26th August 1940 when I went with my Dad to the crash site of a Dornier Do.17Z which had been shot down by fighters earlier in the day at Highams Farm, near Thaxted, and was still smouldering. A souvenir circular panel in my possession reads 'Z Austauschbar 0174241 Do.17.' A few days later, on the morning of 31st August, an aircraft trailing smoke was seen south of the town; this proved to be Hurricane V6628 of 56 Sqdn. which had been in combat over the Colchester area and crashed near High Easter. The pilot, P/O Maurice Mounsdon, baled out, and I recall him being brought to Dr. Hall's surgery in Great Dunmow and being lifted on a stretcher into the building through a window overlooking the High Street.

Soon after that I had a glimpse, through skimpy clouds, of the only formation of German bombers that I saw during the entire Battle of Britain which hit Debden airfield heavily. My final memory of that period is of a stick of bombs dropped across the Great Dunmow area on 19th September, one of which landed ineffectually just over the wall from our house.

At that time, within a 15-mile radius of Great Dunmow town, only two aerodromes were operational, Debden to the north and North Weald to the south-west, but from October 1940 No.2 Sqdn Lysanders arrived at Sawbridgeworth — just over the border into Hertfordshire. They were often to be seen over the area at very low altitude on the way to coastal patrols or ASR operations, as later were their Tomahawks and Mustangs. At nighttime in 1940/41 the sound of enemy aircraft was often heard over our area and the glow in the sky of the devastating fires raging in London could often be seen, even though we were almost 40 miles away.

A significant event in January 1941 was the introduction of the *Aeroplane Spotter*, which I suspect was bought by my brother but was avidly read by me. Up to that time we had little information with which to identify new types, although on our frequent visits to the local Royal Observer Corps post we sometimes struck gold and learnt something to our advantage. I recall seeing an RAF Cierva C.30A, probably in 1941 and from Duxford, hovering over the school playing fields at Braintree County High School. Those playing fields were a boon to our small gang of spotters as we were easily able to pursue our hobby at break-times. The most amazing sight seen from that location, and probably the largest continuous stream of aircraft I have ever seen, was the September 1944 Arnhem Operation when Stirlings, Halifaxes, Albemarles and Dakotas plus Horsa and Hamilcar gliders continuously filled the sky during our lunch-break: but I digress!

On the afternoon of 18th April 1942 I was out with my Dad to another 'incident,' which proved to be the forced landing at Yew Tree Farm, Stebbing of Spitfire W3966 of 65 Sqdn. The pilot escaped when the engine failed and the Spit was sufficiently in one piece for me to be allowed to sit in the cockpit — my very first time in an aeroplane! Great Sampford airfield, another new operational airfield in our area, had only received 65 Sqdn. a few days before the crash.

My first-ever cycle ride to an airfield was the 20-mile round trip to Debden on 26th July 1942, as I had acquired a suitable new bike on my 13th birthday. Up to about that time I had been hampered in my spotting activities by the lack of suitable transportation and optical equipment. A small telescope had come into my possession which enabled me to log several 'EB'-coded Spitfire VBs of 41 Sqdn plus Magister P2459. The very first items in my log were for 5th July 1942: Mustang 1 'XV-T' of 2 Sqdn and Anson N9939. Loggings in that relatively slack period of the war were mainly the low-flying Mustangs plus various trainers such as Tiger Moths, Masters, Oxfords and Ansons, although a Ventura coded 'W' twice put in an appearance in October 1942.

At the end of 1942 the Stirlings of 90 Sqdn moved into the newly-opened Ridgewell airfield and were occasionally to be seen over the area. By that time the USAAF were at Debden, which I visited on 9th January 1943, but on that occasion I logged only a Spitfire VB ('MD-H'), a P-38 Lightning coded '67' of USAAF 336th Fighter Sqdn., and Magister L5954. My next visit there on 8th March was much more fruitful with P-47C Thunderbolts coded '12,' '38,' '58,' '81' and '85' and ten 'MN'-coded Spitfires of 350 (Belgian) Sqdn. The 'grapevine' was active on two crashes at about this time involving the unfinished Stansted airfield; Stirling BF445 of 214 Sqdn., Stradishall, came to grief on 26th February while attempting to land on the obstructed runway, short of fuel and with engine failure. Following that, on 14th May Spitfire VB W3521 belly-landed in a field on the approach after the engine failed in flight.

In May of 1943 things began to warm up on the 'spotting' front when the USAAF B-17 Fortresses moved into both Earl's Colne and Andrewsfield, the latter just a few miles east of our town. My spotting post, on the roof of the police station above the cells, was in a direct line with the Andrewsfield runway, with the B-17s staggering over the town at a very low altitude. Both bases soon re-equipped with the B-26 Marauder, and more of the same type were at Chipping Ongar airfield. I recall a visit with a friend to Andrewsfield at that time when we were very firmly moved from our viewing point by a gun-toting GI — with whom we did not argue. B-17s had also moved into Ridgewell, which added to the local activity, but sightings of Lancasters, Typhoons, Hurricane IIDs, Halifaxes and many other types were now almost daily occurrences. Later in the year I saw my first Albemarle and a rarity, a Defiant, although I also recall another unidentified Defiant, probably in 1941, having difficulty negotiating one of our narrow streets on a Queen Mary trailer.

In September 1943 the B-26s of 386th BG (Bomber Group) moved from Boxted into Great Dunmow airfield, just two miles to the north-east of the town. With four B-26 groups now in action the local activity increased considerably. The gradual build-up of the USAAF in the area soon became a flood, with a P-47 group at Gosfield in December, B-26s at Matching in January 1944, followed by more into Stansted in February, plus P-51s at Rivenhall and A-20s at Wethersfield. I visited Rivenhall on 21st February, where ten of the 363rd FG (Fighter Group's) P-51 Mustangs were logged, and also a P-38 of the 20th FG. Seen in the area that day were Lancaster 'KO-K' of 115 Sqdn, Stirling 'XT-K' of 1657 CU, Oxford V3790 and P-47 Thunderbolts 'MX-Y,' 'MX-T' and 'E4-V' of 78th FG Duxford. Just prior to the Rivenhall visit I went to Debden again on 13th February, where 16 P-47s of 4th FG were logged, plus P-51s 43-12454 ('B6-S') and 43-12472 ('G4-G') and a UC-78, 42-58515. On a visit to Great Dunmow airfield on 2nd March I logged 27 Marauders, and on the next day Debden revealed, in addition to 23 Mustangs and six Thunderbolts of 4th Fighter Group, Mosquito III HJ899/'G', UC-78 43-7483 and UC-61 43-14442. At about that time the A-20s of 409th BG moved into Little Walden and the 394th BG's B-26s into Boreham. P-38 Lightnings from Nuthampstead were often over the area, and the first Tempests (based at Castle Camps) appeared.

During a six-month period from December 1943 there were reports of 11 aircraft crashes within 3-4 miles of Great Dunmow town, some on the 'grapevine,' but others necessitated a visit to the crash site. On 12th December 1943 Mustang IA FD534 of 168 Sqdn. Sawbridgeworth fell at Elmbridge Mill, Little Easton, after colliding with another Mustang. This was followed on 21st January 1944 by the destruction of a B-26 Marauder 'Weasel' of 440 BS, on night exercises from Andrewsfield, at Bigods Wood, just about a mile away from the Mustang crash. On 5th February I went with my father to the village of Tilty, where Mosquito NF.XIII HK454 of 416 Sqdn. Castle Camps had crashed into a wood. The next morning my brother was at the site at Canfield Park where Lancaster DS827 of 115 Sqdn., Witchford, had crashed the previous evening while engaged on a 'Bullseye' exercise: all eight crew sadly died in that very destructive crash. Later in the month, on 23rd February, a Junkers Ju.188 crashed and burned at Holts Farm, near Duck End, shot down by AA fire. Another Marauder, from 585th BS Boreham, crashed soon after take-off at Bishop's Green, south of our town, on 26th March. ATC Cadets Roy Crowe and John Windley, working nearby, received King's Commendations for their rescue work. Then on 4th April I went with my friend Derrick Franklin to the site of a P-47 Thunderbolt crash near the parish church at Takeley. On 20th May a B-26 crashed at Mole Hill Green soon after take-off from Stansted and was destroyed in an explosion which was heard for miles around. On D-Day morning, 6th June, a Mustang from 339th FG Fowlmere crashed south of the town at Sallets Green. Two other crashes which I witnessed (but did not record the dates of) were a Marauder that crash-landed in a field near to Easton Lodge Holt at Little Canfield and a P-38 Lightning, seen from the school bus, which crashed into a field alongside the road near Felstead Railway Station.

After that the area was free of crashes throughout the 1940s, apart from a Spitfire VB BL592 of the Great Dunmow Station Flight that crashed on the edge of the airfield at Blue Gates and the Stirlings mentioned later on 21st November 1944 and 20th March 1945.

An interesting change from the usual B-26s in the Great Dunmow circuit was the unexpected sight on 1st April 1944 of the captured German aircraft of the RAF's 1426 Flight, namely Bf.109G RN228, FW.190 PN999 and a Ju.88. Due to bad weather the flight was delayed at Great Dunmow until departure to Andrewsfield on the 4th. The Bf.109 went unserviceable there, and 1426 Flight did not leave until 7th April, with a P-51 escort *en route* to Earl's Colne. During a specially requested overfly of Rivenhall the Bf.109 had to divert to that airfield with more trouble.

Meanwhile, the 397th BG's B-26s had arrived temporarily at Gosfield on 5th April, moving ten days later to Rivenhall and allowing the A-20s of 410th BG to occupy Gosfield, which I visited on 13 May, logging 29 A-20s. With all three of the A-20 groups and the eight B-26 groups now operational within our local area the spotting potential was almost overwhelming. In addition to our locally based aircraft, literally hundreds of B-17s, B-24s, P-47s, P-51s and many other types of RAF and USAAF aircraft, were to be seen almost on a daily basis. Earlier in the year I had come into possession of a much more powerful telescope from a friend of my father's which added greatly to my enjoyment of the hobby; it is still in my possession, much battered after many years of service. An indication of the scale of 'logged' aircraft was that in May of 1944 I had a total of 660, which increased to 920 in June and to 1,160 in July. Most were 'code letters' due to difficulty in reading the RAF serials in particular, but a fair number of both USAAF and RAF serials are included in the totals. An idea of the variety of non-operational aircraft seen in that period include very frequent USAAF L-5 Sentinels, UC-78 Brasshats and UC-64 Norsemen, numerous Martinets, a Hart variant which I noted as 'SI-N,' a USAAF Proctor (HM362) plus the usual many Ansons, Oxfords, etc. Three HP Harrows ('L,' 'W' and 'E') were over the area on 4th June, and then D-Day was upon us.

That event was quickly followed by the start of the V-1 onslaught but our area, fortunately, did not suffer too badly, with the first V-1 damaging houses at Great Saling near to Andrewsfield on 25th June. Although an occasional V-1 was seen or heard at night, only about 10 fell in our area up to the end of 1944. Unknown to us at the time, a pilot of 501 Sqdn. from Bradwell Bay reported shooting down a V-1 over Great Dunmow on 11th October.

Meanwhile, the hectic summer air activity had continued with an occasional special sighting, e.g. a York prototype on 14th July and the first A-26 Invader (41-39132) newly arrived for trials at Great Dunmow airfield. By the latter part of July the B-26s had moved from Earl's Colne, Chipping Ongar and Boreharn to bases near to the south coast, followed in early August by the Rivenhall group. Matching's B-26s moved to the continent on 10th September, soon followed by those from Stansted and by the A-20s from Little Walden. At the end of September Gosfield and Wethersfield were devoid of A-20s and the last two Marauder groups left from Andrewsfield and Great Dunmow soon after. The local airfields had a short breathing space while various necessary engineering work was carried out, but I counted 25 Albemarles plus some Horsas on the way into Earl's Colne on 30th September — the forerunners of the RAF 38 Group's massive presence in our local area. During the October Halifaxes began to replace the Albemarles, then 1st October brought Albacore 'NH-W' flying north to Bircham Newton in Norfolk and a rare Beaufort coded 'D.' Other unusual types occasionally seen were Sunderlands and Catalinas, probably *en route* to Felixstowe, and I recall a Barracuda escorted by a Hurricane at about that same time.

By then the P-51s of 361st FG had arrived at Little Walden, and on 5th October I saw the first Stirling IVs of 295 Sqdn heading for their new base at Rivenhall, where 570 Sqdn was also to be based. On that same day I logged over 30 Lancasters of 635, 115, 149 and 218 Sqdns., part of a much larger force which passed quite low over our town. The first Stirling of 620 Sqdn. (which, together with 190 Sqdn., was to occupy Great Dunmow airfield) was seen on 7th October although the main force did not start to arrive until the 14th, when a total of 14 Stirlings was logged plus four Whitleys towing Horsa gliders. The complete force of Stirlings, which comprised about 60 aircraft, took several days to arrive — plus well over 100 Horsas. Other Stirlings of 196 and 299 Sqdns. were also arriving at that time at Wethersfield.

The 'grapevine' was busy in October reporting that jets were at Debden. Strange noises had been heard in the sky but it was not until the 14th that I had a quick glimpse of one. On the following day I went to

Debden with schoolmate Geoff Harris but when we got there all we saw were two P-47s, T-6 42-84602, 29 P-51s and A-20 43-8896 'Tenn Lee.' We were just about to give up and go home when a loud roar from the hidden end of the airfield evolved into Meteors 'YQ-K,' 'D,' 'Y' and 'E' of 616 Sqdn., which then took off very noisily. A while later EE227 ('YQ-Y') returned and, on landing, the starboard undercarriage leg collapsed, although the aircraft did not appear to be badly damaged. Incidentally, it was only some time afterwards that we heard that the jets would be known as Meteors.

Also on 14th October, Mustang IIIs of 19 Sqdn. and 315 (Polish) Sqdn. were seen, with others of 65 Sqdn. on the next day. A visit to Andrewsfield on 22nd October revealed an airfield full of Mustangs: I logged a total of 74 of them from six different squadrons. The Mustang squadrons periodically changed bases but right up to the end of the war there was always a very large force at Andrewsfield, with well over 100 aircraft at peak times. With the 38 Group Stirlings often on exercises with the Horsas, we heard of — and sometimes saw — many gliders scattered around the countryside, particularly when sudden bad weather caused them to be released early; PW719 near Great Dunmow airfield on 27th October and RJ156 at Aythorpe Roding on 2nd November were two that I saw. On 21st November the nighttime crash of Stirling LK276 of 190 Sqdn. just west of Great Dunmow town sadly resulted in the loss of an experienced crew.

My records after 4th November 1944 are rather scanty as my next log went missing, but this was still a very busy spotting period. Visits to the west side of Great Dunmow airfield and then to the east side of Stansted were frequent as they could be accomplished quite quickly, even on a bike! Although the B-26s had gone from Stansted there were still plenty of various USAAF types to see at the Base Air Depot. In February 1945 Matching became an ORTU for Halifaxes, Stirlings and Horsas and I made one visit there although little was on view. Later I made a trip which took in Great Sampford, where I was lucky to see a paratroop drop in progress with — I think — Stirlings involved. From there I cycled to Castle Camps where 25 Sqdn. Mosquitos were based, and then to Wratting Common, where I saw many Lancasters of 195 Sqdn. On my homeward journey I intended to go to Little Walden but a guard on the airfield road barrier turned me away and I had to make an unexpected and tiring detour. On 28th February seven Meteors of 616 Sqdn. arrived at Andrewsfield for anti-V-1 activities and were seen on a few occasions. On the afternoon of 3rd March I had my only daylight sighting of a V-1, flying west across the town towards Hertfordshire. Some minutes later a Meteor took off from Andrewsfield in pursuit but I suspect it was too late.

On 20th March 1945 at about 2030 hours I rushed out of the house when I heard an aircraft approaching, just in time to see it in flames and flying very low across the town; it proved to be Stirling LJ930 from Great Dunmow airfield, shot down by a German intruder while returning from a practice drop at Great Sampford airfield. It fell across our narrow river, missing the town, but sadly only one crew-member escaped. A few days afterwards 'Operation Varsity' took place with the 38 Group aircraft from Great Dunmow, Rivenhall, Wethersfield, Earl's Colne & Matching all involved plus USAAF C-47s operating out of Boreharn and Chipping Ongar and RAF Dakotas out of Gosfield and Birch. They were part of a force of 1,591 tugs and 1,350 gliders involved in the Rhine-crossing operation.

In May the war in Europe was over at last, and at about that time I made a trip to Hatfield and Radlett which proved to be disappointing, although many Halifaxes were to be seen at the latter airfield. By the end of May the Ridgewell B-17s had departed to the States but RAF Transport Command set up a staging post at Boreham. Between 7th May and at least 8th December 1945 some 250 movements to and from liberated Europe were made — mainly by Dakotas but some by Liberators and Warwicks. From 4th June 1945 the Ansons, Dominies and Proctors of No.1 Delivery Flight were based at Andrewsfield until the unit was disbanded in the September — although the Proctor P6252 was still there in October. The Walruses and Spitfires of 276 Sqdn had arrived at Andrewsfield on 8th June, assisted by Dakotas KN281 and KG658. Although the Spitfires soon moved on, an occasional sighting of a Walrus was made until all nine aircraft, plus Anson NK325, departed on 22nd August destined for Kjevic in Norway. Once again the sound of Meteors was heard on 23rd June when eight aircraft of 512 Sqdn. arrived at Andrewsfield. On the next day six of the Meteors, with Mustangs of 133 Wing, were airborne for an air display at North Weald for the Royal Observer Corps.

On the afternoon of 23rd June, a long trip with school friend Ron Lee proved to be a partial disappointment. We took in the 4th FG at Debden, the 78th FG at Duxford and the 339th FG at Fowlmere where we logged plenty, but when we got to our final airfield (Nuthampstead) we were told that all the based B-17s had departed to the USA on the previous day. We then had a long, tiring ride of about 20 miles home. Journeys were then curtailed due to imminent School Certificate exams, although an interesting visit with several schoolmates to the 'Britain's Aircraft' Exhibition in Oxford Street was fitted in. School Cert. results proved to be not as good as had been hoped for: a pass in 'Aircraft Spotting' would have helped!

Civilian airliners then started to appear, including BOAC Dakotas G-AGNB & G-AGNC on 26th July, with ABA's Dakota SE-BAB on 4th August and DDL's Fw. Condor OY-DEM on 4th September, probably *en route* to Northolt. By the autumn of 1945 several of the local airfields were closing, while Sawbridgeworth's operational aircraft had departed by spring/summer 1944. Stansted transferred to the RAF in August 1945, Debden and North Weald were temporarily without aircraft after September, Matching closed in October and both Little Walden and Andrewsfield followed in November. Towards the end of the year our local Scout Troop received permission to visit Great Dunmow airfield and we were able to inspect a Halifax, a Horsa and an Oxford. By the 14th January 1946 the Halifaxes of 620 Sqdn. had completed a move to Palestine and Great Dunmow airfield's operational role came to an end. The same applied to Rivenhall, and by March 296 Sqdn. had been disbanded at Earl's Colne and 297 Sqdn. moved to Tarrant Rushton. Meanwhile the Mosquitos at Castle Camps had relocated to Boxted, near Colchester, during January.

My first airfield visit of 1946 was to Hatfield on 17th February, where I logged the prototype Dove G-AGPJ and just two Mosquitos, LR378 and LR534. Dakotas KJ973, KN433 and OY-DCE were seen overflying, and two days later OY-DCA put in an appearance, with SE-BAT the day after. A journey was made to Cambridge with Derrick Franklin on 10th March, by way of Stradishall; the airfield seemed deserted, but we were startled by the take-off of a York (51 Sqdn?) just as we were about to cross the main runway! Cambridge revealed six Tiger Moths and six Auster Vs (TW496, 497, 500 & 507, MZ187 and RT489) of 22 FTS, plus Auster RT483. Also present were Proctors G-AGTB & 'HBI, Tigers 'CDG & 'GYV and Autocrat 'HAW of Marshall's Flying School. Dakotas FD870, 944, 607 & 605(?), KG331, 390, 616 and 677 plus Miles Falcon G-ADLI and two more Proctors, R7497 & R7499, completed the day's log.

March, April and early May saw many aircraft over our area, Mosquitos, Dakotas and Oxfords predominating (including the Royal Navy's PG934 & PH144), also Air Taxis' Proctor G-AGYA. My next outing was again to Cambridge on 12th May, where additional aircraft logged included Tiger Moths G-AGYW, 'HLS and DF204, Proctor HM281 and Dakota KJ983. An interesting one low across our town on 12th May was a Royal Navy Stinson Reliant FK815 heading east. Two more Danish aircraft, Dakota OY-DBE on 15th May and DC-4 OY-DFI on 1st June led up to an escape for me from the office for a few days and my longest cycle ride to date.

On 8th June 1946 I set out early from Great Dunmow to visit my aunt in Esher, Surrey, via a planned airfield route. The weather was not too kind but progress was good. I had a quick look at the LAMS Halifaxes at Stansted and then to Panshanger where Tiger Moth G-AHIZ, Hornet Moth G-AEET and Moth Minor G-AFNJ were the only aircraft visible. Thence to Hatfield, where I saw only Autocrat G-AGXT, and then on to Radlett — where I logged nothing. But things changed for the better near

Mill Hill (apart from the weather), when many formations of the Victory Fly Past were seen in cloudy conditions, an unexpected bonus! My next stop was Hendon where, by climbing the railway embankment I was able to see a USAF Fairchild Cornell, and I also noted Morton's Rapide G-AGWP (but I can't recall whether it was actually on the airfield).

At Heston, my next stop, I recall a Fairey Spearfish and a Northrop P-61 Black Widow plus various light aircraft, and so on to the tented camp which was to become London Airport. On that first visit Lancasters and Lancastrians were noted along with Dakota PH-TCP, but little else. Finally to Hanworth Air Park where Piper J/3 Cub G-AFIZ, Taylor Cub G-AEIK and Autocrat G-AGYG accompanied a bunch of Proctors, Field's G-AHAZ & 'HGA plus NP394, NP177, NP193, MX453 & MX455. After about 7 to 8 hours I was pleased to get to Esher for a rest.

On the next day a shorter trip to Wisley revealed Vickers Vikings G-AGOM, G-AHOS & G-AHOT and then it was on to Brooklands, where Plus D G-AHCI was logged. On 10th June I cycled to London Airport; logging my first Constellation, NC88846, and then on to Staines to see brother John where he was stationed with the Army. I am unable to recall now whether I cycled back to Essex, but I suspect I took my bike on the train; but altogether it had been an eye-opening trip and I was anxious to do more.

In the next month at Dunmow, Dakotas KG403, G-AGZC and G-AGHU were seen amongst many more, also Liberator KN835 and Viking G-AGOL low over the town. Then it was back by train to Esher on 12th July and to Wisley (by bike) on the 13th, where I was pleased to see Messerschmitt Me.163B VF241 plus BOAC Warwick 5 G-AGLD and Anson G-AHUD. Hanworth on the 14th gave me GAL Cygnet G-AGAX, Morton's Consul G-AHJX and Proctors G-AHNA, G-AHXA and NP230. At Heston, Siebel 204D PH-NAV awaited me along with Oxfords LX537 & 538. My first visit to Northolt gave me Dakota VT-CDZ of Dalmia Jain Airways plus many other Dakotas. Next, London Airport was much busier than my previous visit with DC-4 YV-C-AJI, Constellations PP-PCC & G-AHEJ and several Lancastrians.

DC-4 OY-DFO, Yorks MW272 & MW173, Autocrat OO-ANL and Dakota EI-ACL featured among those overflying in July/August. My friends Derrick Franklin & Bernard Walsh and I went to Broxbourne aerodrome by bicycle on 18th August for our very first flight — 10 minutes for 10 shillings (50p) each in Proctor G-AHLW. It took a lot longer than that to get back home! While there I logged Hornet Moth G-ADOT, Proctors G-AGZL & G-AIAC, Tiger Moth G-AHMF and Plus D G-AHEI. All the Proctors and the Tiger were destroyed in a disastrous hangar fire about a year later. A further visit to Broxbourne on 25th August added Comper Swift G-ABPR, but I couldn't afford another flight.

My next sortie on 31st August 1946 included Elstree for the first time, where one LAMS Halifax, Proctors G-AIAD & NP223 and three Autocrats were logged. *En route* were seen Anson G-AGWA and Avro 19 G-AHIF, and then it was on to Northolt, where various BEA Dakotas, Vikings and Rapide G-AHKS were seen along with Railway Air Services Avro 19 G-AHIK. Heston revealed several additions to my records, while London Airport had another LAMS Halifax, G-AHZO, plus Dakotas, Yorks and Lancastrians. Another airfield not previously visited was Langley, which had Lancastrian G-AGWH and York G-AHEW, then back to Hanworth, where I saw the VEF J-12 YL-ABS and added Proctors G-AHMS, 'HTN and 'HVI, and then on to Esher to my very hospitable aunt and her family. On the next day I saw the United Whalers' Walrus G-AHFN over Chobham and then on 2nd September the Indian National Airways Viking VT-AZA at Wisley. Later in the day two New Zealand Proctors, ZK-AKI & 'AKQ were at Hanworth, plus Lockheed 12A G-AGTL and Whitney Straight G-AEVA. Another LAMS Halifax, G-AHZN, was at London Airport with York ZS-ATP and Constellation G-AHEN. My first visit to Croydon was on 3rd September, the highlights being Percival Q.6 G-AHTA and Dragon G-AECZ amongst the Dakotas, Rapides and Proctors.

On 5th September I set out on another long journey. Over the Guildford area I saw the Southampton Air Services DC-2 G-AGBH, while at Farnborough the only aircraft logged was Tudor 8 G-AGST. Blackbushe had, amongst other types, Ju.52/3M VN718, while Woodley revealed Aerovans G-AHXH & G-AGWO and Messenger RG327. At my next stop, White Waltham, three Moth Minors, Hornet Moth G-ADNB, two Magisters, Rapide G-AGWC and the Lockheed 14H G-AGBG of British Aviation Services were added to my log. London Airport had Liberator AL507 and the FAMA York LV-XGP, Heston revealed the new Chrislea Ace G-AHLG plus some more Proctors and a Consul, while finally at Hanworth there was nothing new.

I had a rest day on 6th September but saw Proctor OO-USA overflying Esher, and then it was back to the usual haunts on the 7th with Proctor G-AHVD seen at Hanworth, Beech D.17 G-AHXJ at Heston, and Constellations NC88855 and NC88861 logged at London Airport. My final look at the area was on the 8th, on my way home to Essex, with Tipsy Trainer G-AFJT at Heston and DC-3 NC54227 at Heathrow. The Debden Battle of Britain show which I attended on 14th September included a number of Ansons, Lancaster PB926, Hastings TG508 and other items, but was completely overshadowed by the SBAC Show at Radlett on the following day. I cycled there with Derrick Franklin and although we had to watch the activities from a bridge, it was well worthwhile. There were over 50 different British aircraft on view, although visibility was rather restricted from our angle. Highlights were perhaps the AW.52G, DH.108, Westland Welkin, Firebrand, Seafang, Attacker, Sea Fury etc. — altogether a very interesting day.

After that it was back to the grind, but with plenty of aircraft across the area, including Beech 18 NC80014, Liberators EV884 & KG909, Vikings OY-DLO and 'DLI — not forgetting the fuselage of the Percival Merganser G-AHMH seen on a lorry passing through Great Dunmow on 12th December. Earlier, on 29th October, Anson G-AIFA of Straight Aviation Training appeared over the area and I learned that the company was carrying out navigation training from Chipping Ongar airfield principally for Dutch personnel. The Ansons seemed to be very frequently in use, continuing until at least 22nd April 1947, and included G-AIEZ, 'IFB, 'IFD, 'IOA and 'IOB. The Home Counties Flying Club with their Fairchild Argus also used the airfield.

The severe winter of 1946/47 quite badly affected our part of Essex, and restricted airfield visits along with many other activities. At that time I was in a rather boring job and heading towards conscription, so I decided to apply for an Aircrew Test. Dad took me by car to the Romford RAF Recruitment Centre through masses of piled-up snow, and sometime in March I attended for the test at North Weald. My maths proved to be not good enough but, as I had decided that I would join the RAF, I volunteered for five years in the RAF Police — possibly with a view to later joining the civil police. (With my father and an uncle having been police inspectors and a sister in the wartime Women's Auxiliary Police it seemed to be the right course at the time, but five years or so later it proved not to be!) My entry into the RAF was delayed due to the problems caused by the bad winter, but meanwhile spotting continued with Viking OY-DLA on 9th March, Halifax G-AHZL *Port of Oslo* at Stansted on 22nd March and G-AHZJ *Port of Marseille* on 4th April, with G-AIWT on the 17th. A visit to Southend Airport on the 20th gave me Puss Moth G-ABKZ and Vega Gull G-AEXV and on 5th May Stansted had Halifaxes G-AIWJ and G-AHZK *Port of Naples*.

On 15th May, about a month before my 18th birthday, I left home with some trepidation for my new life, which was slightly brightened by Rapide G-AHGH at Hendon and HP Halton G-AHDY at Radlett, seen while *en route* to Cardington. Square-bashing and spud-bashing followed, but only eight days later, I was surprisingly on my way home on Whitsun leave, and saw Halton G-AHDT at Radlett! A visit to Broxbourne netted Proctor G-AIDT on the 26th and then it was back to Cardington for drill, weapons training, bags of 'bull' and getting very fit for the next nine weeks. It was a glorious summer with only about two rainy days, on which we drilled in the massive airship hangar. Aircraft didn't seem to be very plentiful and I logged only KZ.III OY-DMA on 22nd June and Proctor G-AHVG on 13th July. Whilst at home on leave,

Vikings OY-DLU and 'DLE appeared on 31st July and 1st August, and at Stansted on the 4th August were Halifaxes G-AIWK and 'JPK plus Sparrowhawk G-ADNL, which was a surprise.

Back to Cardington for our final few days and then past Radlett again to see Halton G-AHDL on 13th August, and to Stansted on the next day for Stirling V OO-XAC of Trans-Air, Belgium and Alpha Airways' Halifax ZS-BTA. Then it was off on another trip to Esher (with the bike on the train) and to Hanworth on the 15th and to Heston to see Reliant G-AFVT and Cierva C.30A G-AHMJ, amongst many others. London Airport, almost a year after my last visit, was busier, with Liberators G-AHYF & 'HYG, Constellation NC86530, several foreign Dakotas and two Yorks, LV-XGN & ZS-ATU. A visit on the next day netted DC-3 N79009, DC-4s ZS-AUB, N48762 & NC49524 plus DC-4Ms CF-TEL & 'TEO, a bunch of Constellations and many Dakotas. On to Northolt where EI-ADG & 'ADJ and 15 BEA Vikings were logged, plus Dakota OK-WDZ, Lockheed 14 CF-TCD and many more. Hirtenberg HS.9A G-AGAK was over Esher on 17th August: this was on the day I cycled to Croydon, listed some 60-plus aircraft and met up with my brother, then stationed in that area. We had a flight, my second, in the Newman Aircraft Proctor G-AJTP, which was interesting. Among those present were Argus OO-FAF, Hudson OO-API, Avro 19 OO-APG, Proctor ZS-BSR, Goeland F-BCCB and Lodestar ZS-BAH, to mention but a few. Wisley on the 18th had Vikings G-AIVM & 'IVO, Air India's VT-CLY & 'CLZ plus LV-XFI & 'CFJ. Then it was back home to Essex and the Royal Air Force.

On 21st August 1947 I had to report to No.1 RAF Police Wing Headquarters at Staverton in Gloucestershire to commence my RAF Police training. I had no idea until I arrived that civil aircraft were based there, and had a welcome surprise with Cessna C.34 G-AFBY and Hawk Trainer 3 G-AJDR. Over the next few days Tiger Moth G-ADIH, Autocrats G-AJDW & 'GXV and Plus D 'HUM appeared, and then I was posted for a few days' 'on the job' training to Duxford. That seemed like a good place to go, but in my few days there I do not recall seeing any aircraft apart from an overflying Viking, G-AHOP. I suspect that the resident squadrons were temporarily in Germany. On my way back to Staverton I saw the Merchantman G-AILJ over the Reading area. Our Police Course was part of the RAF contingent in the Battle of Britain march-past in Cheltenham on 14th September and a few days later — I believe the 17th — I was part of a group of trainees sent to Netheravon, Wilts. We night-stopped there and on the next day carried out traffic control duties for a large Airborne Forces paradrop over Salisbury Plain, involving Hastings, Halifaxes, Dakotas, Horsas and Hamilcars. It was very difficult to stay focussed on the road traffic!

The police training continued alongside the visiting aircraft, of which I logged 16, mainly in October, including Argus G-AJAT, Tomtit G-AFTA,

Gemini G-AJZK, BA Swallow G-AFGE and Rapide EI-ADP. During December I was on embarkation leave, destined for the Middle East, so on the 14th I visited my brother in the Croydon area, where the airport produced DH Flamingo G-AFYH, Dove G-AJZT and six Consuls among the types seen. The day after Boxing Day I had to report to the Transit Unit at RAF Burtonwood and for 19 days experienced the delights of winter in the Warrington area, seeing only two aircraft, Messenger G-AJOC and Dakota EI-ACT.

Departure on 17th January 1948 was from Liverpool — to the strains of *Now is the Hour* — on HMT *Samaria*, a 19,597 gross ton liner in its last year as a trooper. We crossed the Bay of Biscay to the delights of hammock swinging and Housey-Housey and in a Force 8 gale, which was most uncomfortable. We anchored off Gibraltar and then again in Malta's Grand Harbour, where I recall a Fiat G-12 climbing out of Luqa airfield. Then it was on to Port Said, where we disembarked after 11 days at sea. We went by train, on which one of our party always had to be stationed (armed) at the rear to repel boarders and/or thieves —one of my mates had his watch slashed off his wrist. We stopped at Ismailia railway station, mainly remembered by the lurid titles of the literature on sale, and on to El Hamra Transit Camp near to RAF Kasfareet. The main pleasure there, in tented accommodation, was testing the strength of Stella beer, keeping clear of very large ants and watching films in the open-air cinema. The only actual duty we did was to be part of an armed raid on a nearby small village to retrieve a mass of stolen radio equipment. One important event was seeing BOAC Sandringham G-AGJM flying quite low near Kasfareet on 5th February. By the 11th our next postings were confirmed and, with two of my mates, I was on my way back to Malta via Port Said, and on the journey passed Fayid airfield in the distance where several Lancasters were visible.

We travelled on HMT *Otranto* on the three-day trip to Malta. When we arrived we were unable to move into the Grand Harbour due to heavy weather and had to transfer, across a precarious gangplank, onto a corvette with all our gear. Then a landing craft took us into the harbour and finally we took a lorry to the Luqa Transit Unit. On the next day we transferred to our new unit, No.14 Provost Flight based in Valletta, Malta's capital. We lived in civilian lodgings, where we had bed and washing facilities for which we paid 1/- per day (5p) out of our 1/6d allowance. The showers were about 50 yards away, our mess hall about 100 yards and our Flight Office about 400 yards away, but it was generally agreed that it was one of the better postings in the Middle East Command. Although based in Valletta, usually on street patrols, I was often at Luqa and able to see what it offered in the way of aircraft. No.38 Sqdn. was the main unit with ASR Lancasters, but the airfield was also available for airline and private movements.

The British Aviation Services Lodestar G-AJAW and the Chartair Consul G-AIKO were my first sightings at Luqa on 16th February. Chartair operated flights on behalf of Air Malta and also used Consuls G-AIUR, 'JLL and 'IKX. York MW140, Tudor VX202, three Iraqi Rapides, YI-ABF, 'BG & 'BH, and BOAC Dakota G-AGKB took me up to the end of February. At 397 MU Safi I came across the remains of Dakota G-AGKD, which had crashed in December 1946. Although I had to go occasionally to the Royal Navy airfield at Hal Far, I have no recollection of seeing any aircraft there, or from the various carriers seen in the Grand Harbour, HMS *Ocean* and, I believe, HMS *Hermes*, as well as one from the US Navy which came in during my stay on the island. Proctor G-AHWX was always very securely tied down at Luqa and seemed to be a mystery aircraft as I don't think I ever saw it flying at all.

March and April 1948 brought a few new types: on 3rd March, Dakotas G-AGKE & G-AGKI and Air India Viking VT-CRC, and a French NC.701 No.16 on the 9th with Airwork's Viking G-AJFP on the 21st, and Anson VL336, Lancashire Aircraft Corporation's Halifax G-AIHY and two Skyways DC-4s, G-AJPM & G-AJPN, all on 2nd April. It was at about that time that 37 Sqdn. took over from 38 Sqdn. at Luqa. I have a memory, but no note, of what I think was a B-25 Mitchell arriving at Luqa with a French Admiral aboard, escorted by some Bell Kingcobras, possibly during May? Only Dakota F-BEFJ and Airwork Viking G-AJFT were logged in June followed by 'JFS on 15th July, when Constellation PH-TET also arrived. BEA Viking G-AHPN, British-American Air Services Halifax G-AKBB, Dove VR-TBB and Dakota ZS-BWX all appeared in July, followed in August by DC-4 G-AJPL, Vikings G-AKTU, G-AIVJ, G-AJFS and G-AIXR, Fiat G.12 I-DALB and Dakotas ZS-BCA and G-AGKJ.

There were at times long gaps in my visits to Luqa, but during September and up to mid-October they produced a total of 24 new sightings. These included SM.95 I-DALJ and Fiat G.12s I-DALC & 'LD, Doves G-AKST & 'JLW, Dakotas G-AGKC & 'GNE, VR-HDQ of Hong Kong Airways, ZS-BTO & 'BTN and PH-TFB, Haltons G-AHDO & 'HDW, BEA Viking G-AIVK, Hunting's G-AHPJ & 'HPI, and Airwork's 'IXS. Avro 19 G-AGPB was at Luqa on 30th September, followed the next day by the interesting Theseus-Lincoln RE418, Hastings TG507 and Proctor HM458 of the Middle East Communications Flight. Finally, I logged Halifax G-AHWN and Skyways' York G-AHLV, which was delayed by a major engine change on 12th October. It was probably about that time when my brother wrote to tell me about the formation of Air-Britain, so I sent off the remittance and just scraped in as Founder Member No.249.

On 8th November my stay in Malta took a turn for the worse, and I was confined to the Military Hospital at Imtarfa with severe skin trouble.

I was not 'ill' but was only allowed out on a few occasions before the end of the year, and eventually a decision was made that my condition would not improve unless I returned to the UK. After many weeks I was allowed out to arrange clearance from my unit, when I logged Dakota G-AKAY of Sivewright Airways and also ZS-AVO, before boarding a small hospital ship, the *El Nil*, on 18th February, after a year and four days on the island. The voyage home ended at Southampton, where we saw the SS *Queen Elizabeth* and, on the approaches, a mass of six BOAC Sunderlands, two Sandringhams and four Solents. Next stop was the RAF Hospital at Uxbridge which enabled me to see SM.95 I-DALN on 26th February and Vikings G-AJBW & 'BY and Consul 'JXE on the 28th. I was then sent on leave, so I went to see my brother at Croydon from 10th-12th March and logged 79 new aircraft, including Beech D.18s NC100E, N79848 and VR-HED, Super Ace G-AKUV, Sokol OK-CIS, four Ansons, 11 Proctors and 30 Rapides etc. On 15th March I passed Langley airfield where I saw Vikings G-AGRP, 'GRV, 'HOV & 'HOW, and on that day had to report to RAF Innsworth at Gloucester, from where I was sent on leave for a further six weeks!

At London Airport on 22nd March I logged 26 new aircraft including my first Languedocs, F-BATT and F-BCUE, Convair 240 PH-TEI and four Dutch Dakotas, plus three Constellations and Tudor G-AGRG. Stansted on the 24th gave me Halifaxes G-AKGO, PP291 & PP324. Hermes 2 G-AGUB appeared over home on 7th April and a visit to Gatwick on the 12th added Halifax G-AHYI, Geminis and Consuls, and a number of military types difficult to log. Then to Northolt on 15th April, where I had a flight (my third), this time in the Lancashire Aircraft Corporation's Rapide G-AKNV, 15 shillings (75p) over central London. At Northolt US Navy R-5D 50850, C-47B 43-48316, DC-4 SE-BBC, and Convair 240 HB-IRV were among the 30 or so logged. Then to London Airport again on the 18th, where Bristol 170 G-AIMA and Tudor G-AKCD were among those present. Then it was time to report back to the RAF Police Wing, which had moved from Staverton to Pershore, Worcs. Whilst there I logged Proctor 3 G-AKXK of the Worcester School of Flying, and on 23rd April I arrived at my new posting to Air Ministry PM2 in Exhibition Road, South Kensington. This involved some clerical work, but mainly running the Officers' Bar in the building, a job I was not particularly happy in although a small consolation was that many aircraft flew past the window into London Airport. Some of these I was able to log, including Short Sealand G-AKNO on 5th May.

During the remainder of 1949 my airfield visits seem to have eased off, but Croydon on 20th August had Vultee Valiant NX54084, DH.86B G-ADUF and Proctor G-AJTP. In the latter I had a flight (my 4th) accompanied by Nora, my wife-to-be, which is one possible explanation for the lack of concentration on aviation matters!

Now to go beyond the 1940s, because I must mention that in August 1950 our Air Ministry Department moved to Bromyard Avenue in Acton. We were accommodated at RAF West Drayton and so travelled in every day to a job much more to my liking with no bar work! I soon discovered that the Air-Britain HQ was only a stone's throw away, situated in Mrs Farmer's house, where 'Mac' MacGeorge ruled as Hon. Gen. Sec., and where I spent a number of happy evenings stuffing things in envelopes etc. to help the cause.

I hope you will bear with me if I stray a bit further. In February 1950 I received notice of a posting to Germany and then spent a total of six weeks on embarkation leave and kicking my heels before being told to report back to my old unit. I was not then called for another Germany posting until June 1951, arriving at Bückeburg town towards the end of the month. Here I was posted to Bückeburg Airfield — which was at that time the airport for Hannover — in July 1951 as NCO i/c No.1 Airport Security Section, which involved checking all service personnel on and off flights, amongst other tasks. I could not have wished for a better posting, although there were times when things were rather slack. Unfortunately, after about two months I was posted on to the Hamburg area.

The following is a fairly comprehensive list of sightings of the based aircraft and visitors:

17th July 1951: Dakota G-ALXM, Anson PH764, Meteor WB118.
18th July: Bristol 170 G-AICS (BEA), Anson TX237, Meteor VZ577 ('B-B'), VZ982 ('A-F'), VW378, C-47B 44-77226, Dakota PH-TAY.
19th July: Tiger Moth T6909, C-47 42-100768, Ansons PH708, TX225, TX157, TX227, Meteors VS970 ('A-A'), VZ599, VZ601, VZ611 ('B-Z'), WA710 ('A-W'), WB113 ('B-T'), EG213 ('MN-T', Belgian).
20th July: Anson VM328, Meteor VZ590 ('B-E'), C-47A 42-100912, C-47B 44-77049.
21st July: Devon VP957.
23rd July: C-47 44-77049 & 43-48328.
24th July: Auster VF615 ('XM-P'), Dakota KN386.
26th July: Valetta VX525 & VX573 ('C-A').
27th July: Auster VF559, Vampire WA396, Meteor VS978 ('A-R') & WA739.
30th July: VZ580 Meteor ('B-G') & WB114, plus a Viking of the King's Flight with the then Princess Royal.
31st July: Tiger Moth T8258, Meteors VS970 ('A-L'), VE587 ('B-D') & VZ607 ('B-H').
1st August: Anson PH725, Finnair DC-3 OH-LCF.
2nd August: Meteor VS974 ('B-X'), Dominie V-2 (GX796, R.Neth.AF), Vampire VZ301 ('L-F'), Tiger Moth N9279, Anson G-ALUR (Crewsair Ltd. — cabin area filled with large tank of exotic fish).

3rd August: Tiger Moth N6635.

5th August: Anson PH531.

6th August: Anson PH700.

7th August: Ansons PH667, PH710, PH537 & PH588.

8th August: Vampire WA143 ('T-B').

10th August: Tiger Moth T6394, Meteor WB143 ('B-U').

11th August: Anson PH841, Vampire WA149 ('L-P'), Meteors VW365 ('B-C') & VW371 ('B-F').

12th August: Ansons PH591, PH647 & PH838, Devon VP961.

14th August: Devon VP974. Anson VM391, BEA Dart-Dakota G-ALXN (on its first cargo flight from Northolt), C-117A Skytrain 45-2548.

16th August: Auster VX123.

17th August: Devon VP960 (in which I had an hour's flight a few days later), Valetta VX494, Meteors VS983 ('A-G'), WA685, VZ596, C-47 43-15344.

18th August: C-47 43-48076.

21st August: Meteor VS984 ('A-H'), Valetta VX574, Dakota K-16 (OT-CWG, R.Belgian AF).

24th August: Tiger Moth T6107, Dominie V-3 (R.Neth AF).

25th August: Ansons TX165 & VM327, Auster AOP.7 VX108, Harvard B-1 (FT362, R.Neth AF).

26th August: York WW581 (Lancashire Aircraft Corpn's G-AGNW), Dakotas CBK20 & CBK78 (Turkish).

27th August: Vampire WA195.

28th August: Valetta VX559, C-47A 42-100847.

29th August: Anson TX256, Devon WB534, Meteor T.7 WG939.

30th August: Tiger Moth N9440, Valetta VW163.

31st August: Auster AOP.6 VF492 ('XM-G'), Proctor RM223.

1st September: Meteor PR.10 VS975 ('A-N').

2nd September: Vampire WA143 ('L-C').

3rd September: Auster VF527.

4th September: Meteor VS977 ('A-P'), Anson 21s VV247, VV248.

5th September: Anson 21 VV257 ('FAG-C') & TX221, Oxford 21/224 (R.Danish AF).

7th September: Vampire VX973 ('X-Z'), Meteors VS979 ('A-S') & VS981 ('A-E') of 541 Sqdn.

9th September: Anson PH540.

10th September: B-26 Invader 44-35885, Mosquito T.2 VA883, Anson PH830.

12th September: Ansons PH647 & PH839, Dakota K-28 (OT-CNO, R.Belg AF).

13th September: Ansons PH815 & TX184, BEA Dakota G-ALTT.

14th September: Dakota G-AHCV, York MW327, Anson TX159, Vampire VX462 ('T-Y'), C-47 43-15221.

15th September: C-47s 43-15133, 43-15505, 43-47988, C-54E 44-9060,
  Mosquito B.35 VP197, Mosquito MA-2 ('B2-B', R.Neth.AF),
  Meteor T.7 WE782 ('T-Z').
16th September: Dakota KN628, Meteor WB156 ('B-U'), C-47 43-49098.
17th September: Vampire WA340, Valetta WD161 ('NU-D'), Anson
  VL351.
18th September: Meteor VZ603 ('B-A'), Vampire WA357 ('E-A'),
  Mosquito MA-4 ('B2-D')(R.Neth.AF), Harvards FT211 ('B-11 5') &
  FS913 ('B-13 6') (R.Neth.AF).

I was scheduled to go on leave on 20th September, flying to Northolt on Valetta WD161 on its return flight from Warsaw. Then I heard that Anson VL351 was leaving on the 18th for Tangmere, and received permission from my CO to travel, and had a 1 hr 50 min flight to Amsterdam. At Schiphol I logged Autocrat PH-OTO, Dakotas PH-TBP, 'TCL, 'TCY, 'TDW & 'TDZ, DC-4 PH-TDL, Constellations PH-TDI, 'TFE & 'TFF, Convair 240s PH-TEA & 'TED, and Curtiss C-46 4X-AQE. After a late lunch, we left in the Anson, passing quite close to Tunbridge Wells as dusk was falling and reaching Tangmere at about 2100 hours after a further 2 hours; then home, eventually, to Essex.

On my return to Bückeburg, by way of the North Sea trooping ferry from Harwich to the Hook of Holland, I was greeted with the news about my new posting and moved to No.104 Police Flight at Uetersen airfield on 10th October 1951. No aircraft were based at the airfield, but I did see three visitors, Tiger Moth R5041 on 5th February 1952, Cessna L-19A 51-7348 on 8th May and Norseman OH-NOA on 26th May. From Uetersen I was occasionally detailed for armed escort duty on arms and ammunition runs to the various 2nd TAF airfields. I visited Fassberg during a four-day trip on 25th March 1952, where Nos.14, 98 and 112 Sqdn. Vampires were based, and then on to Celle to more Vampires of Nos.16 and 145 Sqdns. From there to Butzweilerhof, which was still under construction, and finally to Wildenrath on the 27th where yet more Vampires were due within a few days. We then back-tracked to all the same airfields, arriving at Uetersen in time for a late lunch on the 29th. Another journey of that nature started on 18th April to Jever, where Nos.93 and 112 Squadron's Vampires were based, but this took three days due to a lorry breakdown.

While engaged on an SIB enquiry at Jever on 3rd August my colleague and I were instructed to go to the US enclave at Bremerhaven where the body of an airman, believed to be British, had been found. From the serial number on the shirt and navigator's brevet on the flying suit we were able to establish that this unfortunate man came from Meteor WD607 of 141 Sqdn, which was in collision with another Meteor over the North Sea more than two months earlier on 20th May 1952.

Definitely my final aviation memory of that period relates to 11th March 1952, when I was Duty NCO in our Flight Office at Uetersen and received a call from the German Police that a British aircraft had crashed on the approach to Hamburg Airport. I logged the information and thought little more of it, although I did eventually learn that it was Freddie Laker's York G-AMGL flying under the Surrey Flying Services name. By a strange coincidence, some 15 or so years later while cupboards at British United Airways at Gatwick Airport were being emptied, I managed to rescue a set of photographs of 'MGL's crash which were just about to be scrapped!

CHAPTER 19

PORTSMOUTH AERO CLUB AND BEYOND

by

TOMMY THOMPSON

(The author's personal notes concerning the continuation of his aviation activities after the period discussed read as follows: "I continued to fly at Portsmouth Aero Club and also for Wright Rain in a Twin Comanche and, later, for a private owner with an Aztec C, until 1967, when an opportunity arose for me to join the DH Hatfield team; this was to set up an Ops. Dept. with the growing sales of 125s and Tridents (but for the first 3 months to do the previous four months' Jeppesen amendments for the pilots, or so it seemed). The remaining 19 years were much more enjoyable and took me all over the world in various right-hand seats, and — when anno domini demanded it — as a working passenger on sales trips." — Ed.)

I suppose that my introduction to civil flying began when I was asked to join the Westland Aircraft flight test team at Yeovil in March 1945. Previously, in 1941, I had been in a Blenheim squadron and had had a forced landing in Portugal on the way to the Middle East; I had escaped from this with the assistance of the Royal Navy, and had then returned to the UK.

On 'rest' I was posted to 13 M.U. Henlow as a u/t test pilot on Hurricanes and Hampdens with, as a special treat, an occasional ride in a Vickers Virginia still busily engaged on dropping test parachutes until it blew away in a high wind in 1942. By that time I had graduated on to Whitleys Mks.I-V and moved to 7 Air Gunnery School Stormy Down in Wales, where there was also lots of flying in Defiants, Masters, Ansons and Lysanders, towing drogues and spotting downed aircrew in the Bristol Channel.

The increasing Whitley hours somehow landed me with a posting to 9 MU, a Horsa glider towing-unit at Cosford. Later, in October 1943, a number of gliders were towed to all the Scottish airfields to try and fool the Germans that there was an intention to invade Norway. This was rather expensive as the winter weather wrecked most of the gliders, and of the remaining four only two of them survived their journeys back down south behind their USAF tugs.

My only contribution to Hitler's war effort in the early days of the exercise was to get caught out in very bad weather and a shortage of daylight, resulting in an emergency arrival in a very small field. We were heading across from East Fortune towards Carlisle, but by Hawick the clouds came down and we were forced into a valley, which after some time became a sort of T-junction. As we had on a lot of port drift I guessed we were to the south of the track to Carlisle, and so decided to turn right. This valley went on endlessly, but eventually we came out of the hills near Lanark and the flatter ground offered a few possible landing areas. The chosen one at Newhouse (now in about the middle of the M8) was just long enough for a landing but was not enough to take off from; this took Whitley BD444 out of the war for a whole week while the all-Thompson crew of two dug away a three-foot high bank to give access to another small field: this then allowed me to fly her back to base at Kirkbride, thereby avoiding any further awkward questions.

Glider delivery continued apace with the approach of D-Day, but afterwards I felt that with 500 hours on type I was due for a change, and found a vacancy at 33 MU Lyneham on Spitfires and Seafires being accepted into service; for the next 10 months and 273 hours I gained experience on nearly every Mark up to the Mk.XXI and the three different Seafires.

It was the Command practice to detach its pilots for a short period to a factory to catch up with the firm's pilots' latest methods and production problems. My posting was to Westland Aircraft at Yeovil and their satellite factory at Yeovilton, and my three weeks under Hal Penrose, James Ramsden and Pete Garner were some of the most pleasant yet hard-working times I had in my career, particularly when Hal asked me to stay on permanently.

As a result I became the resident test pilot at their small Yeovilton factory, commuting from Yeovil when required in our recently-acquired Auster 5 TW516 or the Company Rapide G-AHLF. The factory received new and rebuilt wings, fuselages, engines, tails and other fittings from a number of local production units around the area and these were assembled into new Mk.IX series Spitfires.

From a flight-testing point of view the prime snag encountered was the profile of the ailerons which, when paired up in an aircraft, could produce a violent wing-low tendency in flight which could not be readily anticipated beforehand. However Westlands had a genius called Jack (whose peacetime occupation had been as a market gardener) who had been discovered to have a 'feel' for the ups and downs in the metal trailing edges of Spitfires. Jack would inspect the ailerons before a first flight, then cycle round to the Airfield Controllers' van and take up position further down the side of the duty runway ready to attend rapidly to any trim faults on the first flights. The pilot would taxi out and take off, possibly only to discover that both hands were needed to hold the aircraft level as it gained speed in a rather shaky quick circuit and short landing near Jack.

A hand held up, fingers extended and pointing to the offending low wing, indicated the degree of out of trim, and Jack would hammer away as he saw fit and then hold up his hammer and made for the runway edge so that the aircraft could take off again. This performance could be repeated several times in a bad case, but two taps was par for the Spitfire before it could be flown into its full test sequence. The multi-sourcing of Spitfire parts assembled at Yeovilton required a greater number of proving flights than did the Seafires coming down the production line at Yeovil.

The boss of the flight hangar at Yeovil was Oliver Reed, who had spent his working life at Westlands and demanded a high standard of work from all his men — and got it. Another well-known character was 'Fred', a 6 ft 3 in giant whose strength I was particularly glad of when I landed Auster TW516 near the flight line in an unexpected wind and he and others rushed out to hang onto the struts while I taxied into the hangar.

After the end of the European war Spitfire contracts were expected to tail off although Seafire XVIIs were still required for the Pacific fleet, but with the capitulation of the Japanese even they started to have a lower priority for the next year — but I still did over 200 hours up to my demobilisation in August 1946.

A month prior to this I had met a local contractor who wanted to buy an Auster Autocrat and be flown around the West Country looking for concrete 'pill boxes' etc. that could be blown up and removed for local authorities and farmers. I collected Autocrat G-AHHT from Rearsby on the 3rd July via a somewhat roundabout route, starting with the ferry of Seafire 17 SX354 from Yeovil to Culham, and then hitching a lift in the back of Firefly PP554 from Culham to Rearsby. 'HHT then proceeded to Madley to pick up the new owner and then I flew him home to Weston-super-Mare.

For the next month I flew him all over south-west England in my spare time up to demob day, and then regularly until he had secured demolition contracts which more than paid for the Auster. The aircraft was based at either Yeovil or Weston-super-Mare for a nominal sum as there were no exorbitant landing fees or handling charges to contend with. I preferred Weston as there were no sheep to damage the aircraft. When one of the RAF pilots on temporary attachment to Yeovil had a lady friend, an ATA pilot, she used to visit him occasionally at weekends in a Fairchild Argus; that was until one Sunday when the airfield was closed and the sheep were able to roam free and munch the tasty elevator fabric of the Argus! Oliver Reed, ever the 'gent', decreed that the elevator should be recovered and doped adequately so that she could depart slightly late on the Monday — with a somewhat red face and elevator to match!

At the end of September, when the farmer decided to learn to fly 'HHT, I thought that would be the last I should see of her, and so it proved until 2002 when I saw her again at Popham in the able hands of Ambrose Barber, who had re-engined her as a J/1N. I discovered that she lived in a small hangar on a hillside ski slope north of the South Downs near Petersfield, from which I have since enjoyed several journeys around the local strips.

Returning home to Portsmouth in October 1946, I found that active steps were being taken by the former members of the prewar Aero Club to reclaim their old hangar and large clubhouse from Airspeed, who had taken over the buildings for wartime Oxford production and drawing offices; all these were due to be returned to the Club before the end of that year. The original Chief Flying Instructor, Sqdn.. Ldr. Harry Mitchell, had returned from RAF instructional duties and was negotiating with the Hunting Group to supply two Tiger Moths. All this came to fruition when I had a telephone call to go to the Ship Inn at nearby Langstone for a meeting of the early members of the Club, at which it was announced that the clubhouse and hangar had been released and that two aircraft were ready for collection at Weston.

A few days later, on the 1st November, the two ferry crews set off in Rapide G-AHEB piloted by Joe Sallis, but bad weather over the Mendips and Bristol Channel forced a return to Portsmouth; however the following day we did get through and found G-AIDA and G-AIDB waiting for us. The former Secretary to the Club, 'Rocky' Guild, was sharing the trip with me, but it became obvious that, as he had not flown during the war, he was badly out of practice and needed constant attention during the return flight. But eventually Portsmouth hove in sight and, on landing, we were greeted by a small crowd of members waiting to raise a glass or two in the Club bar.

Membership increased rapidly and bar profits soared when flying recommenced at the princely sum of £3.00 per hour. After a short while a chef was obtained and meals were served at lunch time, while the bar kept rather elastic hours, particularly at the weekends. Petrol rationing was still in force, of course, and a regular late-night police check point was to be found on most nights a mile up the main road which ran past the Club. To avoid this, one of the club members — who was the traffic manager of a local bus company and who could be out legally at all hours — often volunteered to set off with full headlights followed by several cars without lights. At a road junction a quarter of a mile from the check point the followers would break off, light up and proceed up a road parallel to the main road and pass Paddy still chatting happily to the coppers!

Members liked to fly over to the Aero Club at Cowes, which was then run by Russell Gunton. The field was quite small with a slight uphill slope to the south, and with the prevailing south-west wind some neat landings could be made in the Tigers, but landings to the north, which were infrequent, tended to float on a bit on the downhill slope and could lead to an overshoot by the cautious beginner. The airfield was on the west side of the road leading into Newport and I remember that Saunders Roe had a hangar there and that a Walrus was seen there occasionally.

The Tigers were also used for aerotowing the light gliders of the Southdown Aero Club run by Ron Clear, an Airspeed test pilot with many hours on gliders. They had a tricky little Scud 1, and also a larger Scud 3 owned and rebuilt early in the war by Ron, a popular machine with an easily-moveable seat to meet varying leg lengths. This facility allowed me to be towed off one summer Sunday evening over the town and the South Parade Pier just in time to hear quite clearly the opening tune of Oscar Rabin's band concert; this reminded me that I had got a ticket for it but in the excitement of the offer to fly the glider had forgotten all about it.

Among the new members was an ex-RFC SE.5 pilot who drove a little Humber sports car accompanied by his beautiful Edwardian lady wife. Hervey had a nervous stutter and a braying laugh, but desperately wanted to fly again after 30 years, so one day I took him with me in 'IDA when 'IDB had also just departed for Cowes. He sat upright in the front cockpit gazing around as we gained height, and as we passed 1,000 feet I called to him through the Gosport tube to ask if he would like to take over the controls.

Back came an unexpected crisp voice: "OK, I have control," (no stutter, no laugh) and the machine climbed steadily ahead until I suggested a turn to the south-west, whereupon he turned her smoothly onto the new heading.

Below and to the left was 'IDB, and I could not resist the temptation to say to him: "If 'IDB was a Hun, what would you do?"

Without saying anything he turned the aircraft smartly to the left and dived after the other aircraft, caught up with it rapidly with full throttle and at 50 yards rolled off to starboard after firing an imaginary burst.

"I enjoyed that!" he said.

Even his landing was reasonable, with a few suggestions and little corrections from my ready hands. Yet once back on the ground the stutter and the laugh reappeared. That I found strange, and for some reason it reminded me of a jeweller I knew in Yeovil who was very deaf and could only discuss business with a traveller on the little train that ran from Yeovil Town out to Yeovil Junction. Once the train was in motion he could hear adequately until the train stopped at the junction, and there they sat in silence until the start of the return journey.

A Magister G-AIDF joined the fleet, followed by our first Auster Autocrat, G-AJAS, a month later, which instantly became a favourite for instruction with its closed cabin and greater ability to hear what the instructor was saying to the pupil alongside.

Yet another type was added in June 1947 when Proctor 1 G-AIYH appeared, allowing flights to more distant airfields by the members. I took people to a Tea Patrol at Redhill (no problem then as Gatwick was very quiet, really just a racing circuit surrounding an airstrip). Later that summer I made quick trips to Plymouth, to the Southend Air Show, and to the Lympne Air Races at the end of August. Then in September Westlands had their own airshow and I took two friends down with me, managing to get a short flight with Peter Garner in their S.51 Dragonfly demonstrator. Peter had been on night fighters and for a 'rest' had volunteered for a trip on an armed Hurricane camera-ship but fortunately had not been catapulted off on his trip. He had joined Westlands just before I arrived with the offer of a permanent job after the war, but sadly he lost his life when a Wyvern he was flying had trouble with the rear contra-prop and he had to crashland in a field and broke his neck.

I did several trips with Ron Clear in their Consul demonstrator G-AHEF to Christchurch and Netheravon, where Airspeeds were still involved with the development of the Horsa; indeed they were still being built and tested at Christchurch as late as the 21st June 1949 when I flew in one with Bob Milne on test.

Another Autocrat, G-AIJI, arrived to carry the steady stream of joyriders who either arrived in coaches from the local holiday camps or were picked up on the seafront by 'Jock' in the Club's Dormobile; he liked to advertise the delights of joyriding with free transport to and from the airfield.

The gliding club at Portsmouth was loaned a demonstration Kirby Kite, and those interested were able to fly it whilst towed, as always, by the faithful 'IDA.

The winter of 1947/48 was quiet from a flying point of view in the odd Tiger or Auster, but in March 1948 Bernard Wilson arrived for a short stay at Portsmouth with his Dragon G-AECZ; I believe he was one of the pilots who flew Dragons and Rapides around the isolated Scottish Islands during the war on Emergency and Communication work. He loaded members into the Dragon and showed them the local area at varying altitudes, and it was during one such flight that I was able to take a closer look at a large shield with thick bushes around the perimeter, and inside it a five-pointed star and crescent (also in bushes), which formed the Portsmouth Borough Badge on the side of a hill to the north of the airfield. A later visit revealed that the area had been planted out by the Men of the Trees Society and that they had recently had three small memorial stones erected to commemorate two RAF members — and one Army member — of the Society who had lost their lives during the 1939-45 war.

Another new although elderly owner asked me to fly him in his Auster 5 G-AIPE. Charlie Bendall was a great character and farmer with a large family; one son was still an RAF instructor, another was a Petty Officer in the Navy, another was a Sergeant in the Army, and his two charming daughters were both Air Stewardesses in BOAC. The farm had just a 250-yard strip with a six-foot fence at both ends, and the larger Lycoming engine was a distinct advantage, particularly as Charlie was 18+ stone and the pilot found it necessary to put one arm round his shoulder in level flight so that they could both sit comfortably. For six months we made regular flights to the Aero Clubs at Cowes, Thruxton, Shoreham, Woodley, Cheltenham, Christchurch, Yeovil, Weston-super-Mare and Sandown — to mention but a few! Landing fees did not seem to be demanded as long as you had a cup of tea and a sandwich from the bar.

On a quiet afternoon in May 1948 an Auster with a long-range tank, G-AHSI, landed at Portsmouth with Charles Purley, the Managing Director of LEC Refrigeration, in command; he wanted Harry Mitchell's — and others' — advice on laying out a runway alongside his factory so that he could operate his Auster (and larger aircraft later) for the benefit of the sales dept of his factory. Harry gave him good advice for an hour, then as I was the only other pilot around and Harry could not get away that afternoon it fell to me to fly him back to land on a very rough piece of field. We walked around his fields and selected a good run that could be levelled into the prevailing wind, and then chose a site for a small hangar and petrol store for which his surveyor could finalise the plans after he had approved our ideas. After that we flew back to Portsmouth, and his surveyor later drew up plans for a grass runway which was used for a number of years by a variety of aircraft, up to an Anson which even made a sales trip to Africa.

Vic Behar bought a Magister, G-AITZ, but even when Harry had passed him out to go solo he had trouble getting used to making approaches and landings. As I remember it one had to hold the stick with the right hand and throttle back a bit with the left hand, then pull the trimmer slightly back to prevent the nose dropping too far, then hold the stick with the left hand and slide the lever forward with the right hand to lower the flaps. A quick change had to be made to move the trimmer back with the left hand while the right retained a firm backward grip on the stick, or the nose would drop until the trim lever held the nose at the right approach angle; this could be checked only by looking ahead over the left side of the windscreen and might require a gentle application of engine power. It was all 'go' for Vic but after several phugoid-type approaches he learned to change hands and feel for the knobs and tits with only a cursory glance into the cockpit.

The July 1948 airshow at Hamble featured Ron Clear flying the Olympia sailplane as one of the items, so I duly towed him over there behind the Tiger 'IDB at 4,000 feet and awaited their Aldis lamp 'green', and on receiving it ran in overhead ready for him to release when ready. Then a series of tugs on my tail was followed by the occasional sideways pull on the tail indicating that all was not well with his release mechanism. I banked slowly round and approached the airfield again, only to find that Ron had built up speed and was in formation with me, and I could see him making throat-slitting movements as he widened out to take up the slack in the tow-rope gently. I set course back to Portsmouth and released him from my end at low level when crossing the airfield fence. I landed and went over to where he had stopped and was working on the release mechanism with the 1948 version of WD40. When he was happy to start again we rang Hamble for another slot time (which they were pleased to give) and afterwards they congratulated Ron on his display of glider formation flying which had not been seen before by many people! On the second occasion all went well and his show was very much appreciated, as gliders were not appearing in many shows nor seen in such close proximity to their tug aircraft!

Ron was able to arrange a less exciting flight with him and George Errington, Airspeed's Chief Test Pilot at Christchurch and Portsmouth, in Ambassador G-AGUA after I had ferried their Hornet Moth G-ADUR down to Christchurch. Various private owners seemed to loan their light aircraft to Airspeed's for communication work, including Arguses G-AJAT and 'JSP. Later in the month I went with Bob Milne in Oxford LX720 to Christchurch to fly with Ron in Mosquito VR805. It just happened that the gliding club was having its summer camp on the South Downs near Washington in Sussex, so a few low passes were made to brighten their day.

The month ended with a rather special flight. Ron's Scud 3 glider was in a shed at Christchurch having some work done to it, and he asked me to come down with him on the Saturday, so we decided to bring our mothers for the run in his palatial but ancient Armstrong Siddeley saloon. But, as usual, something went wrong so that another day's work was needed to finish the modification, so we decided that the easiest thing would be to fly back that evening and return the next day. So our trusting mothers were driven over to the main hangar and persuaded to climb into the back seats of the Fairchild 'JAT which was parked inside the folding doors "just to see how comfortable the seats were." The hangar doors were opened and the aircraft was pushed outside "just to start the engine and hear how quiet it was," and they agreed it *was* quiet as we started up and taxied on to the take-off strip outside. They really did enjoy the very smooth trip back to Portsmouth, despite it being augmented by the endless commentary of their sweating sons!

This was of course some time before it was necessary to file flight plans, and Portsmouth only became EGIE in 1960. RT licences were also few and far between in the club world as few aircraft were fitted with radios. When licences were required the test would involve a simple start-up and cross-country patter with a compulsory SOS and a sighting of a boat in distress — which had to be learned and practised beforehand. A group of us from the Portsmouth club prepared for this with a doctor/pilot at the local Mental Hospital, as he was the only one of us who had a tape recorder. We all went up to the test department and took the exam, including the extra few questions about HF radio transmissions to have HF approval added to our licences, and everyone passed.

The airfield grass was cut regularly by a large gang mower until the aerodrome manager decided to buy a large tractor and mower, with a trailer for the grass which could then be dried. A local contractor had set up a grass-drying plant at Thorney Island RAF Station and this idea spread to a number of other airfields in the South. Unfortunately, apart from having two cut runways at Portsmouth, the grass was allowed to grow unchecked. The system was not a great financial success and was discontinued after some months, reverting to regular cutting so that visiting aircraft could use the whole airfield.

Mosquitos had first come to Portsmouth when — prior to the Dams Raid — Airspeeds had been involved in modifying them to carry a smaller spinning mine for use against shipping. The Air Transport Auxiliary had declined to deliver Mossies to such a short field (which had a maximum run of only 800 yards) and left them at Thorney Island for Airspeed's pilots to collect and deliver. Bob Milne and Ron Clear, without prior training, took off and carried out tests to determine the landing characteristics and stalling speeds of each aircraft independently.

The ATA Pilots' Notes gave a maximum speed for undercarriage down as 180 mph and for flaps down 150 mph, while the final approach speed was given as 125 mph with a 112 mph stall. There was a special mention of the nose-up tendency when flaps were lowered, and also a warning that, when wheels and flaps were down, drag increased appreciably, so that the pilot would have to guard against a tendency to undershoot. It had been agreed that Bob should make the first landing from west to east, which required an approach over 60-foot ramparts and a 10-foot railway embankment with a 30-foot signals mast just to the left of the approach path.

Ron watched Bob make a very steady approach and landing, and then turned away for his own approach, which he later admitted he found difficult and bumpy. Afterwards he asked Bob how he made such a steady approach, but Bob laughingly declined, and it was not until some months later that he finally confessed that he had taken off with the roof hatch unlocked and could not shut it properly! However he subsequently found that at 120 mph the hatch opened slightly, causing a draught that ruffled the top of his helmet, so he had set up his approach using the 'draught effect' — maybe the first occurrence of a "head-up display"! — and found it just as reliable as the ASI.

From its inception just after the airfield opened in 1932, the Club flew the early Moths and later trained members of the Civil Air Guard up until the war. The buildings were then taken over to provide the offices for the production of the Airspeed Oxford for the RAF and Commonwealth Air Training scheme, followed by the Horsa gliders for the invasion of Europe. When the Club was able to reopen in 1946 there was a flow of young — and not so young — who wanted to learn to fly, and many of these promoted — and indeed prospered in — aviation until finally on the 31st December 1973 Portsmouth Corporation decided to close the airfield and build the houses and supermarkets which were more financially attractive to them.

Perhaps the greatest credit to the Portsmouth Aero Club, its instructors, members and the many ATC cadets trained there was the occasion of the first flight of the BAe 146 at Hatfield, when the former Portsmouth-trained cadets were involved in the following professional capacities:

Peter Sedgwick — Co-Pilot.
Peter Tait and Neil Smith — DH.125 Escort aircraft.
Brian Synott — Support.

These, and others, had all been senior pilots in the Royal Air Force, mainly as graduates of the Empire Test Pilots' School, and were specially selected by British Aerospace to form a team to test and promote the new 146.

CHAPTER 20

SPOTTING IN THE FORTIES

by

MIKE HOOKS

Much of this book will be reminiscences by pilots and passengers; in those days I never flew except as a member of the Royal Observer Corps, but I was a keen spotter. Apologies therefore to those uninterested in 'reggies' — perhaps a move to another chapter is indicated?!

My first serious spotting log began on 2nd September 1945 with notes on military aircraft seen at Gatwick: Ansons, Austers, Arguses etc. with serial numbers, and other types too distant for the serials to be seen. Among those identified were DH.Flamingo BT312 of the Royal Navy named *Merlin 27* on the nose; I didn't then know that this had originally been intended to be BOAC's G-AFYH *King William* but was in fact rolled off the production line as BT312 *Merlin VI*, going to 782 Squadron of the FAA. It was restored to the civil register on 24th October 1946 but was eventually broken up at Redhill.

Although my log began in September 1945 I had jottings in several notebooks from April 1945 onwards, and I have recently managed to piece these together. There were such oddities as the twin-finned Oxford N6327, Typhoon SW528/'S-HE', Reliant FK878, Liberator TS527/'Q-6G' and a Hudson coded 'MA-M', presumably all seen in the Croydon area where I lived. Occasional visits to Biggin Hill at that time revealed a number of USAAF Dakotas, while a few days' holiday in Bournemouth gave some spotting variety. Various RAF Dakotas at Hurn wore Transport Command codes: FD867/'ODZX', FL516/'ODZR', FL630/'ODZJ', KJ985/'OFZK', KJ868/'OFZT', KK201/'OFZC' and KK206/'OFZA', while similarly-coded Sunderlands at Poole were DD860/'OQZS', JM662/'OQZT', JM665/'OQZW' and ML722/'OQZB' and a York at Hurn was MW108/'OYZB'. Coming home by train on 7th October 1945 passing Eastleigh, I saw several Dauntlesses, one of which was JS998/'ELOC.'

My method of transport was a bike, so visits to Croydon Airport were frequent. I will not bore readers with long lists of Tigers and other types seen there, but for the benefit of those who may want to identify something seen on a specific date here are some oddities with dates in brackets.

1945
Rapide YI-ABD (13/12).
Camouflaged Sabena Lodestar (23/12).

1946
SAI KZ.IV OY-DIZ (20/3).
Free French Maryland (2/4).
Arado 96 — probably in fact a Sipa S.12 (30/4).
Envoy G-AHAC (27/5 & 28/9).
Aerovan G-AGOZ (13/6).
All-silver Maryland (18/6).
Envoy SE-ASN (the former King's Flight G-AEXX) (30/6).
French Bobcat 944 (15/7).
Comte AC.12 HB-AXA (30/7).
Bobcat OK-XBB (4/8).
Ju.52/3M OK-ZBB (5/8).
Frequent Czech military Ju.52/3Ms (but D-3, D-5 and D-7 all on
    15/8).
Halifax VIII G-AGZP (22/8) — does anyone have a photo of this at
    Croydon?
Spitfire PR.XI PM153 in pieces (24/8) (had suffered a broken
    tailwheel there on 10/7 and had been struck off charge on
    10/8).
US Navy Grumman Gosling 32943 (20/10).

1947
Anson 1s VH-AKI, 'ALX and 'ALY (27/4).
Anson ZS-BKM (10/5).
Lockheed 12 NC79820 (13/5).
Rapides PH-RAB, 'RAC and 'RAD (17/5).
Dove ZS-AVH (15/6).
Wayfarer ZS-BOM crash landing (15/6).
Cessna 120 HB-CAA (24/6) (first of the type in Europe — what was
    its fate?).
Lockheed 14 CF-TCM (24/6).
Ethiopian Avro 19 121 (1/7).
Siebel Si.204A EC-ACM (12/8).
Dakotas VR-HDO and 'HPO (20/8).
Portuguese Anson 1 212 (21/8).
Piper Super Cruisers NX3671M *City of the Angels* and NX2365M *City of
    Washington* from New Jersey on a round-the-world reliability flight
    (28/8).
East African Airways Rapides VP-KEC and 'KED (ex-PH-RAC and 'RAD)
    (29/8).
Argus OK-ZEM and Zlin 281 OK-ZVJ (11/9).
MS.571 F-BBGB, Noralpha F-BBCM and Courlis F-BDUG (11/9).
First new Bonanzas NC90568 and '70 seen being assembled
    (13/9).

Spitfire IX MK515/'JX-N' in the car park – perhaps to do with
  Battle of Britain week (13/9).
Fuselages of Queen Bees LF793. '795, '796, '797, '799 and '802
  (13/9).
Fokker F.43 PH-NAM (15/9).

This list is of course far from complete, but may fill a few gaps in logs.

While on the subject of Queen Bees it was interesting to see another batch of fuselages at Redhill on 11th November 1948: LF789, '790, '801, '803 and '831, plus a pair of Tiger Moths, 5436M (ex-N9239) and 5449M (ex-T6286).

Back to 1946 and cycling trips. In April an oddity at Heston was USAAF Black Widow 25496 which I noted as having a green top and black undersides. Its purpose at that time was not known, but I believe it was subsequently said to have been used by Fairey for research into flying control systems: I wonder what happened to it? Heston was always combined with a visit to London Airport at Heathrow, and on 16th April I was delighted to see the first visit of a Panair do Brasil Constellation, PP-PCF. Also there was Lancaster PP746 with a bulged bomb bay. Seen on several occasions at Gatwick — but unfortunately not close enough to photograph — was an olive drab Savoia Marchetti SM.82 coded 'EP': I subsequently discovered that it was VN163 of 84 Group's Communications Flight.

One puzzle which I have never solved was the logging on several occasions of Lancasters with what I described as "Halifax-type" noses — that is to say the smooth nose with glazed front as on the later Halifaxes. I can only assume now that, from a distance, a Lancaster with the front turret removed but retaining the bomb-aimer's transparency might give this impression.

I spent some time with my maternal grandparents at Pagham Beach, near Bognor, a real hotbed of aerial activity, and was lucky to be there on the day of the Victory Flypast over London, 8th June 1946. My notes of that day's activity may be of interest.

I wrote: *"Ten Beaufighters from Thorney Island arrived over Bognor at 1155 and orbited with 31 Mosquitos until setting course at 1210, followed by two orbits by ten Firebrands from Ford at 1215, 40 clipped-wing Spitfires at 1220 and ten Seafire XVIIs with cylindrically-shaped long-range tanks beneath the fuselage. The formations then flew east along the coast collecting other squadrons at Eastbourne and Dungeness. All aircraft returned at about 300 ft between 1310 and 1350 under 10/10ths cloud and heavy rain. Also in the formations were Sea Mosquitos and Fireflies."*

The first postwar air pageant was held at Southampton (Eastleigh) on 22nd June 1946 and provided a good mix of civil and military types in static and flying displays. Making its first, and perhaps only, public appearance was the Cierva W.9 helicopter PX203 with a novel jet efflux pipe substituting for the usual tail rotor (a forerunner of today's NOTARs?), while Cierva autogyro G-AHLE was also shown. Flypasts were made by Sandringham G-AGKX, Viking G-AGOM and Channel Islands Airways Wayfarer G-AGVB.

RAF participation comprised five Lancasters from 83 Sqdn., PB376/'OL-F', SW261/'OL-N', PD285/'OL-N', ME520/'OL-V' and NG482/'OL-A' (the last obviously borrowed from 97 Sqdn.), nine Spitfire XVIs from 164 Sqdn., six Meteors from 56 Sqdn. (including EE284, '369, '391 & '400 and Vampire TG302/'ZY-Y' from 247 Sqdn.. On the ground were Lancasters SW367, SW376, TX264, RF269 and RF301: this last was unusual in being painted blue. From the Navy came Seafire 46 LA542 and 813 Sqdn. with 10 Firebrands, while Vickers sent Spiteful RB523 and Seafang VB895. A small Miles circus comprised Aerovan G-AGWO, Messenger G-AGOY and Gemini G-AGUS, whilst a novelty was Reid & Sigrist Desford G-AGOS. Exhibited on a trolley was Supermarine S.6B N248, the ATC demonstrated Kirby Cadet RA845 and Tiger Moth BB858/'ELOC' (the prewar G-ADOY) was put through its paces.

Visitors (and residents) noted included Auster Vs TJ187 and '672, Autocrats G-AERO, 'GOH, 'GTU and OO-ATY, Proctors G-AGYA, 'GYB, 'GLJ, 'GTC, 'HGT, HM291 and RM189, Tipsy Bs G-AFSC and 'FVN, Cub Coupé 'FXS, Wickos 'FJB and 'GPE, Hawk Major 'DCV, Falcon Six 'FBF, Voyager 'GZW, Reliant 'GZV, Consul 'HJY, York 'GNL and Rapides 'DAE, 'GPH, 'GPI, 'GSH and 'GSK - a nice collection!

In 1946 I was called up for National Service in the RAF, travelling to the awful enlistment centre at Padgate, a site which had already been condemned but which carried on for years. After the usual kitting-out, haircutting, bad food and shouting I was posted to Yatesbury, a square-bashing camp but also the home of No.2 Radio School, situated less than two miles from Yatesbury airfield and its occupants, No.2 EFTS with Tiger Moths.

The camp itself possessed three aircraft, or at least their 'corpses': wingless Halifax RG364 on the sports field and a pair of Mosquito NF.XVIIs, HK264 and HK301, in a hangar; presumably all three were used for some sort of radio training. The Halifax, formerly with No.1674 Heavy Conversion Unit, had been allocated 5750M on 27th November 1945 but did not wear these marks. Both Mosquitos ended their flying careers at OTUs, No.51 for HK264 and No.54 for HK301 (which was allocated 5695M, again not taken up). I was told of the rear fuselage of Lancaster PD248 with radar-ranging scanner but did not see it.

The first postwar SBAC Display was held at Radlett in September but was not open to the public, so wearing my AC2 uniform I waited near the gate until its guardian was distracted, and walked in easily with other

Service personnel. This was a big show, too big to detail here, and I have written a feature for *Aeroplane* with a complete listing which will be published in 2006 around the 60th anniversary.

The winter of 1946 was one of the worst in living memory, and a number of the RAF sites in the area closed down — but not Yatesbury! As it happened, while on leave I went down with an infection and had to spend some time at home; fortunately we had an understanding doctor!

I was in Pool Flight at Yatesbury until April 1947, so had plenty of opportunity to log most of the EFTS Tigers, and I photographed the wreck of N6659/'FHEU' after it crashed near the White Horse, Oldbury Ring on 11th April about a mile from the airfield, fortunately without fatalities. Quite a lot of interesting aircraft overflew the camp, including a Turkish Beaufighter, Buckmaster RP151 (17/3), Lancastrian 'FH-FE' (20/3) and Tudor G-AGRI (25/3) to name a few, and there were also RAF Yorks going into nearby Lyneham. An unofficial visit there on 23rd March produced Yorks MW192, '203, '234 and '245 plus MW187/'VU-M' of 246 Sqdn., a metallic-blue freighter. Also present were Lancaster PB679 and 61 Sqdn. Lincoln RE500/'QR-B'. A number of Spitfires of various marks were parked, possibly for scrapping, a fate already under way for a pair of former 303 Squadron Mustangs, KM263/'T-PD' and KH735/'W-PD'. These proved very useful since they contained a number of large balsa packing blocks, which found their way into my kit bag for future use!

On 12th April 1947 I was posted to Gloucester, and spent several days at RAF Innsworth before anyone realised that I should have been at the Air Traffic Control Centre, Barnwood, a few miles away. Once there I was put on to shift work, a mere 25 hours a week, which gave me plenty of free time. So I brought my bike from home to enable me to visit a number of nearby RAF stations, plus the Gloster factory airfields at Brockworth and Moreton Valence where a number of new Meteors could be logged. Overflys of interest included the scarlet Meteor G-AIDC (seen on my first day), Welkin DX330 on several occasions, a Dutch Harvard FT160 on the 10th June, a Wellington BK537 with four-bladed propellers at Staverton, and Lancaster RE219 with a yellow panel on the fuselage.

An advantage in being posted to the ATCC was that all aircraft movements coming into the Gloucester sphere of influence — quite a big one — had to come through us, so we dealt with such items as a Mosquito leading six Furies on an overseas delivery flight. Unfortunately I never managed to see any of these, but on one occasion a Lincoln we had been plotting on a cross-country flight had become lost. I had just come off duty when it flew straight over the centre, its massive white fuselage serials providing instant identification, so I was able to go back and get a message passed giving its position!

I was still at the ATCC when a small airshow took place on 6th July 1947 at nearby Staverton; this gave me the opportunity to photograph some of the visitors and residents, which included Cygnet G-AGBN, Mentor 'HKM, Whitney Straight 'FZY, Aerovan 'JOF, Anson 'ITJ, Arguses 'JPB and 'JPC, Geminis 'IHI and 'IRS, Magisters 'HUK, 'JDR and 'JGM as well as various Austers. Also based there was Cessna Airmaster G-AFBY, but unfortunately it was not possible to reach the other side of the airfield, from where Dowty operated some interesting types such as the aforementioned Wellington and Welkin.

My log book at this time also contained other things the RAF required one to know: a list of forms such as 1250 (identity card), 295 (leave), 252 (charge sheet), 624 (sick report) and so on, but more important was a drawing I made of the Sten gun, with complete instructions on dismantling (which could be done in 30 seconds) and re-assembly (which took a little longer). A similar sketch showed the Mills HE.36 hand grenade, the average throw of which was required to be about 30 yards using a four-second fuse. Practising on dummies I fell hopelessly short, and so it was a great relief to hear — on the day before our live throw — that it was cancelled after some faulty grenades had exploded prematurely!

A crafty visit to Brockworth on 3rd September revealed Gloster's hack Rapide G-AHRH and Gladiator N5903. I believe parts of the latter were eventually used in the restoration of G-AMRK, but it is interesting to note that N5903 was registered G-GLAD in January 1995 to be rebuilt as N2276 for The Fighter Collection, Duxford.

Although I didn't see it, there was a Battle of Britain flypast over London on 15th September and I noted the participants. Group 1 (at 162 mph) comprised a Hurricane and nine Lancasters from Wyton: Group 2 (at 190 mph) was three Lancasters from Stradishall: Group 3 (at 220 mph) contained 36 Mosquitos, nine from West Malling (25, 29 and 85 Sqdns.), 18 from Odiham (4, 21, 107, 23 and 264 Sqdns.), nine from Thorney Island (36, 109, and 139 Sqdns.), nine Spitfires from Middle Wallop (595 and 691 Sqdns.), nine Seafires from Ford (807 Sqdn.), nine USAAF Mustangs from Middle Wallop and six Czech Spitfires from Odiham: Group 4 (at 290 mph) had six Hornets from Horsham St. Faith (64 and 65 Sqdns.), 12 Tempests from Duxford (3 and 80 Sqdn.s), nine Meteors from Bentwaters (245, 263 and 257 Sqdns.), nine Meteors from Duxford (266, 222 and 74 Sqdns.) and nine Vampires from West Malling (54, 72 and 247 Sqdns.). The height over London was 2,000 ft, the spacing between aircraft one span, and between groups 100 yds. Getting that lot together must have been a masterpiece of planning.

Biggin Hill held its Battle of Britain display on 20th September with Spitfires and Harvards of 600 and 615 Sqdns., six Tiger Moths of the

London UAS and other assorted types, the rarest being a Storch, VX154, coded 'HB', while a welcome but unusual sight was Walrus G-AIZG.

I was still at the ATCC in 1948. By April, Gloster were turning out Meteors for the Netherlands and Argentina, maybe the reason for Dutch Harvard FT455 being at Brockworth on 14th April. A visit to Tangmere on 7th June produced Sea Mosquitos TW257/'LP590', TW283/'LP591', TW286/'LP599' and TW292/'LP295' in addition to the based Meteors and Vampires.

A day to remember that year was 23rd June, when I cycled to No.20 MU, Aston Down. A friendly Station Warrant Officer (there were such things!) said it was a pity I had chosen that day since there was to be an AOC's inspection, otherwise they could have given me a flight! Forewarned to keep my head down, I was let loose in the airfield's perimeter park where aircraft were stored: 108 Tempests of three marks, 30 Lancasters, seven Lincolns and a pair of Wellingtons — and I logged all the serials! The active part of the airfield had Ansons, Oxfords and Mosquitos of 1689 Flight, and for the benefit of those interested in tying serials to codes they were: Oxfords EB739/'F-9X', HM185/'R-9X', RR327/'N-9X', RR332/'O-9X' and RR333/'P-9X', Ansons VL335/'9XH', VM330/'9XK' and VM383/'9XJ' (codes on these displayed as shown) and Mosquito VP346/'T-9X'. An oddity among five dismantled Austers was TJ707 with prototype markings. A very worthwhile visit, but why didn't I take any photos?

A Staverton display on 3rd July was entertaining, although Swallow G-AFGE smashed its prop on nosing over, but a rather more ambitious show was held at Filton on 17th July with its resident squadrons, 501 with Spitfires & Harvards and 16 RFS with Tiger Moths. Performing were Seafire 47s LA545/'CH-110' & LA555/'CH-105' and Brigand RH809, although 19 other Brigands could be seen in the distance. Eight days later I counted 31 Brigands but only logged TX374 and RH749, but a 'scoop', since I had heard no previous mention of it, was Phoebus-Lincoln RA643.

On 18th August I travelled to Kirkham near Preston to be demobbed, but the only aircraft there was a Typhoon in a hangar — I often wonder which one it was. Part of my demob leave was spent in the Isle of Wight, memorable because I tore my demob trousers trying to climb a wall near the Saro factory to see the SR/A1 (which I saw later anyway). On the slipway at Cowes were Walruses G-AHFM, 'HFN and 'HFO, while 'HTO was still marked as W2688; Z1763 and one other were hangared. Also on the slipway were Sunderlands EJ152 (being scrapped), and RN297.

At that time Cowes still had a small active airfield, and a display on 22nd August produced no less than 18 Austers, 10 Messengers, three Geminis, five Proctors and five Rapides, plus many other civil types, including the Wiltshire School of Flying's Dragon G-AECZ and the one-off Newbury Eon glider tug G-AKBC which later met its end in a hedge at Lympne in a pilotless take-off while towing a glider; the glider pilot's comments would have been worth hearing! Around this time at Cowes I had the delightful experience of seeing a Rapide looped (I think it was G-ALAX), when the sound of the wind in the wires had to heard to be believed.

While the SBAC Display at Farnborough in September is too large to mention here, several interesting types could be seen on the airfield around that time. Airacobra AH574 and Hotspur gliders BT889 and HH610 were all 'hooked', the latter having their noses ballasted with concrete and strengthened keels with no wheels. Rotting away was Barracuda DR126, which had been used as a catapult dummy, while Hornets VA965 and '966 were in poor shape. A Junkers Ju.90, '9V-BK' (Air Min 57) had yet to be buried on site, while a Boston and Turbinlite Havoc could not be identified.

Finally out of the Service, my travels were somewhat less exotic, but Croydon was still a magnet, of course. A visit to Gatwick on 11th November produced the sad sight of Spartan 1 G-ABXO, Spartan 2 G-ABTR, Monocoupe G-AADG, Gipsy Moth G-EBQX and Porterfield G-AEOK all being scrapped near Southern Aircraft, although of these the last appeared to be substantially complete.

The Royal Aeronautical Garden Party held at White Waltham on 8th May 1949 attracted over 100 visiting aircraft. These included the newly-arrived Spitfire G-AISU in primer (better known today as the BBMF's AB910), a pair of American Cubs (NC6400N and N79818), a good selection of the usual Miles, Percival and Auster types, plus some prewar goodies like the Avro Club Cadet G-ACHP and Avian G-ACKE.

A pleasant Redhill 'At Home' day on 9th July provided a number of visitors, the most unusual of which was Piper Super Cruiser VP-KFS (ex-ZS-BNS) and no less than 19 Miles aircraft, many of which were based there, including the Lycoming-powered Aerovan 6 G-AKHF.

On 6th August I was surprised to see derelict Beaufort ML672 at Hamble and gather it was owned by Air Service Training, but for what purpose is not known. On the same day on the water or hardstanding at Hythe were Hythe flying boats (converted Sunderlands) G-AGER, 'GEU, 'GHZ, 'GIA, 'GJJ to 'JN, 'GKY and 'HEO. Twelve days later I was pleased to see nine Indian Tempest 2s (HA596 to '600, '607, '609, '610 and '612) at Langley, while a further visit there on 18th September produced Egyptian Furies L916, '917, '919 and '923 and Iraqi Furies 248, 256, 247, 242 and 249: many years later the last of these was to become, first VH-ISS, then N54SF.

At the Thruxton air races on 21st August, Auster V M6147 was seen on a truck; it should have been marked 6147M but does not appear in Bruce

Robertson's *British Military Aircraft Serials 1978-1987*. Also at Thruxton was Sikorsky R-6 KN844.

On a visit to London Airport on 18th September I was surprised to see a small collection of military aircraft — maybe for a Garden Party — fenced off in an enclosure; they were Hastings TG521, Lincoln RE400/'EM-E', Meteor IV VT287, Prentice VR230/'FB-RE' and Spitfire XVI TE335/'RCA-N'.

So to the end of my 1940s notes, with apologies to those who think we spotters are 'anoraks', but without this attention to detail many authors would be unable to flesh out bare facts in their books.

Cessna 120 HB-CAA (probably the first in Europe) at Croydon on 24th June 1947. Photo: Mike Hooks.

Piper Super Cruiser VP-KFS at the Redhill 'At Home' on 9th July 1949. Photo: Mike Hooks.

Spitfire G-AISU (now better known as AB910 of the BoB Memorial Flight) at White Waltham on 8th May 1949. Photo: Mike Hooks.

Avro Avian G-ACKE seen at White Waltham on 8th May 1949. Photo: Mike Hooks.

The remains of Beaufort ML872 at Hamble on 6th August 1949.
Photo: Mike Hooks.

Death throes at Gatwick, 11th November 1949: Seen are G-AEOK
(Porterfield), G-ABTR (Spartan 2) and G-EBQX (Gipsy Moth).
Photo: Mike Hooks.

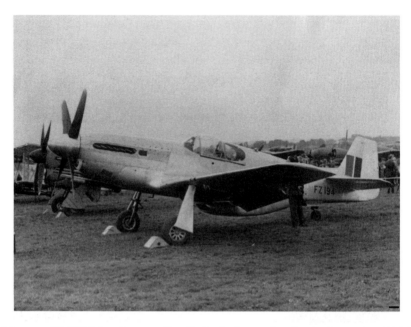

Mustang III FZ194 at the very first BoB display at Hendon in September 1945.
Photo: Mike Stroud.

Heinkel He.162A w/n 120086 (AirMin62) was on display in Hyde Park in
September 1945. Photo: Mike Stroud.

In 1946 Proctor DX231 of Metropolitan Communications Squadrron force-landed in Hyde Park *en route* to Hendon. Photo: Mike Stroud.

Lancaster L7580 ('O for Orange') was in Trafalgar Square in March 1942 for 'Wings for Victory' week. Photo: Mike Stroud.

Miles Aerovan G-AILF, fitted with skis for possible use in Canada, had plenty of opportunities to use them in the UK in early 1947.
Photo: Mike Stroud.

An overview of the 1947 Radlett RAeS Garden Party. A solitary 'copper' looks out over a veritable sea of aircraft. Photo: Mike Stroud.

An overview of Miles' last Open Day at Woodley in 1947.
Photo: Mike Stroud.

Dakota KK279, personal aircraft of Air Marshal Coningham, was painted
pale blue overall and was at Woodley in February 1947.
Photo: Mike Stroud.

Klemm 132A shows its unusual lettering at Elstree, July 1947.
Photo: Mike Stroud.

The mysterious Gemini VR-GGG at Elstree, April 1947.
Photo: via Mike Stroud.

The 1949 SBAC Show at Farnborough. In the foreground can be seen
Apollo G-AIYN and Comet G-ALVG. Photo: Mike Stroud.

G-ADNO, the DH TK.2, took part in the Southend Air Race in August 1947.
Photo: Mike Stroud.

Halifax C.8 visited Luqa on 4th April 1948. Photo: Reg Havers.

Turkish Air Force Dakota CBK20 was seen at Bückeberg, Germany, on 26th August 1951. Photo: Reg Havers.

CHAPTER 21

THE MEMORABLE FORTIES

by

MIKE STROUD

Prewar

If she were here today, my mother would tell you that there was an inevitability that I would end up in the aviation business, mainly brought about by my being taken to the Hendon Air Pageant in June 1931 when she was 8 months pregnant. As you can imagine, I couldn't see much from where I was, but I suppose one could be charitable and accept that the appropriate vibes were probably triggered, and anyway it's a nice Irish story. She later told me that she had once flown in a small aeroplane (presumably with Alan Cobham in the 1920s) but was too scared to enjoy it.

We lived in Hampstead, North-West London, not all that far from Hendon Aerodrome, and some of my earliest memories include seeing aircraft over Central London writing *Persil* in the sky and others towing banners proclaiming *Bile Beans*. I have since assumed that the former were the skywriting SE.5s of Major Savage, which I think were based at Hendon, and the latter Avro 504s banner-towing, probably from Croydon. Around the same time (the mid-1930s), I remember seeing large lumbering formations of aircraft over Central London, some of which were dark green and thus likely to be Fairey Hendons, Handley Page Heyfords and possibly Virginia bombers; these were taking part in the Empire Air Day celebrations, which I think were held each year on 24th May. One could assume that the smaller silver aeroplanes, which preceded and followed the 'heavies', were Harts, Demons and Furies.

In the late 1930s, as war fever grew, I can remember seeing silver-coloured aircraft flying around over London at night while searchlights tried to pinpoint them. This was done as part of well-publicised Air Raid Precaution exercises, and my feeling is that these were the Croydon-based Dragons, Rapides and even DH.86s contracted to operate as mock enemy raiders.

In the immediate period just before the outbreak of war, we went on holiday to Tankerton, a fashionable resort on the North Kent coast, and during our week there took an excursion to *Dreamland* in Ramsgate. We travelled on the top deck of a bus and on the way passed alongside an airfield with green/brown camouflaged Whitleys randomly parked, and I am inclined to assume that this was Manston. I was not into aviation at that time, and only recognised the aircraft because, like most boys, I had a similarly-coloured Dinky Toy Whitley along with a Spitfire, Hurricane and Blenheim.

I also have a recollection of seeing a large airship off Ramsgate, which I assume was the Graf Zeppelin cruising up and down the North Sea, just a few miles out to sea from the then secret Dover radar station, on what would now be recognised as 'signal interception' missions.

1939-1944

Like many other children, I was conned by my mother into being evacuated, and set off on the morning of Friday 1st September 1939 for the safety of the country. Having assembled at All Souls' School, we left South Hampstead LMS station and travelled for what seemed like hours to a secret and distant destination. We were then transferred to buses, and the observant knew that we were some distance from London because the buses were green instead of red. We eventually arrived at a small village, where we were 'auctioned' off, with the girls being picked first and then the boys with much greater reluctance. I was most unlucky, as the woman who took me in was clearly doing it for the money, and I had a most unhappy time there playing 'second fiddle' to her children, very much a second-class citizen. However, after a few days I began to put two and two together and worked out where we were: not, as you might have thought, in deepest Yorkshire, but ludicrously near my home in Abbots Langley, virtually a suburb of Watford, and certainly not more than a few minutes' flying time by a German bomber from my home in North London: so much for the planners. Eventually I persuaded my mother to take me back to London and returned in October on the day that *HMS Royal Oak* was sunk in Scapa Flow.

In 1940 I decided to take aviation more seriously and, like a lot of others, bought myself *Aircraft Recognition* by Saville-Sneath published by Penguin (which I still have to this day). Thus my knowledge of the subject gradually grew and I was quite *au fait* with all but the latest types, which never flew across London anyway. Like many others I soon joined the readers of *The Aeroplane Spotter,* which I relied on implicitly to keep me informed, and gave the newsagent an undeserved hard time if it didn't turn up every other Thursday morning. I still have a full set of the *Spotter* and still refer to them from time to time, even though the wartime paper was of poor quality and the pages have since turned brittle.

As a frequent visitor to the West End of London I soon worked out that there were aircraft to be seen. One of these was the Lancaster L7580/'EM-O for Orange' of 207 Sqdn. displayed in Trafalgar Square along with a Spitfire and Hurricane as a draw during *Wings for Victory* week in March 1942, but which stayed on for a great deal longer. I see from photographs now in my collection that Londoners donated no less than £102 million towards the capital's declared target of £150 million to buy planes for the RAF.

In February 1943 I visited the Stirling N3669/'LS-H' of 15 Sqdn. parked on a bomb site near St. Paul's Cathedral, with costs shown on a placard as £40,000 for the aircraft, £2,500 for a Merlin engine and £350 for a propeller. Bombs were valued as £355 for an 8,000 lb one (which I don't think a Stirling could carry), £405 for 3 x 4,000 lb, £605 for 6 x 2,000 lb or 12 x 1,000 lb, £585 for 24 x 500 lb, £630 for 48 x 250 lb and £2,455 for 3,000 incendiary bombs. N3669 (formerly H-Harry, E-Easy and D-Dog of 7 Sqdn.) was credited with 67 operational sorties, five of which were on mine-laying duties, but unusually wore its bomb-score markings on the port side of the fuselage aft of the wing.

In 1942 we moved house, but not very far, only in fact to St. Johns Wood, and my new school was only a short distance from Regents Park and the London Zoo. The school certainly used some of the sports facilities in the park, and it was on my way back from these activities that I witnessed my first proper air crash. On 6th October 1943 I saw a Dakota threading its way through the London balloon barrage on its way back to Hendon. Unfortunately the aircraft hit a balloon cable, which sliced off the wing outboard of the engine, and the pilot attempted to crash-land on the nearest open space, which was Regents Park. But even a Dakota could not fly with such extensive damage, and the stricken aircraft crashed into the tea pavilion, killing all nine persons on board. The flimsy Victorian building had been used to store 'urban' unexploded bombs, all of which blew up simultaneously. This was my first 'cop' inasmuch it was the first aircraft I saw for which I now have a serial number: the unfortunate Dakota was FD899 of 512 Sqdn..

One particular wartime memory I will never forget was the huge number of aircraft I saw on my way to school every morning. It was quite usual to see virtually hundreds of B-17s and B-24s crossing London on their way to the continent in the summer of 1944. The Liberators were particularly colourful, as were the by now predominantly silver Fortresses. Another memory is of the sky full of Mustangs circling near Boxted during a visit to my father, who was stationed with the Army in Colchester at that time.

On the downside was the V-1 campaign, beginning on 13th June (only eight days after D-Day), which brought me closest to death during the whole war. With my mother and my newly-born sister, we were on our way to visit an aunt who lived in the shadow of the Empire State cinema in Kilburn (at that time the biggest in Europe). We were halfway there when the air-raid siren sounded, but decided to press on, as my sister would soon need feeding. A bit further on things began to hot up, and we decided to turn back for home, and on the way had to crouch in someone's front garden as a V-1 in the terminal glide mode whistled across just over our heads. Only seconds later we heard an almighty explosion and saw the rising column of dust. An hour later we were told by phone that a house had received a direct hit and that both the occupants, my aunt and her friend, had been killed. By the time the launching sites were overrun in September, almost 6,000 'Doodlebugs' had been launched against Southern England. So for my immediate family, a typical lucky escape!

1945

In the autumn of 1944 I somehow managed to win a London County Council scholarship to what was then the Westminster Technical Institute in Vincent Square near Victoria Station, and began my training as a chef there by the end of the year. By early 1945 there was much domestic unrest between my parents as to whether I should continue with schooling or not, and ultimately I got fed up with the arguing and lost interest in the two-year course. As a result I started playing truant, and my chosen sanctuary was the long grass on the eastern edge of Hendon Aerodrome. I used my dinner money to pay the fare on the No.113 bus, alighted at Bunns Bridge, and slipped between the houses and under the railway arch to watch the comings and goings at the back of the airfield. (roughly where the RAF Museum now is). Here I saw many interesting aircraft including a silver biplane in US Navy markings, which I thought was a Swordfish but in fact turned out to be a Stearman used as an Embassy hack. I saw quite a few Dakotas with the Dutch orange triangle on the nose (24 Sqdn.?) and clearly remember seeing a camouflaged Hornet Moth with its British civil registration underlined in red, white and blue. However, for some reason I do not appear to have taken any notes, which I now regret.

I carried on playing hookey for a few weeks, and then resumed my studies when my parents' views coalesced. I also resumed my spotting, and even managed a visit to Bovingdon where the Americans, in anticipation of peace, were busily giving things away. I was presented with a North Atlantic Route Guide (a sort of USAAF *Pooley*) which I later gave to Harry Holmes, together with a Mae West lifejacket which I kept for years. I seem to remember there were many B-17s and C-47s there, plus the first P-38 I ever saw on the ground. Little did I realise that ten years later I was going to work there for the USAF down among the *Gooneybirds*, along with the late, great Arthur Pearcy.

In June 1945, with the ink hardly dry on the Unconditional Surrender document signed on Luneburg Heath, the Ministry of Information, in league with the Ministry of Aircraft Production, organised *Britain's Aircraft Exhibition*, which opened on 21st June on the bombed site of the John Lewis department store in Oxford Street. The intention was to allow the public to see more closely the aircraft and weapons built during the war, and as it was open from 10 am to 8 pm seven days a week, it aroused 'immense public interest' (according to *The Aeroplane* of 29th June). Nine complete aircraft were displayed — Auster AOP.IV MT243, Beaufighter TF.X LZ126, Mosquito B.XVI MM137, Firefly FR.I MB627, Tempest F.V SN112, Spitfire LF.IX PL403, Walrus HD922 (sitting in its own little pond), Gloster E28/39 W4041/'G' and much-decorated Halifax B.III LV907/'NP-F' *Friday the 13th* of 158 Sqdn. (the nose art from this is currently on display in the RAF Museum. There was also a sectioned Lancaster fuselage, a Horsa fuselage and a Wellington wing — showing the geodetic construction. This gave me my first close contact with aircraft and I visited the exhibition several times, savouring the smell of the aircraft laced with bombsite dust. The event was so popular that I believe the closing date was deferred several times.

In September I went to my first air show; this was the very first Battle of Britain Anniversary Display held at Hendon on 15th September. On that day over 90 RAF airfields were opened to the public and the service mounted a big flypast over London and the Home Counties. 25 squadrons took part in the flypast, including Beaufighters and Mosquitos of Coastal Command, Typhoons, Tempests, Mustangs and Spitfires (12 flown by BoB pilots) of Fighter Command, who also provided two squadrons of Meteors. At Hendon 10,000 people turned up to see 37 different types of aircraft on show, which included examples of the Albemarle, Bloch 220, Beaufort, Storch, Hotspur, Lodestar, Me.108, Miles Monarch, Siebel 204, Stinson L-5, Sikorsky R-4, an RAF Fortress, a Warwick carrying a lifeboat, the Mitchell FR209 (with 75 mm gun) and a midnight-blue US Navy Grumman Goose. The 'hot ship' of the show was a Meteor and *The Aeroplane* recorded: *"A quiet, almost conversational voice from the loudspeakers announced that a Meteor was approaching from the north. Almost simultaneously a Meteor F. Mk III screamed across the aerodrome at roughly 20 ft, going into a near-vertical rocket climb at the end of it, then, calmly straightening out, flew in an inverted position for a minute. After repeating this performance several times, the Meteor disappeared among the clouds."*

I had never seen anything like this before, and was so transfixed watching it that I forgot to record the serial, although I did note that it was coded 'HB-W'. Years later, in 1980, I discovered that the pilot had been my friend and British Aerospace colleague AVM Harold Bird-Wilson. He kindly allowed me to check his log book and so, after 45 years, I was able to identify the Meteor as EE357 of 1335 Conversion Unit at Debden; as in the case of the crashing Dakota, I had gained another retrospective serial number for my log.

The day after the Hendon Air Show I was off to London's Hyde Park where, following the *Britain's Aircraft Exhibition*, the 'authorities' had presumably decided to mount a German equivalent from 16th to 22nd

September, housed in a fenced-off enclosure near Marble Arch. Here eight Luftwaffe aircraft were displayed, comprising: Storch w/n 2008 coded 'CV+KB', FW.190A-6 w/n 550214, He.162A-2 w/n 120086, Ju.88G-6 w/n 622838, Me.108B w/n 1547, Me.110G-5 w/n 420031, Me.163B-1 w/n 191454 coded '11', and DFS Grunau Baby 'LN-SS'. This was the precursor to a much more ambitious event entitled *Exhibition of German Aircraft and Equipment* held at RAE Farnborough in October and November 1945, which unfortunately I never visited. Not wishing to be left out, the Science Museum mounted *An Exhibition of German Aeronautical Developments* early in 1946; this I did visit and found it included two Fieseler Fi.103 flying bombs, one piloted and one normal, FW.190A, FA.330 Rotokite, Heinkel He.162, Me.109G and a Me.163B, some of which were almost certainly the same aircraft exhibited in Hyde Park in the September.

On Saturday 22nd September I watched Geoffrey de Havilland give a sizzling display of jet aerobatics over 'The Cockpit' area of Hyde Park near the Serpentine. This was the first disclosure of the Vampire to the public and once again left me with a lasting impression of speed and agility never achieved by piston engine types.

1946

By March 1946 I had left school and was working in the kitchens of the Connaught Hotel in Carlos Place, just off Grosvenor Square, as a trainee chef. This was a very tough regime involving long hours, and I think I worked 90 hours a week with a couple off in mid-morning and again in mid-afternoon; this was some time before the trade unions got a grip on the catering industry and reduced the working week to 40 hours. It was during one of these breaks that I spotted the Proctor III DX231 of the Metropolitan Communication Squadron on the ground in Hyde Park, not far from Speaker's Corner. I subsequently learned that the aircraft was on a flight from Holmsley South in Hampshire to Hendon, but never discovered why it force-landed. God knows how it got down without hitting anything, but it did, and I imagine it was transported by road back to Hendon.

In the spring of 1946 it was announced that there would be Victory Celebrations (including a parade and flypast in and over London) on 8th June, with the focal point in Trafalgar Square. The event was intended to signify the end of the second World War to the 'man in the street' and show the politicians' gratitude to the men and women of the fighting services for their efforts; how better than by a grand parade? I had intended to watch the parade and flypast in Trafalgar Square, but it was dull and raining when the day dawned and, although it dried up for a while, it started raining more heavily by lunchtime, so I stayed at home and never saw any of it. The flypast began at 1 pm in low cloud and heavy rain and comprised 308 aircraft from 35 squadrons, led by a lone Hurricane. Associated with the flypast were two Sunderland flying boats of 230 Sqdn., newly back from the Far East and moored on the Thames. More significantly there was an Exhibition of British Aircraft held in Green Park from 8th to 16th June, which I visited at least a couple of times; this was intended as the RAF's, Fleet Air Arm's and Airborne Forces' contribution to the festivities. On display were 22 complete aircraft, which included Oxford N6424, Horsa RN817, Auster AOP.V MT363, Lancaster ND677/'G', Firebrand EK746, Beaufighter RD773, Tiger Moth T7307/'FD-RK', Mosquito KA189, Vampire TG277, Swordfish LS326, Firefly TW688, Gladiator L8032, Meteor EE233, Halifax PP227, Hurricane LF743/'UH-F', Tempest NV758, Sea Fury SR666, Sea Otter RD919, Spitfire PS909, Seafire LA547, Wellington LP679 and Lysander T1671.

On 9th June, the day after the Victory Flypast, the weather was significantly better, and so I set off to attend the United Services Flying Club Housewarming & Flying Display at Elstree Aerodrome. *The Aeroplane* reported that there were 25 visitors, but I logged 34 aircraft including the Avian G-ACKE, Swallow G-AEOW, Dragon G-ADDI, Hawk Major G-ADCV, Redwing G-ABNX, 15 Autocrats (including the Temple Press's G-AERO), Grunau Baby, Kirby Cadet and Gull gliders, and this time the Meteor F.III EE254 represented the 'hot ship'. It was on this day I made my first flight, with a ten shilling joyride in the red and cream Autocrat G-AGXT of Grosvenor Square Garages Ltd., and it is amazing how many people who later became my friends flew in this aircraft on that day. I know for sure that Tim Wrixon and Maurice Gates were amongst them.

At the end of June the RAE Farnborough staged a three-day event to celebrate the remarkable progress made by the British Aircraft Industry in the year since the end of hostilities. The exhibition was held on the north side of the airfield near the big hangars ('A' Shed) and the control tower. The organisers persuaded manufacturers to send more than 40 of the latest types of aircraft, many of which had only recently flown, and most of which I had certainly not seen before. My memory tells me there were no barriers between the aircraft and the public and I have an uneasy memory of the BSAAC York *Star Venture* starting up while surrounded by crowds of people. There was a two-hour flying display, and the highlight for me was a spirited demonstration of the Martin-Baker MB.5 flown by Jan Zurakowski. It was the only time I ever saw it, and the final fate of this machine remains the subject of much speculation to this day. All the new airliners were there, including the Consul, Dove, Tudor, Freighter, Aerovan, Marathon, Viking and the Sandringham & Seaford flying boats. As the show was held on the north side of the airfield, all sorts of interesting aeroplanes were visible just beyond the barrier. Ever the opportunist, I had a crafty look inside the Barracuda DR126, actually sat in the Seafire RX173 and — even more outrageously — sat in the hooked Bell Airacobra AH574, without let or hindrance. A number of other residents were visible and I particularly remember the Lancaster LL780/'G' which I think had 20 mm gun turrets, the Mitchell FR209 with the 75 mm gun, and the Junkers 290A AirMin57 parked on the hill opposite — where the modern SBAC shows are held. I also visited the so-called Black Sheds (just below the present site of the FAST Museum) and was surprised to find they contained quite a few Messerschmitt Me.108s (or possibly Nord Pingouins). At the end of a wonderful day, I walked back to Farnborough Station, and left the RAE feeling content and at peace with the new world of aviation I found myself in.

Over the weekend of 31st August and 1st September, the 1946 Folkestone Air Races were staged at Lympne. Rain and strong winds on the Saturday dictated that I visited on the Sunday when the weather was much better, and on that day I witnessed the finals of the Siddeley Trophy, Folkestone Aero Trophy Races and the Lympne High Speed Handicap. This was my first experience of air racing. The High Speed Handicap involved a small but eclectic collection of aircraft flying unusually fast and low, which I found very exciting. The entrants were the Hawker Fury I monoplane NX802 (flown to victory by Bill Humble), DH Hornet PX224 (flown by Clem Pike), Supermarine Seafang XXXI VG475 (flown by Mike Lithgow) and Vampire F.I TG285 (flown by Geoffrey de Havilland). The final heat of the Folkestone Trophy Race attracted the Fairey Firefly Trainer prototype 'F.1', Firefly FR.IV VG979 (later exported to Ethiopia, and flown on that day by Gordon Slade), the Spitfire Trainer G-AIDN, Gull Six G-ADPR (flown by the Percival test pilot Les (?) Carruthers), and the winning all-yellow Walrus G-AHFN flown by John Grierson. My sketchy notes indicate that I also saw Tiger Moth G-AINW, Magister G-AJZH and the altogether rarer GAL Cygnet II G-AGAU.

Unfortunately the day was marred when I fell foul of the Southern Railway ticket inspector on the way back to London. Unknown to me, I had boarded the crack Golden Arrow at Folkestone Harbour station instead of the regular service from Folkestone Central, and an excess of several pounds was demanded, which I could not — and *would not* — pay. It was my first scuffle with the establishment and it went on for months, but in the end I paid up, even though I felt a deep sense of injustice. After all, it was their employee at the Harbour station who put me on that train . . .

In October 1946 I made my first visit to Croydon, when I accompanied my stepfather to the aerodrome. Eventually, he flew off to Le Bourget in the Morton Air Services Consul G-AIDY, but not before buying me a Flying Logbook from the famous news stand in the terminal building. I still have that logbook, which I am pretty certain I will never fill up. Incidentally, the weather worsened during the day and they never made Paris but were diverted to Cormeilles. After having hung about for some hours a further event made the day special for me, when I ventured out of the airport building and took a walk up the Purley Way. Here lying in the grass I came across a derelict fuselage, technically on the airfield but only a foot or two from the footpath. I took a look inside and again savoured the peculiar aroma that derelict aircraft seem to have, presumably a mixture of petrol, paint and wet rot. Later research confirmed that the aircraft was the Lockheed Model 14 Super Electra SP-LMK of LOT and the one-time G-AGAV. The official register says that its overhaul was abandoned in March 1944 due to corrosion and it was scrapped in February 1946.

At the end of 1946 I made the decision that the catering industry was not for me, and I set about finding a job in aviation. As it happened I struck lucky and was 'appointed' the office junior and tea-boy at the London Office of Miles Aircraft at a salary of 35 shillings per week, which was 'peanuts' after my well-paid job at the Connaught Hotel. The Miles sales office was at that time a prolific, busy and exciting place to be; however, it wasn't long before a posse of enterprising ex-service and other types seized their opportunities to exploit the somewhat free-and-easy situation, and in the fullness of time the company went into liquidation, resulting in my first redundancy in the aircraft industry; unfortunately it wasn't the last. The office, at 54 Brook Street in fashionable Mayfair, was an elegant four-storey house bang opposite the posh front entrance of Claridges Hotel, a place I got to know quite well when instructed to ferret out missing executives. I saw a lot of Freddie and Blossom Miles and also Mr. Biro, whose famous ball-pen activities occupied a whole floor in the house. I suppose I had a sense that the whole enterprise was riding on 'cloud nine', but I certainly enjoyed myself.

1947

The spring of 1947 saw some of the worst weather of the 20th century with extreme cold, and I read only the other day that the temperature in the UK did not rise above freezing for six weeks, and when it finally did stop freezing, everywhere was flooded. It seriously affected industry and transport; I seem to remember that coal was rationed, and I can remember taking my sister's pram to the coal yard in Marylebone sidings to queue up for some. Manufacturing industry was badly hit and of course this included the Miles factory at Woodley, which virtually came to a halt.

At around this time John Webb formed the *Reading Sky Observers'*
Club, based on Woodley Aerodrome and, somewhat exotically, the RSOC
Clubhouse consisted of the captured Junkers Ju.52/3M (Air Ministry 104
and onetime D-AUAV) parked on the airfield. In order to support the
venture I joined the Club, even though the possibility of attending the
monthly meetings regularly was impractical. However, I must have done
so from time to time because in due course I won an aircraft recognition
contest and received an invitation to visit the aerodrome on Sunday 15th
February to be taken for a flight.

And thus it was that, after a nightmare trip on trains and buses which
took far longer that I had planned, I got to the airfield by early afternoon
only to see the aircraft already in the sky. However, all was well and I was
rewarded with a flight in the Aerovan G AILF, at that time appropriately
equipped with skis for a projected Canadian sales tour. I flew with the ex-
ETPS test pilot Jimmy Nelson, at that time a Miles sales and
demonstration pilot, and my log book shows that I flew twice that
afternoon over the flooded Thames Valley countryside and came away
happy. Some readers will know that the Sky Observers' Club was
effectively metamorphosed into *Air-Britain* by Charles Cain and Gerry
Pollinger about a year later, and I have been a member of that
organisation ever since.

My log also shows that, once the weather improved, I got around
quite a bit, and among the novelties seen were the grounded Halifax 8
G-AHZM at Elstree (in which I sat many times), the Folland 43/47
Griffon engine test bed P1778 (then based at Hatfield), and something I
can actually prove, the Gemini VR-GGG at Elstree (see photo), which I
photographed. As far as I know, 'VR-G' remains the unactivated
allocation for Gibraltar, and quite why the aircraft had been painted thus
remains a mystery to me. During May I noted at Hatfield the Horsa fitted
with a Comet nose, while another entry for 22nd June tells me I saw 25
Mosquitos, 25 Hornets, 10 Vampires and 13 Doves & Devons on the
aerodrome, along with a Saab Safir, a Halifax and the Folland test bed
which was still in one piece. Wow!

Croydon was always good for exotic aircraft, and in June I saw the
Ethiopian Air Force Anson '121', the BA Swallow G-AEZM, Miles Falcon
OO-FLY and Beech 17 LN-HAG. A subsequent visit produced the Aer
Lingus Gemini EI-ACW and the DC-3 F-BCYF of Air Algerie. In June I
made my very first visit to Heathrow, which at that time was a couple of
marquees with three phone boxes standing outside in the mud alongside
the control tower on the north side; it was here that I 'copped' my first
Constellations, including NC88838 *Clipper Donald McKay* of Pan
American and N90923 of American Overseas Airlines. I also saw DC-3
VP-CAS of Ceylon Airways, Lancaster G-AGUJ of Flight Refuelling, Yorks

ZS-ATR and ZS-BTT of South African Airways and G-AHFH *Star Glitter* of British South American Airways.

In July Miles decided to have a weekend Air Display and 'At Home', primarily for employees, but word soon got round and there was a large crowd by the standards of those days. I caught the train down to Reading, and under blue skies logged 12 types of aircraft including the unmarked Broburn Wanderlust glider. A Tempest 2, the Hurricane LF363 (still in RAF service as a 'hack' with the BoB Flight) and no less than 19 different types of Miles aircraft, from Hawk Major to Marathon, flew at Woodley; there were 14 Aerovans and 19 Geminis, including two Swiss-registered examples, and the one and only public showing of the M.39 Libellula 'U4'. It was undoubtedly the biggest coming together of Miles types ever, but unhappily almost the company's swan song, as a year later Miles went into liquidation.

At the end of July there was an airshow held at Elstree, where rarities included the Avro Avian G-ACKE, Cierva C.30 G-AIOC, DH.86B G-ADVJ of Bond Air Services (joyriding, but once again beyond my budget), no less than three Halifaxes, the Hirtenburg HS.9 G-AGAK, Miles Martlet G-AAYX and the newly-restored Westland Woodpigeon G-AAGH flown by Harald Penrose. Foreigners included the strangely-marked Klemm 32A F.B.C.K.X and the Norecrin F-BBBO. No jets appeared, but two squadrons of Spitfire 16s from 601 and 602 Sqdns. Royal Auxiliary Air Force based at Hendon provided the service contribution. BOAC sent the Short Sandringham G-AHZE *Portsea*.

Next was the air race meeting held at Southend, where once again a shortage of cash forced me to miss out on the chance of a lifetime, to fly in Jack Jones' joyriding Airspeed Courier G-ACVF. As the programme included air races (won by Ron Paine), there was a good turnout of de Havilland and Miles types, with the most exotic aircraft being the de Havilland TK.2 G-ADNO, together with a vast number of visiting Autocrats and Proctors. 'New kid on the block' and race entrant was the prototype Chipmunk CF-DIO-X, while the foreign visitors included the Belgian Air Force Oxford V3775 and Bestmann OO-GAD. Military muscle came in the shape of a squadron of Meteor F.3s, and five Vampires from 54 and 247 Sqdns. at Odiham led by CO Brian Kingaby in the oddly-serialled Vampire VF303 and monogrammed 'BK'. Other oddballs were the Blackburn B.2 G-ACLD, the Chilton DW.1 G-AFSV (wheeled about by Ranald Porteous) and the prototype Chrislea Ace G-AHLG.

On the last day of August 1947 I made my third flight, this time at Croydon Airport, where I bought a joyride with St Christopher's Travelways. For some obscure reason I made no note of the aircraft involved, and this has been a source of puzzlement to me ever since, but I was with my female cousin, so perhaps this was a distraction. For some time I accepted that I flew in Proctor G AJTP, but subsequent discussions with John Havers threw some doubt on this, and it now seems more likely that I flew in the Vega Gull G-AIIT (unrestored as G-AFAU), loaned to St. Christopher Travelways. I do remember that it was silver with green trim, which fits the Vega Gull better but, if I could only prove it, it would add another very desirable type to the number of types I have flown in (currently standing at 168). Incidentally, among the visitors to Croydon on that day was the DC-3 VR-HDQ, destined for Hong Kong Airways.

In those days the Ministry of Civil Aviation celebrated the Battle of Britain by arranging for military aircraft to be exhibited in some airport public enclosures. On a visit to Northolt, designated London Airport while building work went on at Heathrow, I saw Lancaster GR.3 RE175/'XB-P' of 224 Sqdn., Hornet PX280/'YT-A' of 65 Sqdn., Meteor F.3 EE457/'ZD-Q' of 222 Sqdn. and USAF B-17 Fortress 469517, along with many civil airliners, including DC-3s LN-IAG of DNL, EI-ACI of Aer Lingus and HB-IRO of Swissair. Also seen were DC-4s SE-BBG of Swedish Airlines, HB-ILA of Swissair, N76444 of Trans Oceanic Charter Inc. and several Vikings, including EI-ADH and 'ADI of Aer Lingus. The oddest aircraft there on that day was the Trans Canada Airlines Lodestar CF-TCD. Incidentally, in those days the MCA provided so-called 'guided tours' around Northolt in coaches; however these were a total farce, carried out in true 'Goon' style, with the driver — who knew nothing whatever about aviation — doubling as the guide, and always looking for a tip at the end of the tour. His little gems included an opinion that the DC-4 Skymaster could carry 21,000 TONS of fuel, rather than pounds. He was also convinced that the B-17 could carry an atomic bomb. On the other hand you did get to see what was 'over the back' . . .

In September 1946 I wasn't well connected enough to get into the ticket-only Garden Party thrown by the Royal Aeronautical Society at Radlett on the last day of the SBAC Show. However, it was a different story when the event was repeated in September 1947, and my boss Freddie Miles took me totally by surprise by presenting me with that all important tag on a string. I took the Green Line bus that passed the Radlett factory gates and, on arrival, was somewhat amused to see a number of clearly important people trying to negotiate entry into the show. Proudly displaying the coveted badge I entered unhindered with a feeling bordering on superiority.

It was at this point I saw a most remarkable happening: two lads, presumably HP employees, were larking about with a fork lift truck just inside the gates of the factory; one drove the thing while the other stood on the forks, which were constantly going up and down and which must have been incredibly dangerous. I then saw a burly man come around the corner shouting at the boys, who immediately stopped what they were doing; he then got hold of them by the scruff of the neck, one in each hand, and physically ran them out the main gate and onto the pavement and told them never to come back. It turned out to be Sir Frederick Handley Page just being himself, so I was subsequently led to believe; he obviously kept an eagle eye on everything going on his works.

The show itself was conducted in a very genteel manner, with everybody on their best behaviour and access to all the exhibits being made very easy, and all followed by cucumber sandwiches and tea in the tent. I went inside a number of aircraft, and one that stood out was the Shell Petroleum Sea Otter G-AIDM, for it had a beautifully furnished cabin. It was also the only time I ever saw a Proctor (X-2) on floats. I was also able to go inside Tudor G-AGRX and the Viking G-AJJN and there were a number of aircraft there I had never seen before (or for that matter since) such as the Portsmouth Aerocar G-AGTG, the Heston A2/45 VL529, Cierva W.9 PX203, Cunliffe-Owen Concordia G-AKBE and the three TS-serialled General Aircraft GAL.56 swept-wing gliders. I also think it was the only time I ever saw three different marks of Hawker Fury monoplane together. These were the Sabre Fury VP207, Centaurus Fury NX802 and standard Sea Fury TF955. This was the last big airshow at Radlett and the following year the whole thing moved south to Farnborough.

Also observed in September each year, the Battle of Britain celebrations provided air shows at many airfields, together with a static display of aircraft on Horse Guards Parade in London. In 1947 I decided to 'ring the changes' and go to the Biggin Hill show instead of Hendon. Here, I suppose for me, the star of the show was the ex-Aer Lingus Walrus G-AIZG acquired by S/Ldr. R.G. Kellett, the then CO of 615 Sqdn., Royal Auxiliary Air Force, and used as a privately-owned squadron 'hack'. In March 1948 it was sold on, but early in 1949 I was withdrawn from use and spent the next 15 years lying derelict in a field at Thame near Oxford; it was then recovered by Fleet Air Arm personnel and beautifully restored for the FAA Museum at Yeovilton, where it can be seen to this day. Other notable sightings at Biggin Hill were (1) a Halifax towing a Hamilcar, and (2) Sir Harry Broadhurst's monogrammed Fieseler Storch VX154/'HB', happily still with us at Cosford.

Around this time I started attending the monthly meetings of the Aircraft Recognition Society; these were held in the Library of the Royal Aeronautical Society in Hamilton Place and hosted by that legendary total aviation person, Peter Masefield. The format of the meetings was a talk by a noted aeronautical figure, followed by a black & white slide recognition test comprising 30 views of aircraft seen over the UK, or any Russian type. I became quite proficient in recognition and seemed to win something on most of my visits — a silver spoon for the monthly contests, a set of cufflinks now and then, and annually, the coveted Silver Hurricane Trophy donated during the war by Rolls-Royce and considered the premier award for the subject. I recollect that on a number of occasions the Trophy was contested in the Lecture Theatre of the Science Museum on a Saturday afternoon in the spring, and the winners could be heard later on the popular radio show *In Town Tonight* from the studio in Broadcasting House.

Also by this time I had joined the Royal Observer Corps, then a part of Fighter Command, where my prowess at recognising aircraft was a bonus. However, I always preferred to be at the centre of things and served my time at the Group Headquarters at Watford rather than on a post where spotting skill was essential. I spent many happy years in the ROC, and only gave up when the aircraft reporting role was abandoned in favour of the nuclear fallout monitoring role.

1948

By 1948 things had deteriorated at Miles Aircraft, and in due course the company went into liquidation and was split up into what would now be called 'profit centres' (or possibly 'loss centres'). My aviation job then crumbled, but in order to continue working with the company I was obliged to transfer to the CopyCat Division. This made wet process office copying machines in several sizes, also an optical device called the Grant Projector, a sort of glorified enlarging machine which became an essential tool for many advertising agencies.

In the spring of 1948 I discovered that the Green Line 715 route passed the entrance to Broxbourne Aerodrome near Hoddesdon, and I took to visiting the Herts & Essex Flying Club regularly. My notes indicate that the club was equipped with the Autocrats G-AIZV and G-AJEG, five Tiger Moths (including G-AIDT), the Hornet Moth G-ADOT and the Rapide G-AJKY, and I took a number of 10-shilling joyrides in the Austers and the Rapide during that year. The longest runway was only 630 yards long and the airfield closed to flying in 1954 to become a housing estate and an early form of shopping mall.

Occasionally I would visit Hatfield and sometimes forsake the Green Line for a train which travelled through New Southgate on its way north. There, if you hung out of the window in good time, you would pass the fuselage of a Dakota in the grounds of Standard Telephones & Cables works. It took years for me to establish its identity as the C-47A-25-DK 42-93418. I wonder if it is still there? Another DC-3 spotted at Heathrow around that time was NC79100, seen alongside the Bloch 161 Languedoc F-BATB of Air France. Again, I see from my notebook that on a trip to Elstree a week or two later, I saw five Piper J/3C Cubs there including two, NC79800 and NC79818, in the same sequence as the Heathrow

DC-3. The other Cubs were G-AKAA, G-AKNC and what looks like a 'live' L-4 Grasshopper 44-79918. This was before the days of 'warbirds'.

In July the *Daily Express* held its first Air Pageant at Gatwick Airport, at that time undeveloped but with the 'Beehive' left over from its short prewar stint as London's second international airport. I see I took a train from Victoria to Gatwick Racecourse station, my ticket costing five shillings which also included admission to the air show. The display itself was an eye-opener to someone like me, and there were all sorts of novelties there like the Fulton Airphibian flying car NC74104, Goodyear Duck NC5506M, the blue & orange Stinson Reliant NC2311 snatching a man from the ground, and on the military side, formations of Spitfires, Lincolns, Vampires, Dakotas towing Horsas, and Sea Hornets along with single examples of the Halifax, Hadrian glider and an Army(?) Hoverfly. Civil participants included a Skyways York, BOAC Solent, BSAAC Tudor, Air France Languedoc, KLM DC-6 and Airwork & BEA Vikings. Tantalisingly visible across the airfield but not accessible were Stirling OO-XAE, DC-3 ZS-BYX, DH.86 G-ADVJ and the Bristol Freighter F-BENF. Considering how indifferent the weather was, there was a huge crowd, reckoned to be around 80,000.

The next big event in my life was the first SBAC Flying Display and Exhibition, better known as the Farnborough Air Show, and the first to open to the general public. This was held in September on the north side of the airfield and it was still possible to see the Junkers Ju.290 on the hill to the south of the display area. There were many aircraft I had not seen before such as both AW.52s, the Blackburn Firecrest, Cierva Air Horse, Fairey Primer, General Aircraft GAL.61 swept-wing glider, Planet Satellite (which later metamorphosed into the Firth Helicopter), Saro SR/A1 (flying), Short Sealand, Supermarine Seagull, the Nene-Viking (the world's first jet airliner), DH.108, the truly STOL Prestwick Pioneer, and curiously the Westland Pterodactyl plus the all-white 'Griffiths' Hurricane Z3687 used for laminar flow experiments. Believe it or not there were no less than 30 prototypes on show, and the flying display was scheduled to last for 2¾ hours.

On the eighth Anniversary of the Battle of Britain in September, the RAF held an *At Home* at Hendon in very indifferent weather. Although relatively modest, the static show comprised a Tiger Moth, Proctor, Harvard, Anson, Expeditor, Spitfire 16, Dakota and Hoverfly. There were also a number of formation flypasts including Lincolns, Vampires, Spitfires, Mosquitos, Tempests, Meteors, and — for me — my first sight of P-80 Shooting Stars with a formation of 12, which I think were based at Manston. Singletons in the flying display were the Theseus-Lincoln, a Valetta and a Hastings.

My final aeronautical excursion in 1948 was to a National Car Park site near St. Paul's Cathedral in October, where *The Aeroplane* had organised a City Centre to City Centre flight between London and Paris, codenamed *Hare and Tortoise*. The aim of the demonstration was to carry a letter from the Lord Mayor of London to his French equivalent, the President of the Municipal Council of Paris, as fast as possible. The first stage was carried out by the Bristol Sycamore VL958, flown by Bristol pilot Eric Swiss; he dashed to Biggin Hill, where he speedily handed over the letter to Bill Waterton waiting in the Meteor T7 G-AKPK. Bill then flew flat out to Orly, where the letter was handed over to Alan Bristow, waiting in the Westland Sikorsky WS.51 G-AJHW. He then flew to the Place des Invalides where the British Civil Air Attaché handed over the letter to the Parisian Vice-President, the whole exercise having taken just under 47 minutes.

1949

1949 was an odd year for me with everything seeming slightly out of place. My job at CopyCat came to an end in the spring when that part of the old Miles empire also went into liquidation, and because my National Service was looming I had to take any job I could get, which inevitably was out of aviation.

However, I continued to visit airfields with my next air show at Elstree on 18th April, Easter Monday, where the exotica comprised a formation of B-29 Superfortresses (from Marham), the BAC Drone G-ADSB, Comper Swift G-ABPE, Watkinson Dingbat G-AFJA, Zlin Krajanek glider G-ALMP (flown by Laddie Marmol), the Argus G-AKJM, Beech 17 G-AJJJ, the Bibi 550 G-AGSR and four Tiger Moths coded 'RCM-A', 'RCM-C', 'RCM-D' and 'RCM-L', all from 1 RFTS at Panshanger. The *Aeroplane* claimed that 10,000 members of the public turned up, to see among other things the newly-appointed Auster test pilot Ranald Porteous giving his first display for the company. During the Show the Lancaster B.3 TW871 overflew the airfield, and Spitfires from 601 and 604 Sqdns. Royal Auxiliary AF, by now based at North Weald, carried out 'Air Drill', which seemed to mean just wheeling about in the sky . . .

Although the price had now increased to 15 shillings, I did manage to scrape enough money together for another joyride, and that was from Northolt in the Lancashire Aircraft Corporation Rapide G-AJKY. In the days before air traffic control prevailed, the aircraft took about 20-25 minutes to fly from Northolt to Central London and back, and the trip was considered quite good value amongst the *cognoscenti*.

In 1949 the RAeS broke with tradition by separating its annual Garden Party from the SBAC Show, and it organised a grand event at

White Waltham instead, calling it a *Grand Aerostatic Fête*. This was held on 8th May, and the Georgian-style souvenir programme issued for the event included a most attractive reprint of Mr. Green's Great Nassau balloon ascent in Vauxhall Gardens in August 1848. Included in the static display was Supermarine S.6B S1595, while the air show itself included a number of veteran aircraft, including the Blériot and Deperdussin monoplanes, the WW1 Sopwith Pup G-EBKY, some interwar lightplanes such as the Avro Avian G-ACKE, Blackburn Bluebird G-ACLD, Chilton G-AFGH, Percival Gull G-ADPR, Comper Swift G-ABUS, GAL Cygnet G-AFVR, Hawker Tomtit G-AFTA and Hart G-ABMR. For once the rotary wing community were represented and the flying programme included the Cierva C.30 G-AIOC and the new Skeeter G-AJCJ, and the obligatory RAF Sikorsky Hoverfly KK991, the whole being accompanied by the Fairey Aviation Band, who played 'favourite airs throughout the afternoon, including the Lunardi Air March. It was indeed a grand occasion, and I see from my notes that the Avro Tutor G-AKFJ, Beaver G-ALOW, Lockheed 12 G-AGDT, Zaunkoenig VX190, and two Percival Q.6s, G-AEYE and G-AHOM, were in attendance, along with 21 Miles aircraft including the Nighthawk G-AGWT and Sparrowhawk G-ADNL.

A visit to London Airport in the summer of 1949 brought me my first Stratocruisers when I 'copped' N1023V of Pan American and N90941 of American Overseas Airlines, along with the Tudor 5 G-AKBZ *Star Falcon* of British South American Airways and three Air France Languedocs, F-BATT, F-BCUE and F-BCUJ, parked among the many Dakotas and Yorks.

Eagerly anticipated by the spotting fraternity was the second *Daily Express* Air Pageant on 23rd July, held once again at Gatwick. The 1949 novelties were the 15 ft wingspan Wee Bee NX90840, which required the pilot, Karl Montijo, to lie prone on top of the fuselage, and Betty Skelton's Pitts Special NX86401. During the morning Rapides (including G-AKNX from Air Enterprises) and Dakotas (G-AKLL from Hornton and G-AKOZ from Kearsley Airways) gave 10-minute and 40-minute joyrides, all at a cost of 1/- (one shilling) a minute. The afternoon's flying programme was opened by three Spitfires from the Central Gunnery School trailing red, white and blue smoke, who deposited a Prince of Wales Feather in the sky (repeated at the end of the show), then there were flypasts of 6 Meteor F.4s, 6 Vampire F.3s, 3 Sunderland flying boats, 6 Lincolns and 5 Hastings. One of two CFS Tiger Moths (T6274 and DE459) carried out crazy flying and Bernard Lynch demonstrated a live ejection from EE338, Martin-Baker's modified Meteor F.3. The USAF contributed nine B-29s from 98th Bomb Group at Lakenheath and four (by now styled F-80) Shooting Stars. French participation consisted of the Patrouille d'Étampes aerobatic team flying four Stampe SV-4Cs and the SUC.10

Courlis F-BEKQ, while the Dutch Air Force sent an S.11 Instructor flown by well-known Fokker test pilot Gerry Sonderman. Civil items included Ranald Porteous aerobatting in the Autocrat G-AJIZ, the Cierva Skeeter G-AJCJ and Laddie Marmol again in the Krajanek, although the new Lunak had been promised. Civil 'heavies' comprised the BOAC Argonaut G-ALHF, followed by Pan American Stratocruiser N1034V.

One of the expected highlights was the DH.108 but it failed to appear and a Vampire FB.5 took its place. The finale was dubbed *An Airborne Attack on an Enemy Radio Station*, and began with Meteors strafing the target, followed by three Dakotas dropping paratroops. A Halifax dropped a jeep and a gun, as four Dakotas released Horsa gliders. After the ensuing assault, an RAF medical team parachuted into the battlefield and prepared to evacuate casualties with a snatch pick-up of the RAF Hadrian 274521 by a Dakota flying at 100 mph only 12 ft from the ground. The event ended with a downed pilot being rescued by a RAF helicopter, presumably the Hoverfly KN844, and a massed tow-off of the Horsas by Dakotas returning to their base. It was a great day out with plenty of air action. However, the format was never repeated and the *Daily Express* turned its attention to an air race around the South Coast in 1950 and celebrated *50 Years of Flying* at Hendon in 1951.

The 1949 SBAC Show at Farnborough in September followed the same basic format set the previous year and was (for the last time) basically held on the north side of the airfield. Star of the show was undoubtedly the Comet jetliner and the shape of things to come was embodied in the first of the Avro 707 delta research aircraft to appear. Most companies managed to have at least four different types on display and this applied to Auster, Gloster, Handley Page, Hawker and Percival, while Avro had five and de Havilland a magnificent seven. Newcomers included a second Skeeter and production Chipmunks, but it was the last display for the Griffon-powered Supermarine Seagull and certainly for the Cierva Air Horse which crashed at Eastleigh the following June, unfortunately followed a few days later by the Skeeter 2 which shook itself to bits.

The 1949 Battle of Britain Display at North Weald broke new ground by being televised by the BBC and broadcast live on Saturday afternoon. The programme included the usual formations of Tiger Moths, Ansons, Lincolns, PR Mosquitos, Hornets, Vampires, Hastings, Dakotas and Spitfires, some from the resident 601 and 604 Sqdns., along with three PR variants from Benson. New technology was embodied in five brand-new USAF B-50 improved Superfortresses and, due to its proximity at nearby Hatfield, the Comet prototype G-ALVG. I also see from my notes that an anonymous RAF Hadrian glider was snatched by a Dakota, and still on a gliding theme, the Air Cadets' new Slingsby T.21B Sedbergh two-seater was making its debut.

By September 1949 the annual Battle of Britain Exhibition on Horse Guards Parade had settled down to more or less the same format every year. The BoB aircraft were the Hurricane L1592, Spitfire P9444 and the unmarked Messerschmitt Me.109G (actually RN228). The variables, representing the modern RAF, were the Vampire VX953 and Meteor RA476, and the two jets turned up in this role for several years.

It was while awaiting my National Service call-up papers in the autumn of 1949 that I flew in my fifth type of aeroplane (apart from the Autocrat and Aerovan, the others were the disputed Proctor/Vega Gull and the Rapide). I was still serving in the Royal Observer Corps Group Headquarters at Watford and from time to time we received invitations to visit a RAF station on goodwill trips. On this occasion it was No.1 Reserve Flying Training School at Panshanger, and I was flown in the camouflaged Tiger Moth T7862/'RCM-X'. It was my first flight in an open cockpit and, being October, it was none too warm; however, it was exhilarating and I had a bird's eye view of Hatfield Aerodrome, which was very busy at that time with the development of the Comet. Following two years' National Service and after rejoining the ROC, I had quite a few rides in RAF Ansons, but in 1954 I got really lucky and won the draw for a ride in a Fighter Command Communications Squadron Meteor T.7 at Bovingdon: now that was exciting!

While in contention with the authorities over my call-up, I made my first trip overseas and went to Paris with my stepfather who, being a painter, had many friends there. France was still in absolute disarray, with everything rationed including electricity and food, affecting everyone even in the centre of Paris. We more or less camped in Eduardo Paolozzi's artist's studio on the top floor of a house in the Rue Bude on the Île de la Cité, and I found the whole experience very, very different from home and quite exciting. There was a minimal aeronautical connection but I did meet Phillipeaux, who was the designer of some of those very distinctive postwar Air France posters. Naturally I asked if we could visit Le Bourget, and was rewarded with a trip on the old open-back buses which took us to Port de la Villete, and then another direct to the airfield. I see from my notes that I stood on those hallowed terraces and saw the C-46 F-BESL, Goeland F-BAOP, Fiat G.212 I-ESTE, SM.95 I-DALR, Amiot AAC.1 F-BBYF, Dakotas F-BAXR, F-BEFO and F-BEST, and the SE.161 Languedocs F-BATP, F-BATS, F-BATV and F-BCUB. Also visible were three British Consuls and the BEA Vikings G-AHPP and G-AJDI. Little did I realise that I would visit Le Bourget again many times in later years for the Paris Air Show.

And so it was that, despite my service with the ROC, my career in industry, and my total involvement in things aeronautical, I was called up to serve, not as expected with the RAF, but with the *Army*. Because my birthday was in July I should theoretically have joined up in August or September, but because I contested the issue the whole process was delayed. In the end my request was refused and I joined the Royal Signals at Catterick in the deep snow of mid-December, only days before Christmas. And that was where I spent the first year of the fifties. However, there was one bonus to all this: my co-sufferers included one Roy Stephens who had a commercial pilot's licence but whose flat feet had unbelievably robbed him of a career in the RAF. So we palled up, and on Saturday afternoons in the spring and summer of 1950 managed to get away from the camp to visit the ex-WW2 airfield at Croft (sometimes called Neasham); here he would hire the Autocrat G-AJRN, and we would fly around dodging the brand-new Hastings then entering service with 47 Sqdn. at Dishforth: so, as they say, every cloud has a silver lining. I met Roy again at the Biggin Hill Air Fair some years later, by which time he had become a distributor for the Maule series of American lightplanes.

And so we came to the end of the 1940s, a turbulent decade of war and peace, and one requiring a great deal of self-discipline and adjustment for virtually everybody in the country, but which was all to the good of the nation. The British aircraft industry had somehow produced the goods in wartime, albeit with a few failures, and in peace the directions provided by the Brabazon Committee about what aircraft to build postwar were found to be fallible. Political indecision inhibited many promising projects, and we gave up on some things far too easily, such as supersonic research. Then there were the technical cul-de-sacs such as centrifugal jet engines.

For myself I was out of it, not being a military person, but somehow enduring my National Service. I suppose I soon found my own level and made the best of it, spending 1950 on the staff at Catterick, followed by a year at the War Office in Whitehall. Ironically, the latter turned into an aviation job when I was put in charge of decoding air combat reports streaming in from Korea. In those days the RAF did not have its own communications network and therefore relied on the Army for such things. I was demobilised in December 1951 wondering just how I would get back into aviation, but could never have forecast exactly the way things would turn out. If really interested, the curious reader can discover some of what transpired in the sister publications *Tails of the Fifties* and *More Tails of the Fifties* . . .

CHAPTER 22

POSTWAR AIR RALLYING
PART 1: The Madrid Air Rally

by

P.A. CHABOREL

(Originally published in The Light Plane and Private Owner *for June 1947)*

The idea of holding an air rally in Spain was first suggested by the Duke of Almodovar to the British delegates attending the first postwar meeting of the *Fédération Aéronautique Internationale* held in London during September 1946. Considerable interest was shown in this, and 18th—21st April 1947 was finally selected as the most suitable period. Invitations were sent to Members and Associate Members of the Royal Aero Club, and a total of 52 guests in 19 aircraft (Proctors, Austers, Messengers, an Airspeed Consul and a Lockheed 12) finally arrived at Madrid.

In company with Mr. D.C. Ward-Campbell, I attended the Rally in the Proctor G-AHZY, operated by Intava Ltd., and one of the main objects of our trip was to review the aviation servicing facilities available in France and Spain at the opening of the 1947 private flying season.

We left Gatwick on 16th April, and proceeded via Dungeness and Boulogne to Paris (Toussus-le-Noble) where inward Customs were cleared. An excellent lunch at a reasonable price was obtained at the airport restaurant. Some delay was experienced before our flight plan was approved by the authorities. This also happened on our return trip and apparently is confined only to the Paris Zone, as no difficulties were experienced elsewhere in France in obtaining clearance from Flying Control.

After landing at Tours (St. Symphorien) we proceeded to Bordeaux (Merignac), our first overnight stop. The following morning, 17th April, our proposed route via Biarritz and Logrono had to be abandoned due to unfavourable weather. Instead we flew via Toulouse (Blagnac), where outward Customs were cleared and on to Barcelona (Muntadas) via Perpignan (Llabanere).

On landing at Barcelona (Muntadas) all necessary formalities were completed with speed and efficiency, but bad weather prevented our proceeding direct to Madrid.

Zero hour for the arrival of the guests at Madrid was 12.00 hours on 18th April. Although the weather gradually cleared during the morning, we were not able to leave until the early afternoon. After lunching at the airport restaurant, clearance was obtained for our flight to Madrid via Saragossa.

The grandeur of the mountain scenery on this section of the route defies description. We followed the valley of the Ebro to Saragossa, and then along the Henares to Madrid, where we had the distinction of being the first visiting aircraft to land at the Barajas Airport, although we were followed closely by Messrs. Bay and Frewer in their Proctor. A large and enthusiastic crowd of spectators had assembled on the airport, and the Spanish Press were out in force. After taxying to our allotted parking position, we were warmly welcomed by the Duke of Almodovar, the Spanish Minister of Civil Aviation, the President of the Madrid Aero Club and many other officials connected with the Rally.

Then we commenced to experience true Spanish hospitality. On entering the airport building each guest was handed an envelope containing all official invitations, details of hotel accommodation, general information and even sketch plans for our guidance. Tea and light refreshments were served in the restaurant, after which the guests were driven to the Palace Hotel, Madrid, where an official reception and supper was held in our honour by the Presidents of the *Federación Aeronáutica Nacional de España* and the Aero Club of Madrid.

In accordance with Spanish custom, this did not commence until late in the evening and lasted until well past midnight, when the more energetic members of the party proceeded to investigate the night life of Madrid.

An early start was scheduled on 19th April for the flight to Seville. Perfect weather was experienced and all pilots were briefed on this section of the flight by the British Air Attaché, Group Captain A.C.P. Carver, who accompanied the party to Seville in the Embassy Avro XIX. Our route passed over the ancient city of Toledo where the best Spanish is reputed to be spoken.

We flew at 7,000 feet over the Toledo Mountains and the Sierra Morena range and landed at the military airfield by courtesy of the Spanish Air Force, who also kindly provided efficient maintenance facilities. After an official welcome by our hosts, the Royal Aero Club of Andalusia, we were driven to Seville, where the annual *Feria* was in full progress. This was an unforgettable experience, as a more typical display of Spanish national costumes could not be desired.

After lunch, which was given by the Presidents of the *Federación Aeronáutica Nacional de España* and the Royal Aero Club of Andalusia, we were invited to attend a bullfight as the guests of the Duke of Almodovar.

The Andalusian Palace Hotel was fixed as the rendezvous for the early part of the evening, after which we returned to the *Feria* for a tour of the illuminations followed by a cold supper and Andalusian entertainment —

provided by our hosts, the Royal Aero Club of Andalusia. We were privileged to watch some of the finest exponents of Spanish folk dancing, and their perfect rhythm, emphasised by the accompaniment of castanets and guitars, was a fitting climax to the day's activities.

In the early hours of the morning we proceeded by coach to Jerez, the centre of the sherry trade. At approximately 05.00 hours a tired but very happy party of British guests was unloaded at the hotel. While rooms were being allotted and baggage sorted out, drinks and light refreshments were served. Full marks for the hotel service! In view of the strenuous round of visits experienced the previous day, we were left undisturbed until 13.00 hours, when the whole party was invited by the Duke of Almodovar to lunch at the famous Bodegas of Sanchez Romate. This was the highlight of the Rally, and a better way of spending a Sunday afternoon could not be imagined than by listening to experts explaining some of the mysteries of the sherry trade and very properly illustrating the more difficult points with liberal samples.

Lunch was attended by more than 100 guests, who sat at a long table laid between a lofty alley of sherry casks in a cool warehouse with a hard earthen floor. A speech of welcome was delivered by the Duke of Almodovar and Wing Commander Michaelson's reply on behalf of the guests struck exactly the right note. Mr. A.D. Duncan then proposed toasts for the host and hostess, after which the party motored to Cadiz — the historic port of Spain on the Atlantic seaboard.

The evening was left free, and on returning to the hotel at Jerez each guest received a souvenir parcel from the Duke of Almodovar containing bottles of sherry and Spanish brandy: also a leather cigarette case.

The following morning we were driven to Seville (Tablada) for our return flight to Madrid. Thereafter the party split into various groups for the trip to England via Logroño or Barcelona. We chose the latter route and flew direct from Madrid across the mountains. A strong crosswind was blowing, which made landing a tricky business as there is only one runway at Barcelona (Muntadas). The weather was breaking up, so we decided to remain for the night.

An early start was proposed for the morning of 22nd April, but we delayed our departure when news was received that a Vega Gull (G-AFEA) piloted by Dr. Little was badly damaged on landing at Saragossa late the previous evening.

We returned via Marseille (Marignane) and Lyon (Bron) where an overnight stop was made. We were planning to continue via Dijon (Longvic) but unfavourable weather compelled us to fly via Roanne and Nevers along the valley of the Loire to Paris. Lunch was again taken at the airport restaurant, and after some delay clearance was obtained for our return fight to Gatwick, which was accomplished without incident.

PART 2: The Derby International Air Rally

(almost certainly) by

S.O. BRADSHAW

(Originally published in The Light Plane and Private Owner *for August 1947)*

Britain's first postwar International Air Rally was held at Derby Airport on 20th and 21st June 1947. Organised by the Derby Aero Club in conjunction with Derby Corporation and Rolls Royce Ltd., the Rally was a huge success. Despite a bus strike which paralysed local communications, over 13,000 people attended the airport for the air display. Of the 200 visiting aircraft, 34 were foreign visitors. These included a Cessna 120 (HB-CAA) from Switzerland, a KZ.II and numerous KZ.IIIs and VIIs from Denmark and Sweden, a gaggle of Piper Cubs from the Ghent Aviation Club, a Bücker Bestmann and a Lockheed 12A from Ghent.

By the kind cooperation of Messrs. Intava Ltd. we were able to attend the Rally in their Proctor V, G-AHZY, flown by Eric Marshall. Taking off from Gatwick airport in the evening of Thursday 19th June, we arrived at Lympne to find eight aircraft of the Wolverhampton Flying Club already in occupation as a welcoming committee. These eight aircraft had arrived earlier on Thursday and were led by Ron Paine and L.E. Barley. The rest of Thursday evening was spent in the splendour of the Lympne Country Club, and we stayed the night in the Majestic Hotel, Folkestone, all eagerly anticipating the dawn.

The following morning we were all awake bright and early, and undaunted by a 'duff' Met forecast. We had no sooner stepped from our taxis when the sound of the first arrival was heard, and a few moments later Guy Fecheyr's Bücker Bestmann, OO-GAD, came into view. Handshakes all round, and the first visitor to Britain's first international air rally had arrived. Next to arrive was an Me.108 Taifun, OY-DMI, from Denmark. This machine was flown by Paul Nielson of Kastrup, Copenhagen. Soon the sky was full of arriving aircraft: Piper Cubs from Ghent, KZ Larks from Le Zoute (where they had spent the previous night) and Austers from Belgium. By noon all the expected aircraft had arrived, except two which had been forced to make forced landings at Lille and Le Zoute respectively, luckily without incident. The only mishap of the arrival was a young Dane, who fell while jumping onto a moving car and had to have several stitches in his head.

While the customs formalities were in progress the weather rapidly closed in and it was decided to abandon the plans and get the visitors off to Derby as quickly as possible. Unfortunately, however, despite the fact that the International Air Rally had received publicity in both this and other magazines some months in advance, the powers-that-be at Lympne seemed not to have the haziest idea as to why there were so many foreign aircraft at Lympne, and there were no more personnel on duty than on a normal day. This caused long delays, both in customs clearance and in refuelling, with the result that only a few aircraft were able to take off before the weather clamped down completely. Due to the speed with which the clouds descended, several aircraft were caught aloft; of these a Belgian Auster Arrow was lost and had to make a forced landing in a field at Denton Green near Sevenoaks. However, both the occupants were OK. Other aircraft caught by the storm were the Fairchild Argus (OO-GAO), which had to descend at Bovingdon, and George Hanet's Lockheed 12, which came down at deserted Hawkinge when he failed to find Lympne in the murk. With the weather down to the tree tops we all had no alternative other than to adjourn to the Lympne Country Club for a fine lunch. Great credit for the arrangements at Lympne must go to Major and Mrs. Ann Attree for the fine way they stepped into the breach and arranged food, transport and accommodation for the 60-odd foreign visitors. Friday evening was spent in the bar of the Majestic Hotel, Folkestone, which helped to keep our thoughts off the cocktail party then in progress at Derby. In the deplorable absence of a Royal Aero Club official, members of the Wolverhampton Aero Club, under the leadership of Messrs. Ron Paine and L. Barley, acted as hosts and were ably assisted by Paul Chaborel and Eric Marshall.

In common with our foreign visitors, your humble reporter awoke early on Saturday morning with the usual heavy hangover. However 9 am found us all present and correct at the airport and by 9.30 am the first aircraft were leaving for Derby. All the aircraft got away smartly except the Piper Cub OO-PCR; this aircraft was fitted with an experimental curved propeller and, whilst taking off, the metal capping of this wooden propeller sheared, causing the aircraft to vibrate and to come down, smashing the undercarriage. The aircraft was flown by Monsieur Brabundre and a friend, and M. Brabundre and his co-pilot continued to Derby in Intava's Consul G-AIDX.

An interesting visitor passing through Lympne on Saturday morning was Hugh Kennedy, late of Miles and now of Raceways Ltd., flying a Gemini. We ourselves left Lympne at 11 am, after most of the aircraft had got away, and travelled to Luton in Auster Autocrat G-AHHT owned by Don Everall of the Wolverhampton Flying Club. At Luton we found several of the visiting Austers and Larks busily re-fuelling. Bad weather made the flight to Luton difficult and gave us some quite dicey moments over Ashford. However, once north of the Thames the weather cleared completely and the visibility became excellent. For the remainder of the journey to Derby from Luton we are indebted to Peter Bayliss, who kindly gave us a lift in his Miles Mentor (G-AHKM). Arriving at Derby Airport at 12.45 after an uneventful flight of 30 minutes, we joined the longest queue of circuiting aircraft we have seen — Larks, Ansons, Magisters, a Swift, Dominies, Messengers, and numerous Autocrats. However, we were soon down and received a warm welcome from the appropriate committee.

Lunch was taken at Burnaston House, the residence of Mrs. R. Harben, and which also serves as the Officers' Mess of the Reserve Flying School now in operation at Derby under the administration of Air Schools Ltd. Lunch over, we adjourned to the adjoining airfield to watch the fine flying display which had been arranged for the occasion.

The display was opened by Lord Nathan, Minister of Civil Aviation, and the first event was the race for the *Harben Memorial Trophy*. This consisted of five Miles Magisters, the pilots being instructors of Air Schools Ltd. The race was won by F/Lt. J. Findlay, and the second and third places went to S/Ldr. R. Porteous and F/Lt. Loveridge respectively. The race was followed by a demonstration of glider aerobatics given by two Eon Olympia gliders flown by Mr. Walter Morrison and Mrs. Ann Douglas. Other highlights of the Air Display were the antics of S/Ldr. Porteous flying the Miles Sparrowhawk (G-ADNL) and the taxying Blériot monoplane of 1909 vintage now part of the famous Shuttleworth Collection. The demonstration of the usual Meteor, Trent-Meteor, Nene-Lancastrian and Theseus-Lincoln caused no mean attention and aroused much interest from our foreign visitors. Personal planes demonstrated during the display included the Globe Swifts, Cessna 120, DH Chipmunk, Miles Messenger and Gemini, the Reid & Sigrist Desford (G-AGOS), and the Chilton monoplane. Great laughter was caused by S/Ldr. Porteous' taxying of the diminutive Chilton; with engine ticking over, he simply lifted the tail on his shoulder and walked forward. The display was rounded off by a grand flypast of all visiting aircraft, in which we flew in the KZ.VII OY-SAI.

We were particularly impressed by the large crowds present and by the tidy, attractive way the visiting aircraft were dispersed around the perimeter. The evening was finished off in the usual way, giving joyrides, and for this two ancient Ansons and a Dominie were kept working until dark. We ourselves adjourned to the fine banquet given to our foreign guests by Messrs. Rolls-Royce Ltd., in co-operation with the Derby Aero Club and Derby Corporation. The banquet and ball was held at the Rolls-Royce Welfare Hall in Derby and we were pleased to see many of our old friends present; these included Mr. L. Satterthwaite, Civil Air Attaché of the US Embassy, Col. Preston of the Royal Aero Club, Alex Duncan (Aviation Manager of R.K. Dundas Ltd.), Mr. Whitney Straight, W/Cdr. Roxburgh and many others too numerous to mention.

Alas, the evening went all too soon, and at 2 am in the morning we returned to our hotel tired, happy and hangovered.

6 am Sunday morning found the airport a hive of activity, with the continental visitors busily preparing their aircraft for the return trip. First away were the Danish visitors, who hoped to make Copenhagen the same night. Last to leave was George Hanet's Lockheed 12A, which left at midday.

We left Derby at 2 pm in the Intava Consul and flew to Lympne to see that all the foreign aircraft had cleared customs OK. Tea was taken in the clubhouse of the Cinque Ports Flying Club and we returned to Gatwick the same evening.

Britain's first postwar International Rally had ended — a complete success. Congratulations to all concerned and to those who contributed to its magnificence.

PART 3: The Deauville Rally

by

P. A. CHABOREL

(Originally published in The Light Plane and Private Owner *for September 1947)*

More than 220 Members and Associate Members of the Royal Aero Club attended the Deauville Air Rally in 68 privately-owned aircraft and several charter aircraft, which made an impressive display at the St. Gatien airfield.

Excellent weather was experienced throughout the Rally, which was held on 12th and 13th July 1947. Contrary to the usual practice at air meetings, practically all the participants landed within the period scheduled and were therefore able to enjoy the entire programme which had been prepared by our ever-generous host, M. Andre (President of the Society of Hotels & Casino at Deauville), supported by the Mayor of Trouville. The importance attached to the Deauville Air Rally by the French Civil Aviation authorities was demonstrated by the welcome attendance of Baron de la Grange (President of the Aero Club de France) and M. Dome (President of the Féderation des Sports Aeriens). Great credit is also due to Colonel R.L. Preston CBE and Mr. Duncan Delahoyde of the Royal Aero Club for the groundwork and organisation behind the scenes, which ensured that all participants were not troubled with many of the minor details and formalities which are often experienced at air meetings.

In company with Mr. W. Brodie, I flew in the Esso Aviation Proctor G-AHZY from Gatwick via Dungeness and Boulogne to Deauville (St. Gatien), our flying time being 1 hour 35 minutes. Visibility was excellent and the flight along the French coast most enjoyable. Shortly after clearing Dieppe a French Armée de l'Air Nord 1200 formated alongside, and after the usual exchange of greetings we parted and followed our respective courses.

Compared to the Rally in 1946, the airfield at St. Gatien has been improved considerably, but it is felt that further clearance of the approaches to the metal mesh runways might be advisable. The ground organisation worked without a hitch, the French Customs and Immigration formalities being carried out rapidly and with a minimum of inconvenience to all concerned.

The participants were then provided with all necessary invitations and asked to write down their first impressions on arriving at Deauville. The result of this original competition was announced during the Gala dinner at the Casino on Saturday evening, some of the more amusing efforts being read out beforehand. Mr. Alex Duncan of R.K. Dundas Ltd. was awarded the *'Oscar'* by submitting a very neat phrase to the effect that his aircraft always flew best when it headed for France.

Hotel and transport facilities were arranged with the customary smoothness experienced at the Deauville Rally, which can rightly be regarded as the highlight of the International Aviation Fixture List. After a late lunch at the Royal Hotel, the remainder of the day was spent in preparing for the Gala dinner, either by acquiring a reserve of sleep or else by making last-minute purchases to rectify deficiencies revealed when hastily prepared suitcases were unpacked.

A reception was given by the French-English Society at Trouville on Sunday. Visitors were welcomed by the Mayor and a short address was delivered by the Duke of Fitz-James. After lunch at the Hotel du Golf, most of the guests adjourned to the races or to the beach.

Excellent food, good wine, two bands, dancing and a real party spirit combined to make both Gala dinners on the. Saturday and Sunday evenings a pleasant reminder of prewar days. Nor must mention be omitted of the firework displays which occurred during dinner.

Thereafter the Casino gaming rooms attracted many guests, some of whom were successful at the tables. Others, less fortunate, sought consolation at the bars or else adjourned to the only night club, *Chez Brummel*, which kept going until the last guests had departed. This never occurs before 07.00 hours, as two members of the Royal Aero Club will testify who were seen returning to the Royal Hotel early Monday morning in evening dress. Shortly afterwards they emerged from the hotel prepared for an early morning swim, which may have dispelled their tiredness but did not clear the sea mist and low cloud, which delayed departures until 11.00 hours. Thereafter a steady stream of aircraft returned to England, and as usual the various officials at Lympne and Gatwick were quick, courteous and efficient when dealing with the tired but happy Deauville contingent.

The unstinted hospitality and entertainment bestowed by our hosts will long remain a happy memory, particularly as there is every indication that we are about to experience a period of even greater austerity in England with restricted foreign travel. As such the chances of attempting to repay a little of the kindness extended by our numerous friends on the Continent must remain in abeyance for the time being. Mais, *un de ces jours* . . .

CHAPTER 23

A BRIEF FLYING PROFILE OF MAJOR M. SOMERTON-RAYNER TD AAC

(We are very grateful for permission to publish this account, which first appeared in the 1990 Army Air Corps Journal, by courtesy of the magazine's editor at the time, Col. Tim Deane.— Ed.)

There are those who say that Mike Somerton-Rayner — known as S-R — was never born, he has always been here. A former editor of the Journal once maintained that the Corps was split between powder-blue *poseurs* and real pilots. He nominated S-R as a copybook example of the latter. "*Poseurs* ease the stick forward — real pilots dive" was one quote . . .

Being qualified as a civil engineer, Mike applied to join the Sappers for his National Service in 1952. He soon learnt the first rule of the service — if you wish to serve at the North Pole, volunteer for the South. He was posted to the Gunners, with not a bulldozer in sight.

Still not convinced, he volunteered for field artillery and Air OP — in order to indulge his love of flying. He was posted to ack-ack at Tonfonau.

Boredom set in quickly on his release leave from National Service, so he phoned the Adjutant, rejoined the army and was made weekend duty officer — all in one easy movement.

A spell playing with trains in the Royal Pioneer Corps followed, and the first real opportunity to indulge his love of flying. Military duty took second place to gliding at Long Mynd, Lasham and Tonfonau.

He bought the first of many aircraft — a glider from the RAF — for £5 (he gave it back to the RAF on being posted to Malaya).

And so to 121 Course at the Light Aircraft School RAF at Middle Wallop in 1955. Students today will be reassured to learn that the original five Chipmunks are still in service today *(or, rather, they were when this article was written – Ed.).*

Life was bliss with as much flying as he wanted. Austers of all marks were flown, and even Balliols and Ansons with the RAF Squadron based on No.1 Hangar.

He wanted a posting to Malaya, so applied for Germany, and was posted to Malaya. He had leant the form.

Malaya with 656 Squadron, was marvellous: a hundred hours a month with detachments to Thailand, and even India for a month. Also a chance to fly Tiger Moths with the club at Ipoh.

Pay was air-dropped to plantations and mines — to stop the terrorists pinching it. It didn't always go according to plan: he once came back with £12,500 (equivalent to over £100,000 today) hooked to the tail.

A flight not to be forgotten was from Grik to Ipoh with an unwelcome cargo — a dead terrorist in transparent sheeting — strapped upright to the passenger seat by willing Gurkhas.

He managed to get his hands on a Catalina flying gold to Hong Kong and Macau, and also had a go on Stinsons at Clark Base in the Philippines.

He bought an old Auster III that had been with the Squadron during the war, rebuilt one wing, found a Tiger Moth engine in a monsoon drain, and set off from Ipoh to Middle Wallop. The six-week return trip included a night in Baghdad jail — the Iraqis had shot the Prime Minister responsible for his clearance. *(This Auster, still the only one of its type on the British Register, was allotted the registration G-AREI on its arrival in Britain in 1961, and is currently still airworthy in the ownership of Richard Webber in Devon — Ed.)*

S-R attended the last conversion course to Skeeter helicopters; they told the four students — known as the "Temperance Four" — that if you can fly the Skeeter you can fly anything. On again to an instructors' course at Ternhill. Mike blames the poor flying of some senior officers on himself — he taught them to fly! He then teamed up with other extroverts to fly with the Blue Eagles Bell 47 helicopter display team.

In 1969 'chinagraph' wars were raising their ugly head in the army, so Mike decided to race to Australia in a borrowed Army Auster (XR241) — but that is another story. There were those who thought that he would never come back, but Australia was too rough — even for S-R.

On his return, they threatened him with a ground tour, so he left the army, but not quite: he joined the TA. In the eleven years he flew with Netheravon-based 653 Squadron he flew everywhere, including a trip to Kenya in a Beaver.

On the 30th May 2000 S-R had a problem when taking off the AAC's Tiger Moth (G-AHMN, N6985) at Middle Wallop in something of a crosswind, and as a result he crashed close to the fence between the airfield and the Museum of Army Flying. Unfortunately he had chosen not to wear a 'bone dome', and as a direct result of the crash he suffered brain damage which hospitalised him long-term and eventually resulted in his death in 2003. It was very sad that he was therefore unable to fulfil his last remaining ambition, which was to hold a party at Middle Wallop on his 90th birthday — and give a flying display for the students.

CHAPTER 23

SOME MEMORIES OF A COMPANY PILOT
(1940-1960)

by

DUNCAN SIMPSON

(Duncan Simpson first joined Hawker Aircraft Ltd. as a test pilot in 1954 and became Chief Test Pilot at Hawker Siddeley Aviation, Dunsfold, from 1970-1978. From 1978-1992 he was Deputy Director of SBAC (the Society of British Aerospace Companies — Ed.)

Those of us who have lived through the past 80 years must agree that we have been privileged to see remarkable advances in aviation, so perhaps I may be allowed to reminisce on flying some interesting types during the forties and fifties when I was with the Hawker Aircraft Company.

In order to do this I must first go back to the twenties, because when I joined Hawker Aircraft Ltd. in 1954 my initiation into the Company included flying the Hawker Tomtit (G-AFTA) and the Hart (G-ABMR); both these aircraft emerged during 1928, the Hart founding the great series of Hawker designs which were to equip the Royal Air Force in the 1930s.

The Tomtit was a delightful aeroplane: it handled well and had a spacious and comfortable cockpit. Only a limited number were produced for the RAF, who chose the Tiger Moth as their primary trainer; personally, I judged the Tomtit to be the much superior aircraft. But perhaps Hawkers were much too involved with the contemporary Hart and its derivatives and the Fury.

The Company retained the 13th Hart off the production line, and it continued to fly as a demonstration aircraft for 40 years before eventually being donated to the RAF Museum, where it now hangs in the new building in a prime position. I flew the Hart for 18 of those years, and always felt that it was something special — part of our aviation heritage. Over 2,000 Harts and variants were built, quite apart from the magnificent Furies which equipped RAF units before the war, so it was no wonder that Sydney Camm regarded the Hart as his favourite design.

In its early days the Hart was faster that the contemporary fighters, and the take-off and climb performance was impressive even at the reduced engine settings which we used later on. I had one nasty experience in 1956 when flying down to the West Country for a Battle of Britain air display; the weather deteriorated in the Salisbury area to such an extent that the cloud was covering the hills, and I had just turned round to return to Dunsfold when the engine stopped. I was already at low level and began to lose height with the propeller motionless, leaving a thin trail of smoke behind me, so I had no option but to continue straight ahead and land up a hillside, missing telephone wires and some trees. It was a very short landing roll and no damage was visible; in fact it subsequently became clear that what had brought the engine to an abrupt seizure was a complete supercharger failure. Eventually a Flight Sergeant and his crew arrived from Boscombe Down and was delighted to find a Hart to look after, as he had worked with them on the North-West frontier; I knew that the aircraft would be more than well cared for until we could retrieve it.

It took three years to find a replacement Rolls-Royce Kestrel, and during that time I took the opportunity to restore the aircraft to represent J9941, which had served on 'B' Flight No. 57 Squadron. This was chosen for a variety of reasons, mainly because it was 'borrowed' from the Squadron in 1932 to show at the Paris salon, a project in which Sir Sydney took a close interest. Later on I had the pleasure of flying J9941 up to Marham for the Colour Presentation to No. 57 Squadron by HRH Princess Marina.

The Hart was a responsibility which I really enjoyed, and I am pleased that it is now safely in the Museum for all to see. I shall never forget the flying — the performance, the abundance of fresh air, the crackle of the Kestrel's exhausts, the vibration of the flying wires, and the visits by Sir Sydney to Dunsfold to look at his masterpiece.

I must now move on to 1935 when the Hurricane first flew. Over 14,000 were built and its story has been well told — its service in France, the Battle of Britain and in every theatre in WW2. On the same day that I flew the Hart, 12th November 1954, I was encouraged to get into the last Hurricane to be built (PZ865, G-AMAU) and fly it. I had just flown across in the Rapide from Dunsfold to the grass airfield at Langley, where we kept the Hart and Hurricane at the time. This Hurricane made its first flight from Langley in 1944, then later it was moved to Dunsfold and remained there until I delivered it to theBattle of Britain Memorial Flight (BBMF) in 1972. The aeroplane was very strong, solid and reliable, and was relatively straightforward to fly and very docile. Fortunately I had completed my basic training in the Air Force on Harvards — probably the best trainer ever built to prepare the way for the big piston fighters.

The Hawker pilots continued to fly the Tomtit, Hart and Hurricane around the air show circuit until 1972, and must have given pleasure to thousands of spectators, young and old. All three are still in existence today, the Tomtit airworthy at the Shuttleworth Collection, the Hart in the Hendon Museum and the Hurricane ('The Last of the Many') still with the BBMF.

My next challenge at Hawker's was to fly the Sea Fury, which was being rebuilt at Blackpool for Burma, Cuba and target-towing in Germany. Our resident test pilot was on leave and I was 'asked' to go up to Blackpool to continue the Sea Fury testing. So off I went, with the Pilot's Notes in one hand and the Flight Test Schedule in the other. I had to be my own instructor, adviser and general caretaker to tackle the formidable Sea Fury, really the ultimate single-seat fighter.

Once again the Harvard — flown so many years before — played its part. The 2,500 hp Centaurus in the Sea Fury provided magnificent performance, the take-off was spectacular, and care was required to keep the aeroplane pointing straight down the runway. But once in the air the Fury handled beautifully, with spring-tab flying controls perfectly balanced, and it proved a great favourite with pilots in the Royal Navy and all others who flew it. Once the earlier oil system problems had been ironed out (with some difficulty) the Centaurus engine proved reliable and robust. My last flight in a Fury was in TF956, the first production FB.11, which I handed over to the Royal Navy Historic Flight at Yeovilton in 1972.

Before moving on I must mention our fleet of communications aeroplanes at Hawker's. The test pilots flew these as their own transport around the country on a variety of tasks, such as between factories at Blackpool, Bitteswell and Langley, and ferrying our Directors and staff as required to wherever they needed to go. This flying involved a considerable degree of adventure and ingenuity to reach our destinations. Weather was inevitably a problem in the UK, and the Rapide (G-AHGC) and Anson (G-AHXK) became frail in heavy weather, although in fine conditions they were delightful — particularly the Rapide. Sitting up front, one had the best of all cockpit vision, although in the rear the basic seating was not quite up to Directorial standards: on one occasion a seat collapsed under the ample person of our Chairman.

On another occasion I was forced to land with a Director at Upper Heyford due to atrocious weather, when we were arrested as spies by the USAF (it was a Strategic Air Command base), and I still have a vision of my Director with a gun being held to his head by a rather aggressive Whitecap. Despite this I was fond of the Rapide, but less so of the Anson although the latter had a VIP interior and was comfortable. We also had a splendid Whitney Straight two-seater (G-AEUJ) which we used ourselves.

Inevitably the day came when our miscellaneous fleet was replaced by a nearly-new DH Dove Mk.8 (G-ASMG), and then we all had to 'pull our socks up' and become real communications pilots: we had to obtain an instrument rating and were obliged to fly on Airways. We all liked the Dove; it had only one feature which worried me, a lack of effective airframe de-icing — the anti-ice system by TKS was totally inadequate.

Our main occupation at Hawker's was in fact the production and development of the Hunter. Before I joined Hawker's I had been fortunate in taking part in the RAF trials of the Hunter Mk.1 and Mk.2 at the Central Fighter Establishment. We had already flown the Swift Mk. 1 in February 1954, and in July we took delivery of our first three Hunters. The Swift was not a success as an air defence fighter, but later it served well in the low-level fighter reconnaisance role. The Hunter 1 had several problems, but it was fast and manoeuvrable, and nothing could prevent it from being developed into one of the most successful fighter aircraft of all time; its attractions led me astray, and I joined the Company after the Mk.1 & 2 trials were complete.

For the rest of the 1950s the Hunter was vastly improved: the 200-series Avon with more thrust, the coming of a variety of weapons, the four-gun 30 mm Aden pack (a triumph of Hawker engineering), overload fuel and a host of other features. It saw service in 21 Air Forces and the Royal Navy, and was the favourite of all who flew it. Every aircraft off the Hawker production line was subject to a seaching Flight Test schedule, being flown to its limits to ensure it functioned — both engine and airframe — in every respect. It would then be prepared for delivery, either to Europe, the Middle East, India, the Far East or to South America; I cannot recall a Hunter returning to Dunsfold on delivery due to unserviceability.

Perhaps a brief reference at this point to some of the other jet fighters which were in service in the late forties and fifties would be appropriate. The Meteor and Vampire were built in large numbers and were successfully exported. Although I was 'brought up' at de Havilland's, the Meteor was, at that time, my first choice. Initially it entered RAF service just in time to catch the V-1 flying bombs — together with the Hawker Tempest it was the only aircraft fast enough to do this. Then the aircraft was steadily developed through the Mk.4 to the Mk.8, which equipped the regular fighter squadrons in Fighter Command in the early fifties. I was lucky enough to complete a Squadron tour on the Meteor 8; it was docile, strong and fast, with two very reliable Rolls-Royce Derwent engines and, together with its FR and PR versions, represented a substantial improvement on the earlier marks.

The Vampire 5 was a delightful little aeroplane to fly, but it was its logical development to the Venom which could not fail to impress. When I first worked on the Venom in the aerodynamics department at Hatfield in 1947, it was known as the 'thin wing Vampire', equipped with the DH Ghost engine of 5,000 lb thrust. As an interceptor fighter the Venom started up quickly and could climb rapidly to well over 50,000 feet; it was very manoeuvrable at all altitudes but had some exciting high Mach number characteristics. The later Mk.4 Venom was an effective ground attack fighter, equipping several squadrons in Germany.

One of the most interesting fighters at the Fighter Establishment in the early fifties was the American F-86 Sabre. Trans-sonic in an almost vertical dive, the Sabre was exceptionally well-equipped and possessed an exemplary set of flying controls powered by a duplicated hydraulic system. Our Sabres were used in comparative trials with our own Swift and Hunter as they entered service, and I know that our British Industry learned a lot from them.

I would now like to digress to the times when I flew some interesting historic machines in the Strathallan Collection near Gleneagles. Sir William Roberts had acquired a fleet of aircraft, one of the first being a Canadian-built Hurricane IIB. This aircraft had taken part in the Battle of Britain film during the sixties and had a reputation for poor handling, so I was asked by David Davies, then Chief Test Pilot of the CAA, to carry out the initial flying with a view to issuing a Permit to Fly (he pleaded that he was short of Hurricane pilots!).

We noted that modifications had been made to the ailerons, so we decided to remove extraneous tabs and start from what we thought was 'square one'. A full account of how the problem was solved is recorded elsewhere, so suffice it to say that the aileron overbalance on the first flight required an immediate landing. An innocuous trailing edge modification had caused the trouble and we 'acquired' a new pair of ailerons from another service; subsequent flying was straightforward and there were no problems about issuing a Permit. The Hurricane continued to fly at Strathallan for some ten years before eventually it was returned to the Canadian Warplane Heritage, where sadly it was destroyed in a disastrous fire.

The next major restoration project was an ex-Canadian Westland Lysander, which took ten years of dedicated work by the engineers before it was ready for a first flight. Needless to say, I had never flown one, but I studied all the available notes on flying and engine handling. The official Pilots' Notes were brief and to the point: take-off, general handling and landing occupied barely three pages. I was particularly taken by the paragraph headed 'General Flying'.

"The controls are not well harmonised, the rudder being light, the ailerons heavy and elevators *too* heavy.

The flying characteristics at very low speeds are such that a foolhardy pilot might be tempted to take liberties to which no aeroplane can with safety be subjected."

In other words, this aeroplane is very docile but it is capable of entering corners of the flight envelope at low speeds which require care and thorough understanding. The independent outer slats/slots, the inboard slats cross-connected and interconnected with the flaps were a masterpiece of Westland (and Handley Page) ingenuity; all these extended automatically with increase of incidence.

The Permit flying went well and I continued to fly the Lysander at local air shows and for the BBC documentary on SOE operations. Eventually the aircraft came south and is now in good hands in the Shuttleworth Collection.

Sir William included some 14 types of vintage flying machines in his collection, so it may be of interest if I comment on some of my favourites.

Perhaps heading the list was DH Leopard Moth G-AIYS. This was one of de Havilland's most attractive light aeroplanes and I am delighted to see it still flying after a complete restoration. It is a comfortable three-seater high-wing monoplane with folding wings, ideal for touring. Although it handled well, I remember feeling distinctly unhappy under strong gusty wind conditions, but it had class and I always wore collar and tie with a blazer when I flew it in public (I was DH-trained, you see!). Another super little DH aeroplane was the Moth Minor — plenty of fresh air and fun.

The Miles Magister in the collection was a particularly fine example. As a basic trainer it was comfortable and handled well. It was interesting to compare it with two later trainers which both had side-by-side seating, the piston-Provost and the Fokker S.11; both these aircraft handled well and were effective basic trainers in their way, but I still rate the Harvard as one of the best, and Strathallan owned a near-relative, the AT-6.

I must also mention the Reid and Sigrist Desford Trainer, a splendid twin-engined light aircraft which had been modified for trials at Farnborough on the 'prone pilot' project. At the time it still sported the extended nose which housed the unfortunate 'test pilot' who had to lie prone on his stomach. The aircraft was a joy to fly, with spring-tab ailerons contributing to its good overall characteristics in the air.

May I complete the Strathallan experience by making brief reference to the General Aircraft Cygnet; this aeroplane, two-seat side-by-side and single-engined, was noted for its lack of performance. I flew it first with a distinguished British Caledonian captain, who explained to me that we hoped to get airborne by lowering flap halfway down the take-off run while at the same time coinciding with a bump in the grass strip! We thus achieved forward flight, but in order to increase speed we continued to fly down Sir William's river at very low level until it seemed prudent to climb: needless to say I never flew it again!

May I now conclude on a happier note, returning to the very first flights that I made during the war. I succeeded in transferring from the Army section of the Cadet Force to the Air Training Corps; I had to start flying somehow, but my transfer was not, as some suggested, because I was reluctant to crawl amongst the whin bushes in the Pentland Hills dressed in a kilt!

I first flew in a Tiger Moth from Drem airfield in 1943, then during the following year I completed a gliding course at East Fortune — sheer bliss! I started on a Dagling device, sitting on a wooden plank with a stick and rudder bar, with no protection whatsoever. I then graduated to a Kirby Cadet, which sported a cockpit; on this aeroplane we did 'high hops' to about 200 ft after being towed off by a winch on the far side of the airfield.

I then applied to join the Air Force late in 1944 but they appeared to have too many pilots, so it was off down to Hatfield to the de Havilland Technical School to get some sense into my head before learning to fly with the RAF in 1949.

I have enjoyed recalling my experiences with a number of classic aeroplanes, and hope that they will have also been of interest to the reader.

A pleasing aerial view of the Hart J9941 (G-ABMR).
Photo: Charles E. Brown.

The Heath Parasol G-AJCK, built by the the South Hants Ultra Light
Aeroplane Club, is seen at Christchurch in 1949. Photo: John Pothecary.

Auster J/1 Autocrat G-AGVP and Taylorcraft Plus D G-AHUG in 1947 outside the High Post Hotel, which had been the prewar clubhouse of the Wiltshire School of Flying. Photo: John Pothecary.

Whitney Straight G-AERV (ex-EM999) after repaint and C. of A., seen at Thruxton in July 1947. Photo: J. Pothecary.

Stinson Voyager G-AGZW (X1050) spent time in France in 1940 and subsequently returned to Old Sarum; it is seen here at Thruxton in 1949. Photo: John Pothecary.

Miles Falcon G-ADFH saw wartime service with RAF station flights at Turnhouse and Northolt. Seen here at Christchurch in 1947, it was broken up in 1954. Photo: John Pothecary.

John Pothecary carries out a fuel flow check on Hornet Moth G-ADKM, autumn 1949. Photo: John Pothecary.

Miles Hawk Trainer 3 (Magister) G-AIUC at Thruxton in 1949. Photo: John Pothecary.

CHAPTER 25

THESE DAYS WILL RETURN . . .

by

JOHN POTHECARY

The title is taken from advertisements placed in aircraft magazines in 1945 by the industry paint manufacturers, depicting gaily-painted Miles and Percival aeroplanes as they were at prewar meetings, and indeed as they appeared for many years once peace was upon us.

Halfway through the decade, censorship was being reduced, *The Aeroplane* and *Flight* reporting in detail about successful British and American aircraft. Fascinating snippets of information were emerging about potential war-winning super-fighters and bombers of the Third Reich.

In the autumn the new Labour Government announced that civil aviation was to be allowed from New Year's Day 1946. Great was the speculation in *Flight* and *Aeroplane* about the form this would take: landplanes or flying boats for the Empire routes? Langstone Harbour (Portsmouth) or Southampton Water for the flying boats? (Poole Harbour had been used during the war). Would gas turbines ever be capable of powering these machines and would supersonic flight become a reality? On the light plane side, would the flying clubs be subsidised again and where were our small power units to come from?

Imperial Airways and British Airways had already amalgamated into British Overseas Airways in 1940, and they were now to have an offshoot in British South American Airways. However disillusionment existed amongst the small internal airlines, Railway Air Services and Scottish Airlines being the major players. Nationalisation loomed, as it did with many industries, and British European Airlines would take over internal and European schedules.

Lord Brabazon had chaired a wartime committee two years earlier to look at the postwar commercial aviation scene, 'feeder-liner', 'Empire' and 'long-range Empire' being some of the categories defined and on which design work would quickly commence. Emerging in the latter half of the decade would be the Bristol Brabazon, Saunders Roe Princess and Tudor, making headlines in the popular press. More successful would be Handley Page's Hermes, DH Dove, Bristol Freighter, Vickers Viking and the elegant Airspeed Ambassador.

Sadly the Hermes prototype G-AGSS crashed on its maiden flight on 2nd December 1945, but 30 were built for civil use and 151 of its military derivative, the Hastings, were built for RAF use. Handley Page also built

40 Marathon four-engined aircraft to a Miles design, which was used by the RAF and civil operators.

Of the principal prewar manufacturers, only Miles and Taylorcraft (whose name was changed to Auster Aircraft in 1946), had plans for major postwar production of civil types. Percival produced 95 Proctor Mk.Vs to a civilian four-seat standard, while Chrislea Aircraft, who had produced the very pretty Airguard in 1939, made 32 examples of their four-seat Ace and Skyjeep.

The internal and European air routes were obliged to buy ex-RAF Rapides, Ansons, Dakotas and even Junkers Ju.52/3Ms from a defeated Germany. BOAC had to plan on Avro Lancastrians, Yorks and Liberators until dollars could be found to buy American aircraft. Flying boats, converted Sunderlands and new production Solents, were the mainstay of the Empire routes, while three Boeing 314 Clippers provided transatlantic services.

The flying clubs and private owners, always impecunious, had set their sights on the vast numbers of training and communications aircraft surplus to RAF requirements, and these would prove to be very unwelcome competition to manufacturers and agents for new aeroplanes.

In late 1945 the Air Ministry offered for sale over 50 aeroplanes, most of which had been impressed into RAF use in 1939-40. Included in the sale were three Vega Gulls, three Miles Hawks and eight Taylorcrafts (including G-AFTN, 'FUB, 'FUD, 'FVA and 'FZH), fourteen Moth Minors, a Stinson Reliant, two Falcons, two Monarchs, two Envoys, a Tipsy B.2, three General Aircraft Cygnets, one Heston Phoenix, four Piper Cubs, one Stinson Voyager, three Whitney Straights and a solitary Rapide. These aeroplanes were initially offered to those persons who had their aeroplanes impressed six years earlier. This sale was held at No.5 Maintenance Unit, RAF Kemble. No Tiger Moths were on offer here as they were still the basic trainer in the Air Force. 166 had been impressed from flying clubs in 1939-40, but at that time W.S. Shackleton Ltd., aircraft brokers, managed to sell 41 overseas before the Air Ministry could get their hands on them! However the first ten Tigers on postwar offer were sold from 6 MU, Brize Norton, together with 16 Proctors from 29 MU at High Ercall.

Eventually I worked on and flew many of these aircraft, and remember in particular the Miles Whitney Straight EM999; it was being overhauled at Thruxton and, after stripping off layers of camouflage paint, I found the prewar owner's nameplate and the name he had given her, *Anky Sim*, cut in aluminium letters and still riveted to the cowling. Mr H.W. Moore paid £50 to get his own aeroplane back; it's C. of A. was renewed by Wiltshire School of Flying on 5th July 1947. Now, 60 years later and after a substantial rebuild, G-AERV will soon be flying again from Durley.

At that time it was difficult to tie up prewar registrations with service serials, hence many acquired new registrations, e.g. Taylorcraft G-AFVA became G-AHAE, 'FVD became 'HBO, 'FZH became 'HEI and 'FTZ became 'HSH, while Monarch G-AFRZ became G-AIDE. When undergoing civilianization it was often impossible to remove evidence of the heavily-painted roundels, the only solution being to re-fabric that area. Another problem was the 'Gas Warning Panel'. In earlier wartime days all British aircraft carried a panel painted with a mixture that would change from green to yellow when contaminated with poison gas. It could not be painted over and so again the only solution was to re-fabric the area. In my collection of old fabric I have an example of this; the date it carries is November 1944, showing that there remained still a threat of gas attack even at that late stage of the war.

One of the Taylorcrafts brought by the Wiltshire Flying Club carried D-Day markings: G-AFVA became HH982 in 1941 and G-AHAE in 1946, and was possibly the only prewar club aircraft to see service in France in 1944. Certainly she gave good service with 651 Sqdn at Old Sarum, as does another survivor of that unit, G-AHXE, which still flies from this WW1 airfield.

On the 1st January 1946 civil flying was allowed to resume from authorized airfields. Few of these fields had radio aids to landing: Standard Beam Approach was installed at Croydon, Bournemouth and Bristol (Whitchurch).

There was to be no financial help for the flying clubs. In prewar days they enjoyed a generous subsidy from the Air Ministry, and as political situations deteriorated in mid-1938 the Government produced their Civil Air Guard scheme. Suitable applicants who would be obliged to offer their services to the country in the event of hostilities were to be trained as pilots, paying only as little as 2/6d per hour (!), the government paying the remainder to the always sorely-pressed clubs.

In the two years before the war, the British aircraft industry was working at near-full capacity, Miles with Magister and Master contracts, de Havilland with Tiger Moth and Flamingo & Albatross airliners; but here was the opportunity to introduce their DH Moth Minor, and more than 100 were produced before production was moved to Australia. Those companies not producing indigenous designs were busy with sub-contract work, hence many flying clubs were obliged to purchase American light aircraft. Piper and Taylorcraft were producing high-wing aircraft with flat-four engines.

A new company was formed in Leicester to manufacture Taylorcrafts and a lineage of Auster types, which would end with the demise of Beagle over thirty years later.

These halcyon days were to come to an end on 1st September 1939, with private flying being banned two days before the outbreak of war, when many other civil aircraft were grounded. In the following year 1,017 powered aircraft and 102 gliders were impressed by the Air Ministry. The transport types went to National Air Communications, an internal and — until July 1940 — a cross-Channel air service; Tiger Moths went to the EFTSs (uniquely, Bristol Club Tigers went to India), while faster private aircraft went to communications flights.

The oldest aeroplanes to be put to wartime use were seven Avro 504Ns. At least two were used for towing gliders from Christchurch and High Post for the Telecommunications Research Unit at Worth Matravers, Dorset; it was from here that Minimoa and Viking gliders were towed 40 miles out to sea before release, in order to determine if radar could pick up wooden aircraft. Other Avros continued until 1942 with the Central Landing Establishment at Ringway, where early paratroop and military glider trials were undertaken.

Sadly many of the Gipsy Moths became decoys on dummy airfields in the early forties, where the elements took their eventual toll. Other machines went to technical training schools or were given to the Air Defence Cadet Corps (later ATC), where many came to an ignominious end, although the Comper Swift G-ABUU which I owned for 24 years had survived six years with the Newcastle Air Training Corps. Compensation was paid to the now bereft owners and, where clubs now closed for the duration had enjoyed a subsidy contract, this was paid until 1942.

The end of 1945 saw little sign of the 'broad sunlit uplands' that Winston Churchill had promised us in a morale-boosting speech of three years earlier. Bread had now been put on ration for the first time, 9 oz per day for adults, 15 oz if you were a manual worker, and this lasted until 1948. Clothes rationing was abolished in March 1949 and petrol in June 1950. It was an era of utility clothes and utility furniture. For small (and bigger) boys there was little or no Meccano, and Hornby trains and model aeroplane kits were hard to find.

Come 1st January 1946 and again 'civil aviation' took to the skies. The weather was not as harsh as in the two succeeding winters, and the *Aeroplane Spotter* was able to report that Marshalls of Cambridge commenced civil flying training with Tiger Moths on that day. Hunting Air Travel made an "air taxi" flight with Proctor G-AGSX, and Cambrian Air Services made the first charter flight in Britain, departing from Cardiff (Pengam Moors) and landing at Bristol (Filton); Taylorcraft Auster V J/1 G-AFWN carried aircraft parts — it had been a prewar aeroplane retained by the makers, and in 1945 it was converted to the prototype Autocrat.

Complementing BOAC, the Government had formed British European Airways and British South American Airways. It was a Lancastrian of the latter, G-AGWG, which made the inaugural flight on

1st January 1946 from the new London Airport at Heathrow, bound for Montevideo.

At this time I was becoming influenced by the writings of Eddie Riding and A.J. Jackson in the *Aeromodeller* and aforesaid *Aeroplane Spotter*. My mind had really been made up at the age of seven by such films as *Hell's Angels* and *Dawn Patrol*; seeing that modern marvel, the airship *Hindenburg,* fly past my home, and being allowed to sit in a Hawker Audax at Old Sarum, only confirmed my aspirations. Perhaps I was hooked on red and silver dope at that tender age. My father tried to discourage me by lurid descriptions of crashing biplanes and triplanes on the Western Front in 1916-1917, but to no avail.

Now an opportunity presented itself. In late 1945 advertisements appeared in the Salisbury paper about the local flying club restarting, and in the Anna Valley Garage showroom was exhibited Auster Autocrat G-AGVP. This garage was one of several in the area which had been busy for the past five years making Spitfires which were subsequently flown from High Post aerodrome, the prewar and postwar home of the Wiltshire School of Flying. My mind was made up, and I sought an interview with James Doren-Webb, proprietor and MD of the School. He kindly agreed to take me on as a weekend worker during the summer (unpaid of course) and so it was that I was put to work on Cessna Airmaster G-AFBY, one of two models of the C.34 on the British register.

The Wiltshire Flying Club was founded in a field midway between RAF Boscombe Down and RAF Old Sarum in 1931. A clubhouse was built and one of the two small hangars had been rescued from the site of the WW1 aerodrome at Stonehenge, where it had been used by the Handley Page flying school. The original equipment of the flying club was one Redwing biplane, and a painting of this machine, G-ABLA, was hanging in the postwar clubhouse and was the inspiration for me to buy the only survivor of the marque some 13 years later. Moths and a Desoutter formed the fleet after the demise of G-ABLA, but the advent of the Civil Air Guard in 1938 meant the purchase of new Piper Cub Coupé and Taylorcraft machines. The Pipers were G-AFSY, G-AFSZ, G-AFVL and G-AFWR, and upon impressment they became HM865, BT440, BT441 & BT442 respectively. They all saw useful war service with the AOP training units at Old Sarum. Of the Taylorcrafts G-AFTY/HL536 was burnt out by misuse of a Very pistol in 1942, and G-AFTN/HL535 survived the war to be sold to Bertram Arden at Exeter, who kept it for many years at his farm near Exeter. Also incarcerated at Exeter were many Pobjoy engines, BA Swallows, and Tiger Moth G-ACDA. The Surrey AL.1 2-seat biplane is still there! Fortunately the Taylorcraft G-AFTN escaped and survives in the museum at Leicester.

In late July I left school and started full-time employment at the aerodrome. It also meant that my bread ration went from 9 oz a day to 15 oz! Bill Watts was the Chief Engineer, an Australian and ex-Royal Flying Corps. He was assisted by Ted Pepper, who after RAF service in the twenties had worked prewar for Phillips & Powis and at Blackburn's during the war. Many were his tales of DH.9s and Wapitis in Mesopotamia and ghosts of Roman soldiers at Old Sarum. My working colleague was Geoff Feltham, recently ex-RAF, who would later leave WSF for the attractions of Boscombe Down and Farnborough, and eventually become Chief Inspector of the Accident Investigation Branch.

It was a delirious summer with a variety of visiting aeroplanes, for example Harold Penrose with his Westland Widgeon G-AAGH (complete with motor horn) plus all varieties of Miles, DH and Percival types. Vickers still operated from High Post, and Spitfires, Spitefuls, Seafangs, Seagulls and Sea Otters could be seen every day, with regular aerobatic displays from Jeffrey Quill and Pat Shea Simmonds. New machines from Boscombe Down, less than a mile away, were much in evidence; I particularly remember a low pass by Tudor 2 G-AGSU, possibly on its departure from Boscombe Down for Woodford. It was only a few days later, on 23rd August, that it crashed as a result of crossed aileron controls, killing the designer Roy Chadwick and his senior test pilot Bill Thorn.

It was the proximity to Boscombe Down and its recently-extended runway that would enforce the closure of High Post at the end of 1946. At that time the flying club fleet comprised the Autocrat G-AGVP, Taylorcraft G-AHAF (which had been the prototype Auster Mk.1 T9120 and, as such, was part of "D" Flight from Old Sarum sent to France in April 1940) and G-AHAE (ex-G-AFVA/HH982), unique in that it retained its original narrow wheels and had only one door — on the starboard side. G-AHKN (ex-LB321) was refurbished in April 1946, but G-AHKO (ex-LB381) did not fly as such until 1947. Magisters G-AIUB and G-AIUA went through the workshops, and Magister G-AHKP joined the fleet in May. One day I was assisting John Isaacs (he of the Fury) in starting this machine; neither of us properly understood the function of the ignition master switch and as a result the propeller bit me, leaving a scar I still carry. Lesson learned! Other Magisters from the early sales were G-AIUC and G-AIUD, which were civilianized at Thruxton in 1947.

The Royal Artillery Aero Club was founded in 1934 at nearby Larkhill and grew up alongside the Wiltshire Flying Club, using their aircraft. In 1946 two Taylorcraft Auster 1s were acquired, and both were overhauled and based at High Post: NB282 became G-AHUG and LB279 became G-AHUH (the latter was delivered in pristine silver with new fabric and postwar markings). Unfortunately 'HUH crashed at Ballard Down, Swanage on 17th July 1949, but G-AHUG is at present on a protracted rebuild. Also kept initially at High Post was a prewar Taylorcraft; impressed into RAF use as late as July 1941, G-AFWM saw service at Old

Sarum and was sold from 5 MU Kemble in March 1946 to the Earl of Cardigan, with its C. of A. renewed on 30th August 1946. It was later kept on the Earl's private landing ground in Savernake Forest. Club aeroplanes at this time were grey with red trim, the Artillery machines were red with dark blue trim and G-AFWM was metallic blue with dark blue lettering.

The first postwar CFI at High Post was Ken Birt (ex-105 Sqdn.) who later moved to Gosport and Hamble, and he was ably assisted by Bert Hawkins, who had learnt to fly with the Civil Air Guard whilst a bus driver with the Wilts & Dorset bus company. The other important member of the staff was 'Dan,' the elderly barman; he was in charge of that delightful custom whereby on achieving his first solo a student would buy a bottle of champagne to be consumed by witnesses. A copy of the photo required for the pilot's licence and Royal Aero Club aviator's certificate was fixed to the bottle, which then graced the bar shelf.

The private pilot had an 'A' licence and a commercial pilot was required to hold a 'B' licence. A navigator required a first-class 'N' certificate, an airline captain a second-class 'N'. For an 'A' licence the usual medical exam was required. The flying requirement was three hours' solo, which could include the flying test; this was flown solo carrying a barograph, and required five figures of eight (rate 1 turns) flown at 800 ft followed by a climb to 2,000 ft and a glide landing to a designated spot on the airfield. There was no written test but ten questions on air law and the *Air Pilot* were posed by a 'Royal Aero Club Observer.' In the early fifties I became a RAeC observer, which I suppose I still am, should you require your record-breaking flight to be officially observed! By September 1939 approximately 24,000 licences had been issued since Lord Brabazon became licensed pilot No.1. The first two postwar years saw another 35,000 issued: mine was 27,486.

To the detriment of new aircraft sales the Air Ministry continued to sell off war-surplus types. Geoff and I were dispatched to the care of the Sergeants' Mess at 51 MU Lichfield, where in six weeks we assembled twelve Magisters for Bert Hawkins to fly back to High Post. I travelled back in the last one, L8086 — later G-AITV. Ferry marks were not applied and the trip was via Brize Norton, then a great field for a comfort stop! It was 15th December 1947 and my first introduction to open-cockpit flying. I found it very cold, but worse was to come in the next few months. RAF Lichfield was packed with stored aircraft, our hangar with about 140 dismantled Magisters, including V1101 which had been very active at the the Battle of Britain air display at Netheravon only two months earlier. The next hangar was full of Oxfords and all the redundant Miles Messengers (including the glossy camouflaged one used by General Montgomery) were nearby. Outside were the Lend-Lease Fortresses and Liberators of Coastal Command, slowly being broken up as Lancasters replaced them in the maritime reconnaissance role, while also present was a lone two-seat Lockheed Lightning in RAF markings but no serial number. This had been on unofficial loan to 5 Group HQ, Bomber Command, and its American serial was 44-23517. Modified to take Loran and Gee navigation sets, it was painted PRU blue, the letters DRA appearing on the tail boom, and is believed to have been used as a target marker and bomber controller. It was first used for night operations on 23rd September 1944 and subsequently used regularly, later migrating to Northolt and eventually returning to the US.

The first postwar year of civil aviation came to a close, as did flying from High Post aerodrome. The approach lights for Boscombe Down's runway encroached almost to the boundary of High Post's undulating grass, and therefore the flying club operations moved 10 miles across the county border to Thruxton (where, although in Hampshire, it was still known as the 'Wiltshire School of Flying').

Thruxton was a disused RAF airfield dating from 1941. Initially used by Army Co-operation units, its major claim to fame was being the base for *Operation Biting*, the first British operational paratroop drop mounted from the UK. On the evening of 27th February 1942, 12 Whitleys (carrying 'C' Company, 2nd Parachute Battalion and an RAF radar expert) departed Thruxton bound for Bruneval in Northern France and its 'Wurtsburg' radar station. The troops were dropped accurately, dismantled vital components and blew up the rest of the buildings. They later withdrew to the beach and were picked up by the Royal Navy. Thruxton was used as a base for smoke-laying Bostons and Blenheims engaged on *Operation Jubilee*, the Dieppe raid on 19th August 1942. During 1944 Thunderbolts of the USAAF 9th Air Force took over the field. By 1945, with the completion of glider operations in Europe, Thruxton was being used as an open-air storage unit for Horsa gliders — 299 of them were there in early 1947.

The only permanent hangar then was a large T2, which soon filled with Austers, Magisters and Proctors, plus a couple of Rapides. Magister G-AGEO arrived in February, covered in a one-inch-thick layer of rain ice from its overnight road journey from Litchfield, such was the weather. Thick snow prevailed at this time and frequently prevented flying, but not hangar work. Our only heating in the hangar was a 45 gallon oil drum burning wood from the rapidly deteriorating Horsas! They had been tied down using large Carver pickets (which made good fencing posts for local farmers), and were also a useful source of nuts and bolts, Perspex and plywood. Slowly being disposed of, wheels went to farm trailers, and many fuselages were turned into caravans. Cold as it was, I can assure you that the burning of Taylorcraft G-AHKN on 26th February 1947 was unintentional, it caught fire whilst being welded by the Chief Engineer.

The extreme cold countrywide had caused a fuel crisis. Coal boats were ice-bound in northern ports, and roads and railways were blocked with snow. On 7th February the Ministry of Fuel & Power ordered electrical power to industry to be cut off entirely in some parts of the country and restricted in others. Householders had to switch off electricity from 9-12 am and 2-4 pm. Snow fell in England every day until 16th March. At the Miles factory at Reading the lack of heat and power severely disrupted work on their new, all-wood aircraft, and delivery was disrupted; severe repercussions would be felt later on.

Spring came to us in April, and with it some newer aeroplanes. Autocrats G-AIGC and G-AIZW joined the Wiltshire club's fleet and the Royal Artillery Aero Club purchased Austers G-AGYI and G-AJAE, which I was to buy from them twenty years later. Mr. W. Schwyn sold his Cessna Airmaster and brought Gemini G-AIWS. Geoffrey Marler bought Messenger G-AJWB. Glenn Kidson kept Gemini G-AKHC at Thruxton and early Chrislea Aces and Skyjeeps were visitors.

The Royal Artillery Aero Club organised a rally on 14th June 1947 for powered aircraft and gliders. From Czechoslovakia came Praga Baby OK-BGA, in which I was lucky enough to get a flight. Individual competitions were given names with Royal Artillery connections, e.g. 'Woolwich' stakes for glider spot-landing, which encouraged Olympia, Weihe, Broburn Wanderlust, Kranich, Minimoa and Kite to enter; they also contended for the glider cross-country, named the 'Ubique' plate. The test of navigation was called the 'Larkhill' chase; most competitors were local aircraft with Proctor 'JMV, Tipsy 'FSC and Tiger Moth 'INU among the visitors. A display by an early Chipmunk and a Vampire demonstration by S/Ldr Zurakowski enlightened the proceedings.

Shortly after this time I went on Sundays to the ATC gliding school at Christchurch. This was my first introduction to Ron Hayter and his dedicated team of instructors, and to an aerodrome which would be almost my entire life in the early fifties. After a succession of 'ground slides,' 'low hops' and 'high hops' I acquired my first aeronautical qualification — the gliding 'A' licence.

Whilst Bournemouth Flying Club still had their prewar clubhouse and hangar at Christchurch, they were not allowed to operate by Airspeed's; this manufacturer was still conducting Horsa trials, for which a Halifax was borrowed from Beaulieu. Mosquito production was the principal military contract and major construction work was directed towards the Ambassador. Vickers Warwick HG341 was used for Centaurus engine trials. The Hornet Moth G-ADUR and Consul G-AHEF were the company communications aircraft. Other interesting visitors at this time were Douglas Dauntless JS998 & JS923 from Eastleigh and Miles M.18 U3 from Reading. Francis Fisher, owner of Bournemouth Aero Club, brought Magister P6366 from Portsmouth, later to be registered G-AICD.

Fairchild Packet 422993 visited on 9th August 1946. Taylorcraft 'A' G-AFJP made its first postwar flight in May 1947. On the 13th of that month Auster 5 TW452 and Proctor DX232 (piloted by Air Commodore Pearce) arrived from 62 Group HQ and gave flights to us ATC cadets. Walter Gibb brought in Wellington RP484 from Filton and later came Beaufighter RD810. Locally-based Swallow G-AEGH and Monarch G-AIDE flew regularly, and Magister G-AIUE made its first civilian flight on 20th June 1947. Civil visitors were banned from Christchurch and the flying control logbooks show examples of itinerant visiting aircraft being ordered off the airfield; often Hurn would not accept them either.

The great day for Christchurch came on 10th July 1947; late in the afternoon Chief Test Pilot George Errington carried out a weather check in Mosquito VP194, and 25 minutes after landing was airborne again the with Ambassador G-AGUA making its first flight.

It was the following year before club flying could start, with the formation of the South Hants Ultra Light Aero Club. Ron Hayter was in charge and the club was based in the gliding school hangar in the SW corner of the field. The Zaunköenig G-ALUA was then on loan for a while, but the principal aeroplane was the Taylorcraft 'A,' G-AFJP. The significant achievement of this club was to build and fly the second example of the Heath Parasol (G-AJCK) in the UK. It was a single-seat monoplane, eventually powered — at the time I flew it — with an Aeronca-JAP J.99 engine. This was made possible by the representations made to the Ministry of Civil Aviation by a small group known as the Ultra Light Aircraft Association. One result of correspondence referred to earlier was a meeting of like minds on 26th October 1946, when Maurice Imray, Edward Mole, Teddy Davis, Arthur Ord-Hume and others formed the first executive committee of the ULAA.

Of these pioneers Group Captain Mole was the most senior. In 1930 when a young Flying Officer, he was stationed at Old Sarum, the School of Army Co-operation, and he paid £52.10s for a Parnall Pixie III which had recently been re-engined with a Bristol Cherub of 34 hp. This aeroplane had taken part in the light aeroplane trials at Lympne five years earlier, and was ingenious in that it could be converted to a biplane when two persons were carried, but unfortunately Edward and colleagues flew it without the benefit of the top wing, and the result was an uncontrolled descent into the Woodford valley.

G/C Mole became the second chairman of the ULAA, and negotiated the return of the 'Permit to Fly' system for ultralight aircraft, at that time defined as 1,000 lb max. AUW and a with a maximum of 40 hp. Initially for single-seat aircraft, the limitations soon allowed two-seat home-built aeroplanes and the limitations have gradually been expanded over the years. It was upon AVM Don Bennett's proposal that the name was changed to the Popular Flying Association in October 1950.

The South Hants Ultra Light Aero Club had meanwhile bought Autocrat G-AIPX into club use in early 1949, but sadly it crashed, fatally, on the airfield on 18th August 1949, an event which led to the closure of SHULAC and the genesis of the Christchurch Aero Club. Operating from a wooden hut in the middle of the aerodrome the club was a partnership between Tommy Marshall and Ted Gould (both Bournemouth motor traders) and used Ted's Taylorcraft G-AHUM. The following decade would see a move back into the prewar club premises with up to 12 aircraft on the fleet and with myself as CFI.

But, back to Thruxton. Having now a gliding licence — albeit only an 'A' — I was old enough for a powered aircraft 'A' licence. Having been given odd dual instruction on many C. of A. test flights it was no great step to master the art of landing an Auster and I was sent solo by Bert Hawkins on 3rd September 1947. (Bert went on to instruct at Christchurch and the Royal Naval College at Plymouth). Within a month I had completed the three hours required for the Pilots 'A' licence. Not only was I old enough to fly solo, I could join the RAF.

So in November I departed Thruxton for the delights of Padgate and beautiful South Cerney. The scheme at that time was to fly as NCO aircrew but also with a basic trade. Flying began on Tiger Moths at a small grass aerodrome, Shellingford in the Vale of White Horse, during early 1948 when snow permitted! At that time seconded glider pilots were coming back to RAF control and pilot training was being cut back and hence an entire course was redundant. Some opted to be navigators and went off to Rhodesia. All was not lost, however, as I enjoyed a fitters' course at St. Athan, which added considerably to my knowledge of Gipsy Majors and gave me an insight into the magnificent Bristol Hercules that I would spend thousands of hours flying behind in later years. Together with the Merlin, Welland and Derwent engines, maintenance training on airframes included a Tiger Moth with G-AEZC still visible under the service paint. Ex-Brooklands, this machine had been used as an instructional airframe since December 1940.

On completion of the course I was posted to the Empire Radio School, Debden. Avro Lincoln *Mercury* was pride of the fleet, but day-to-day tasks included maintaining the school Ansons and Oxfords; our daily exercise was winding the hand starters of their Armstrong Siddeley Cheetah engines. As I had signed on for 'the duration of the present emergency' the time soon came to leave this happy band. Declining tempting offers of Flight Engineer training I returned to Thruxton, as it would be another year before I was old enough to become a licensed aircraft engineer or commercial pilot. The latter was helped by transferring my reserve commitment to 19 Reserve Flying School at Hamble, where I would soon get flying experience on brand new Chipmunks for my CPL and training for my instructor rating.

When I went back to Thruxton it was to meet with Geoff Keable and Keith Sedgwick, Norman Parker and, later, Keith Harvey (PFA Inspector 76), all on the hangar staff. Colin Street had just obtained his PPL, and our commercial flying careers would closely parallel each other, starting with Bristol 170s and ending with BAC 1-11s.

Frank Bradford had joined the instructional staff with Laurie Jennings as a part timer. He was also a part-time test pilot for Elliots of Newbury, and his experience went back to building and flying a Pou du Ciel in 1937. I remember him teaching me forced and precautionary landings in a Moth Minor and a BA Swallow to which he had access. He also allowed me to fly the Newbury Eon, a low-wing tricycle four-seater. Thruxton at the end of the forties was filling up with private and club aircraft, and there had been a few losses: for example, Taylorcraft G-AHAF was damaged beyond repair when it landed on top of G-AHUG on 29th May 1948. On the plus side Chilton G-AESZ made its first postwar flight at Thruxton and Rapide G-AFMA was overhauled and sold to Portugal as CS-AEB.

John 'Joe' Currie came in as Chief Engineer after Ted Pepper left. The Magisters were all completed, and most were sold abroad. With the reduction of RAF flying training and the changeover to the Percival Prentice for basic instruction, Tiger Moths were coming on to the market, and conversion of these and ex-AOP Mk. IV and V Austers was keeping the hangar busy. The Flying School was popular with overseas students, Indians and Jordanians predominating.

In August 1949 the club organised a flying display and air races. Gwynn-Johns, who had held records prewar in parachuting, completed a delayed parachute descent. Laurie Jennings gave a superb demonstration of his Olympia sailplane G-ALNF, and Dakota, Horsa, Spitfires and Vampire comprised the military displays. There were one-class races for Auster Is, Auster Vs and Magisters, but the main event was a handicap race from Thruxton to Totland Bay, IOW and return. D. Jemmett of Wolverhampton in Magister G-AKPE was the winner, with Tommy Rose in a Cygnet second; Hawk Speed Six G-ADGP, Moth Minor G-AFPH, Auster G-AHCR, Hawk G-ADNL, Nighthawk G-AGWT, Falcon G-AECC and Miles M.28 G-AGVX were among the 'also rans'. 'These days' (from our chapter title) had certainly returned, with Dragon G-AECZ (now EI-ABI) giving pleasure flights. The first National Air races had been flown three weeks earlier from Elmdon, J.N. Somers winning the King's Cup with his Gemini.

Early September 1949 saw a vintage Farnborough with a delta-wing Avro 707 being seen for the first time in public following its flying debut on 27th July. The Comet gave its first public display and the opportunity for onlookers to realise how far turbine propulsion had come in a little over eight years since P.E.G. Sayer had taken the Gloster E.28/39 for its first flight on 15th May 1941.

Towards the end of the season came the Battle of Britain shows at many RAF airfields. That year I went as prop-swinger with the Dragon to Northolt, where we collected five 'Rank Starlets', young ladies under contract to Rank Films, and took them to RAF Upper Heyford where we could say they were the star attractions. The following month I travelled in the Dragon to Cherbourg for a club outing. The Taylorcraft G-AHCR flown by Capt. Spencer Smith ended up in a ditch, having force-landed in fog over the Cherbourg peninsula. About this time Ted Gould had a problem with his Taylorcraft G-AHUM and ended up in a hedge at Thruxton (*see the photo section following p.120 in* Tails of the Fifties — | *Ed.*)

My final solo flight of the forties was in Tiger Moth G-ALSH. Wiltshire School of Flying was able to announce that, during 1949, 2,147 hours had been flown. The fleet now comprised the Dragon, five Autocrats, a Tiger Moth and the Taylorcraft G-AHCR, which was offered at £2.10s per hour solo hire.

At the end of the forties a pattern had been established in light aviation for the coming decade. There were to be no dollars for the import of light aeroplanes or their engines: no new aircraft were coming from Miles or Percival, and de Havilland were looking towards only military customers, while Austers continued to produce their rather stereotyped high-wing four-seat machines. The ULAA name was to change to the Popular Flying Association, and the homebuilt movement was, just, on the move.

Ex-service Austers, Tigers and Proctors would keep us busy for years to come. Inflation was not a problem: three pounds an hour for training on Austers and Maggies in 1946 was still the going rate eight years later, and a 10/- pleasure flight could still be had in the mid-fifties.

As to the future, *Flight* contained an article which suggested that Gatwick could become a diversionary aerodrome for London Airport; at that time its longest run was 1,400 yds of grass and it closed at dusk!

As I was writing this brief survey of the late forties I received the news of the death of two close friends from Thruxton days, Keith Sedgwick died in October and Ted Gould in December. Both had built Currie Wots, Keith's with a Pobjoy and Ted's with a Walter.

Sunward they've climbed.

CHAPTER 26

THE BROOKSIDE FLYING GROUP, SHOREHAM — PURE DIY (1947 – 1952 RIP)

by

LEWIS BENJAMIN

"The Life and Death of a Flying Club" was the original title, probably inspired by that hugely enjoyable film of the period, *The Life and Death of Col. Blimp*. Yet strangely enough that subconscious thought was not misplaced: in fact there were definite similarities between that great old soldier and the young Brookside flyers. Both were born of a military mind-set, laced with a rather *olde worlde* sense of duty, and both were to fade away – as old soldiers do, – overtaken by the rush to embrace the rules of a bright new future.

Club pilots 60 years ago were different: not in their flying of course, but in their uncluttered mental approach and directness of action. They were wholeheartedly supported by our friends at the Air Ministry (forerunner of the CAA), and it's hard to appreciate how little beaurocracy intruded. The AM's philosophy was to help, and help they did. They even signed themselves "Your obedient servant" – and meant it. It's now little known, but all pilots then were ranked as captains and recognised to be totally in command. Help, not direction, was the order of the day, and since radio was far from universal there wasn't much help requested — good eyesight was far more useful. A delightful state of affairs; I know one can't turn the clock back, but one itches to do so.

Once in the skies though, the forties' pilots were indistinguishable from today's, for up there nothing has changed since the dawn of flight. No, flying remains a constant, but to spot the differences in outlook one must look back. To start with we all seemed to share the same direction, and things that seem impossible today were once run-of-the-mill. The war was blamed for much, but it could never be blamed for the adventurous spirit that the coming of peace engendered.

You see, there was a refreshing enthusiasm abroad, a direct result of shrugging off the universal military mantle. We were mostly in our twenties, just out of uniform and incredibly innocent and unworldly, swept up straight from school into the discipline of the armed forces with no enlightenment inbetween. As a generation well-versed in training to kill, and able to fly expensive machinery whilst still in our teens, few of us could drive, and to be truthful a lot of us were even unsure where babies came from: I kid you not. And as for 'the other,' don't even think about it, for most of us it simply didn't happen — the babes in the wood had nothing on us!

To compound our lamentable ignorance, we trusted, oh how we trusted, and this trust abounded even between perfect strangers who, on production of a smile, became perfect friends. So you will appreciate that this unpreparedness for civilian life makes the story that follows easier to take in, if not completely understandable.

I had joined the South Coast Flying Club down at Shoreham but had become restless with the slow and cautious approach to getting airborne; there seemed no room to progress to better things, and more importantly, there was the expense of it all. The more I thought about it, the more convinced I became that the cheapest way to get flying was with an aeroplane of one's own. One day at Shoreham I put the idea to Duncan Davis, who was the Club's chairman and a rumbustuous character.

"Excellent idea," he roared. "Count me in to help."

So encouraged I began to scout around, but every avenue I explored had the same dead end: no money. That wasn't really surprising. By now (May 1947) I had now left the RAF and had promptly spent the next six months sitting on a beach in a summer of brilliance such as one could only dream of. I got wonderfully brown, I swam, had parties, danced and made merry. I was 22, I had been in the RAF four years, and I wasn't going to do a thing until I was ready, and whilst I had some gratuity money left and parents who were glad to have me home again, I certainly *wasn't* ready. Two things finally made me think of work as autumn drew on. I'd run out of money, but worse, there was the threat of the then current Control of Engagement Order, which gave layabouts like me a choice between finding work smartly or being conscripted to the coalmines. I capitulated and went to work for a friend who had a wholesaling toy business; there I was the office do-all — I tried to keep the books, collected and sold toys, but my mind was always out of gear. All I could think about was flying and owning my own aeroplane.

Then one night a brilliant idea came to me. What was wrong with a tiny share, I asked myself, as opposed to a larger one like a half or a quarter? There was no more sleep that night for me as I furiously extended my germ of an idea. I was living in Hove at the time, and had come to know Ron Clegg, who lived in nearby Brighton and was a leading light in the Ultra Light Aircraft Association (ULAA, forerunner of the PFA). It was he who encouraged me and suggested that I put an advertisement in the local paper for starters, so I not only put an advertisement in the local paper, the Sussex *Evening Argus*, announcing the first meeting of the Enthusiasts' Flying Club, but I also wrote an article entitled "£1 An Hour Flying Planned." The article was published on 14th November 1947, and as a result the first meeting of the provisionally-named Enthusiasts' Flying Club was held in Southwick on the 20th. I can remember little of that meeting except that it was proposed that we honour the memory of Geoffrey de Havilland junior, who had been killed flying the DH.108 a month or so earlier. In a charming response, his father (Geoffrey senior) urged us to wait for a time and tactfully omitted to mention that the Club we would like him to put his name to had scarcely started.

A fascinating entry in my diary for 10th December reads: "Gave Clegg a lift to Piccadilly — very helpful type." Presumably we were attending a meeting of the ULAA committee at Londonderry House where the legendary Group Captain Edward Mole presided. (An aside: dear Edward, what a remarkable and lovable friend he was to light flying! To our collective shame his tremendous contribution to the postwar scene, and to our PFA movement in particular, has never received the recognition it deserves.)

Further entries in the diary show that we originally sought an ultralight. For instance, the following day I followed up a lead that Edward had given me; the cryptic entry says: "Chased up Holmes and Pilgrim re the Aeronca." After some long-term reflection, I think that this must have been a joint reference to (1) 'Titch' Holmes AFC, who had been a Paris mail pilot prewar, flew VIPs clandestinely into France during the war years, and subsequently insured all the Tiger Club aircraft in its formative years, and (2) A.R. (Tiny) Pilgrim, who kept his Beech Staggerwing G-AJJJ at Denham postwar until he exchanged it for the sole surviving Heston Phoenix G-AESV in 1950.

The entry for 7th January 1948 reads: "Decided Cub was no cop." So obviously we were still ultralight-minded, an attitude confirmed the following day: "Phoned Leeds re Mann's Tipsy (the Yorkshire Aero Club had two Tipsy Bs at the time)." Then, on the 10th January: "Cancelled Tipsy; money backed out." The aircraft had been offered with a new year's C. of A. for £500, but even that was too expensive for us.

In my *Evening Argus* article I had suggested that if we could drum up fifty members at £10 per head we would have enough for an aeroplane with a bit left over for luck and the insurance. But money, even at a tenner a time, was hard to come by. I'm not sure I believe in coincidences, but right on schedule my grandmother died, and with the few hundred pounds that came my way I bought, in quick succession, a big share in the aeroplane, an old open Armstrong Siddeley car of 1931 vintage and a new BSA Bantam 125 cc motor bike.

The Club I eventually founded late in 1947 at Shoreham eventually became known as the Brookside Flying Group, and we operated a Miles Magister which we bought from Rollason's for £325 complete with a year's Certificate of Airworthiness. We did everything ourselves, to the immense joy of the members and the alarm of others. We set up camp on the north side of the airfield and at first Duncan wasn't amused at all.

When I reminded him of his offer of help he grumbled that he didn't think I meant it, but he eventually relented and proved a good friend. Incidentally it was the first community flying club in the South of England. We were beaten to being the first ever only by a short head when Jill Donnisthorpe started a similar club in Reading; at the time neither knew of the other's existence.

The fun we had is a story in itself, but a little background is important to get the feel of club flying in the immediate postwar years. For instance, anyone could instruct and anyone did. Take me for instance. The insurance policy I negotiated was fully comprehensive — it covered any member under instruction or otherwise, and all for only an incredible £70 a year; that would take some beating today. It also listed me, a complete unknown, as the Club's Secretary, and one authorised to check out others. I did so, often, even to putting on my most serious face when, as happened on one occasion, I was called upon to give an A1 qualified Wing Commander instructor an initial check. If 'Wiggie' is still alive and ever reads this, I hope he'll forgive me the indignity of calling for another circuit because I wasn't satisfied with the first.

In those days I kept a small diary, and a browse through it conjures up a picture far removed from present times. In a life that has been dominated by a conviction that one should only look forward, I'm only tempted to glance back encouraged — as if encouragement was necessary — by the words of a screen goddess with whom I was in love at the age of 17, that in looking back one should only remember the good things. Too true!

The Brookside Flying Group was arguably the PFA's first Strut. The Popular Flying Association celebrates its 60th anniversary this year (2006) but in its first few years it was known as the Ultra Light Aircraft Association and my outfit joined the ULAA in 1947. We didn't call it a Strut then for the PFA's word for a branch didn't come into existence until much later, but in all events it was the same association. If ever there was a DIY flying group it was ours. It wasn't all easy going.

That first Strut, if first Strut it was, sought no outside help: we did our own maintenance. In my mind's eye I can still see us pushing our Maggie out of her tatty blister hangar, her silver sides wet with dew, and eyeing her critically. If she looked lopsided we'd boost her ego and sagging wing with a car footpump and so replenish her seeping pneumatics, and when she looked spritely again, there was a wiggle of controls, a count of plugs, and we were away, often flying before the club on the south side of the airfield had even opened. The stillness and innocence of those early morning flights are the sort that memories are made of.

Our Miles Magister G-AKRJ arrived on 17th April 1948, some six weeks after we confirmed our order with Rollasons. Part of the delay could be thus accounted:

25/3/48: "No women, no money" (things must have been desperate). And then:

27/3/48: "Wrote Lord Nathan — protest." (Lord who?).

10/4/48: "ULAA meeting, Londonderry House. Spoke to Col. Preston. Could hardly say we saw eye to eye."

Quite what we were fighting for all those years ago is now obscure. Permission to operate probably, not everyone wanted us. Nothing changes, does it? Certainly there was no trouble with the Air Ministry, then custodians of the airfield. I well recall phoning the department that looked after civil airfields.

The someone at the other end was very supportive. "What do you need?"

"Well, hangarage first, I suppose, our Maggie is due soon."

He countered: "Is there anything suitable on the north side?" (The south side housed the South Coast Flying Club who viewed our arrival with dismay bordering on panic.)

I told him of the two blister hangars; the better one of the two already housed Hamilton's Auster, but the farther one, the one nearest to the old gunnery dome, was empty.

"Sounds the thing," he said: "what's its condition?"

Reply: "There are no side screens, cattle use it, and there is some loose roofing."

There was a pause for thought. "Would £25 a year fit the bill?"

I agreed.

"What else?"

"Well, there's a large hut not far away which would do nicely for a Clubhouse."

The hut (at a guess it was about 35 ft x 30 ft) looked out over the billiard table that was always Shoreham, and was perched just beyond the peri-track and a little stream bridged by a plank (no marks for guessing how the group was named).

"Make it £50," he suggested. "OK?"

His final words could well have marked the zenith of common sense. "Perhaps you would be good enough to let the resident Ministry police know of our arrangement?"

I assured him I would. On the anniversary of that verbal agreement I used to send off £75, at least until 1952 — no reminders, a simple understanding that worked. The police, a friendly lot, promised to keep an eye on things for us.

I guess I won't be the first to reflect how, once upon a time, a few civil servants did so much, so efficiently and for the common good, and yet still have time for a friendly word.

The hut had once been, so the tale goes, the flight office of a Free French fighter squadron. I recall I painted our name in vast white letters on its side, and even until the 1980s the faded inscription could still be seen on a part of the old hut where it had been repositioned alongside the railway line; then the last time I looked, I looked in vain. I shrugged; it amazed me that that little bit of history had lasted so long.

But we had fun, we had tragedy too, and bought another Maggie, G-AKRM, to replace the first. We instructed, sent off solos, no one was paid, no one was qualified in the bureaucratic sense, and no one suffered. We occasionally took orphans under our wing. People would just leave them with us. For instance an Aeronca stayed for ages, and it was joined at times by a Fairchild Argus and a DH Rapide.

One last entry, on 29/4/48: "Obtained some 1,300 gallons for three months. We all retired to the (looks like) *Hobbled Goose* to celebrate."

At a time when motorists were strictly rationed, sometimes to only a gallon or two a week, this was a princely allocation. Before making the application I had blithely calculated an annual utilization of 500 hours (in retrospect I don't think we ever bettered 200). I multiplied that by seven, as she was a thirsty beast. It did look an awful lot, so with trepidation I visited the Allocating Officer and put my case. He nodded, thought it wouldn't be enough, and upped it. On reflection we must have been living in cloud cuckoo land but it all happened.

Characters were drawn to our Club like Moths to Woburn. One, I recall, turned up at Shoreham early in 1949 in the Percival Proctor G-AIIP (correction: two turned up.) "Come and have a flight/fright," said the first one, Mick Conry. The second appeared to be his personal pilot, a Persian nicknamed Sinbad. I'd known Mick some time, albeit vaguely. I doubt he held a licence right then, which would account for Sinbad's presence. Mick had earned some infamy a year or two back, having crashed a BAC Drone, and the poor fellow had come off badly. He wasn't a hero, but he was treated with a degree of awe at his audacity in even flying the thing. The crash investigators conceded that the near-glider, underpowered with its Scott motorcycle engine, hadn't been in an airworthy condition. Apparently that was a calculated understatement, as rumour also had it that they had found a bicycle chain and a dead rat in the petrol tank. There was more, but it made a good story at the time.

The Proctor flight, a series of erratic circuits and bumps, was highly different. I thanked them, grateful to be down in one piece, and off they flew to adventures new. Once in a while I wonder what happened to Mick; whatever it was it would have had an Errol Flynn ring about it.

* * * * * * * *

Memories are a bit like characters, they hang around to be recalled with delight at the touch of a log book. One such moment arrived a year earlier.

We hadn't had our Maggie a week before we decided to aerobat it.

"What will it do?" we asked the only person we knew who'd flown one.

Poor Chadwick (he who had collected it for us from Rollasons of Croydon) was a bit nervous in recommending too much. He was a steady fellow, ex-ATA, and I doubt he'd done much experimenting with the aircraft he'd ferried.

"Well," he began, "it doesn't like spinning but it does everything else." If he'd had the nerve he'd have added "I think."

The year was now 1948, we were young and the spring sunshine brought Shoreham's lush green billiard table of grass to life inviting us to aviate, nay, willing us to get airborne with an urgency that left us breathless.

Our Group's Magister G-AKRJ sat happily just the other side of the little brook beyond our clubroom over on the north side of Shoreham, isolated from the well-established South Coast Flying Club by a nearly unused airfield. All ours. There was no Air Traffic, one just sniffed the grass-scented air and took off, usually from where one clambered aboard.

G-AKRJ, clad in a simple all-over silver respray, still had the Gosport tube system of intercom, but even in 1948 there was the beginning of a shortage of helmet tubes. I recall I had bought a bundle of 30 pairs from Phil's surplus radio shop off Leicester Square for 1s/6d a pair.

"Don't know what they are for," said Phil.

I didn't enlighten him, I figured he'd only have asked more the next time. I sold them on at 3/6 a time, my first business venture, if you discount my distribution of laboriously written copies of a disreputable Byron poem at the age of 14.

This isn't really a digression, for the shortage of Gosports led to our first experiment with electric hats. To start with we lashed two huge Leclanché cells into the locker behind the rear seat. (Leclanché cells? Well, I haven't seen one now in 50 years, but they resembled mortar shells and weighed nearly as much, gave out 1½ volts — or was it 3 volts? — just about for ever. People were throwing them out around then as better doorbell systems took their place. Ours — free of course — were probably young in the first World War.) We had yet to wire in the new-fangled electric hats, i.e. standard RAF helmets, so the proposed trip was intercomless, the usual pair of Gosports short.

We promptly took off, a shared trip, this one, the understanding being that I'd do ten minutes' aeros and then 'Baggy' Woodward in the back seat would do his stint. It was a lovely day. Sufficient height, a quick swing 180° either way, and nose down for the first loop. The Maggie felt heavy as I heaved back. As we went over the top there was a heavy clunk. I levelled out at the same time Baggy yelled. I throttled back and Baggy's excited voice came forward.

"Something hit me."

I thought, a bird? What on earth could have hit him?

His breathless voice added: "It hit me on the head, I think it's on the floor." Then a far-away voice yelled: "I can see it. I'm undoing my straps, keep it steady."

With a twisting of the head I couldn't repeat today, I peered back and saw his head reappear; he was holding up a black object I recognised, one of the two black cells.

His face was wreathed in a wide grin. "It came through the hole behind my head," he explained. "Hang on while I do my straps up again." Baggy's thumbs-up encouraged me to proceed.

Nose down, I put on speed and again pulled through. There was a second resounding bang. I levelled out and waited for Baggy's voice.

"Bloody hell," he yelled above the slipstream, "it's the other one. I'll pick it up." Then, "Got it!" he shouted triumphantly.

Now presumably he held a cell in each hand. The two loops were easy, thought I, let's go for a slow roll. I dived the Maggie firmly to about 120 mph, when the air shrieked over the cockpit in protest. Then, up came the nose — I paused with it just above the horizon, an artistic touch, that — and moved the stick firmly to the left and a little forward. I got on ten degrees, clearly heard two thumps and the stick went solid: I couldn't move it in any direction. Bewildered, I throttled back and became aware of someone shouting. The stick eased central and stayed there. I didn't force it but something must be awfully wrong, there was still this strange resistance. The shouting was renewed.

"Stop, stop," Baggy was yelling, "I haven't done my straps up."

We flew back; Baggy had a cell again in each hand, ready to drop them at a moment's notice to grab the controls, but I flew gently: he wasn't the only shaken pilot. And yes, we scrapped the cells idea. Providing you can get Gosport tubes the old way is the best.

* * * * * * * * *

A few months later, there was another diary entry. The log book records the date as September 11th 1948, and the remarks column suggests it was a glorious day. A young woman hesitantly approached our Group with a strange request. She carried a sleeping baby in her arms and told us the baby had developed whooping cough. Somewhere, somehow, she had heard that altitude cured whooping cough, tops of mountains and suchlike, and asked if it was true. None of us could answer her for sure, but we assured her that, if we could offer help, she'd come to the right place. Her glance upwards and back to our faces said it all: no time like the present, we all agreed.

The still-sleeping child was cocooned in blankets and placed on Joan Wood's lap in the open front cockpit up near the warmth of the engine. I climbed into the rear and carefully took off, and climbed and climbed and climbed. At 9,000 feet both Joan and I were frozen, but the baby, who had rosy cheeks and was cosy in the blankets, slept peacefully. My log book reveals the baby's name to be Pat Lock, but boy or girl heaven knows, and I've often wondered what happened to him or her and whether the mother told him or her about us one day. We cruised for a while at this, for us, great height, and then slowly drifted downwards in big gentle spirals into warmer air, the engine noise now muted and rhythmic; it lulled our senses while Pat slept on.

Back safely on the ground Mrs. Lock received her still sleepy child back with heartfelt murmurs of thanks and the Group members clustered round happily. Young Pat hadn't coughed the entire trip. Wasn't that proof enough of a cure? We thought so.

It was only later that the thought of publicity entered into our minds, and Joan Wood offered to go around the next day to see the Locks and to report straight away to the *Evening Argus*.

A couple of days later, Joan returned, somewhat subdued.

"Is Pat better?" we asked excitedly.

She just shook her head and said: "'Fraid not; you see, it seems not only has Pat still got whooping cough but the doctor says the child now has pneumonia as well."

* * * * * * * * * *

One thing general aviation at our end seldom had was the use of a radio. I can't recall any light postwar aircraft with it as standard. No doubt commercial flights used them and even then it was confined to the heavies. Local, and, indeed, European taxi and freight flights flew cheerfully around obeying the simple rules of sound airmanship. Joining circuits was an established procedure dictated by the signals square and an eye open for an Aldis lamp. There was also a universal understanding that pilots commanded their aircraft. Air Traffic was there to assist. Naturally one obeyed their directions whilst within their orbit: it made sense. For example, one could ask what the weather would be like at one's destination, and if it was likely to be 'duff' the controller would only suggest that perhaps it wasn't a good time to aviate; but the decision was always the pilot's.

Along with a draughty cockpit bare of radio there wasn't much in the way of navigational help. A forties pilot relied on compass and a well-worn wartime half-million map indecently nude of overprinting. True, there were occasional prohibited areas to fly around, usually small, mostly firing ranges. Even airfields *en route* were overflown at 2,000 feet. I seem to recall that below that height we had to give the circuit a three-mile clearance. Generally we drew a line to our destination with ten-minute interval marks and set off to follow it. While a simple and obvious method in fine weather, if the weather looked 'duff' we could fly with certainty up and down railway lines because our maps showed every line clearly marked single or double track — they went everywhere. Nowadays they are a forgotten species and those that are left are outdated by ADF and GPS. Incidentally we always flew between 1,000 and 1,500 feet along the right-hand side of any track — road, rail or river — essential to avoid the fellow coming the other way. Interesting to note we automatically adopted the European right of the road in spite of mere drivers below keeping to their left.

One flight, non-radio and in this case with little help from the map, comes to mind, as for me it conjures up the spirit of flying then. My log book records it was in the June of 1948.

I was asked by Danny Taylor, who suddenly felt like visiting his friends and family in Scotland, if I'd fly him up there, and would yesterday be too soon? Danny was a tiny man who ran an amusement arcade in Brighton, and he and his sister-in-law, Eileen, were firm supporters of our small club. As usual it was a case of 'no sooner said than done'.

We flew north in our open two-seater, and after stops for fuel at Sywell and Yeadon we pressed on into the gathering dusk above Yorkshire. By now, I'd flown off the South of England map, and although I hadn't been able to find a North of England map before we left, Danny's logic that you couldn't miss the Firth of Forth appealed to me, and we left without one.

Darkness closed gently about us. There was a full moon and the evening was beautifully still. The land beneath us was ghostly in its pale whiteness, and our Maggie flew herself and her contented passengers into a dreamy state. Sure enough, some two hours after leaving Yorkshire we saw the Firth of Forth in the moon's reflected light, found the bridge, and turned westwards to Grangemouth, our destination.

I had reckoned to arrive in the early evening, but we'd stopped for a chicken supper at Yeadon and it had put our timing back a bit. It was dark over the airfield, but I could just discern the even darker triangle of runways below, but as I dropped lower I saw too the big white crosses painted on the ends of them: unserviceable.

Just after the war airfield runways were often used to store munitions, bombs and the like, so no way was I going to land blind on one of them. I eased the throttle and set up an approach on the runway up-moon, aiming to land on the grass alongside. The Maggie sank softly below the tree line, and the moon, low on the horizon, vanished, leaving us in Stygian blackness. The grass couldn't have been 80 feet beneath us, so I closed the throttle and eased the stick into, first, a glide, and then when I thought the moment was right, eased the stick further back . . . and back, and finally right back.

But nothing happened. I could see nothing, there was no instrument lighting, nothing. All I was aware of was the rhythmic bark of the engine up front ticking over. I held the stick fully back and waited. Still nothing happened. Perplexed, I shut off the engine. The black stillness of the night embraced us.

A voice from the back said: "Are we down?"

"I don't know," I said.

We sat there a bit longer and the voice said: "I'll climb out and see."

I said: "Be careful," then there was a sound of Danny undoing his harness and fumbling around.

"I think we are down," he said. "I'm going to jump."

I waited with bated breath. He was only a little bloke, even shorter than me, and the wheat we'd landed in came up to his chest.

From afar came voices and flaming torches as Danny's friends and family ploughed their way to our rescue. I slept soundly that night in a showman's caravan, woken only once when someone implored me to stop Danny, who couldn't fly, from going on another flight. The full moon was overhead now and probably affecting Danny as much as the whisky.

* * * * * * * * *

Sadly the Brookside Flying group drifted into oblivion in 1952. It had been four years of fun, and yet the memories of those community flyers linger still. For at Shoreham there is now a delightful Museum and Archive run by David Dunstall that exists to preserve and keep fresh the history of that very old aerodrome (the first one to be licensed in the UK, incidentally).

And if you ask the custodians, they will gladly show you the records of the old club, full of photos and personalities of all those years ago. Do give the Archives a visit; you'll enjoy the place, and do ask — assuming you care — about the club's very own ghost, a beautiful red-headed girl who haunted our clubhouse for a while. As if at times flying wasn't alarming enough . . . but then they don't make ghosts like they used to.

CHAPTER 27

A NOSTALGIC TRIP THROUGH THE 1940S — WHO NEEDED A CAR ANYWAY?

by

PETER AMOS

My wife says that I have always been old — well, I couldn't help having been christened on the same day as the R.101 airship crashed: 5th October 1930! On reflection, this was not a very auspicious start to what was ultimately to be a career in aviation and a lifelong interest in most things aeronautical!

Anyway, the future (in my considered opinion, for what that's worth!) has little or nothing to offer us 'oldies' in the way of common sense in general and aviation in particular, so let's enjoy what treasured memories that we have while we can.

Where to start this trip was the big problem, so I have cheated a little by just creeping over the line to 3rd September 1939 — was it really 66 years ago? Even though I was a nine-year-old boy, I can now still vividly recall that fateful moment at 11.15 am on Sunday 3rd September 1939 as we listened to the wireless ('radio' for the benefit of our younger readers) in the 'front' room (one didn't have 'lounges' in those days) to hear the Prime Minister, Neville Chamberlain, make his historic 'Speech to The Nation':

"I am speaking to you from the Cabinet Room at 10 Downing Street. This morning the British Ambassador in Berlin handed the German Government an official note stating that, unless we heard from them by eleven o'clock that they were prepared at once to withdraw their troops from Poland, a state of war would exist between us. I have to tell you now that no such undertaking has been received, and consequently this country is at war with Germany etc, etc."

I remember that no one spoke. My father had been in the army in WWI and was too old to get involved in another one, but he alone knew only too well what it meant. However, none of us could have known then just what a long drawn-out struggle for our survival was to lie ahead. Soon after the fateful announcement, the siren sounded — for the first time, but certainly not the last — and, although this turned out to be a false alarm it was a taste of things to come. We went back to what we had been doing — there was little enough that could be done about it at the time anyway.

My home was in Merstham, Surrey, a village just north of Redhill and a few miles south-west of Kenley Aerodrome on the North Downs, where on 20th May 1939 I had been to see the Empire Air Day display along with my long-suffering father, who had no interest in aeroplanes but who had been 'persuaded' by an enthusiastic son to take him! I still have the programme, and one lasting memory of the show, apart from the flying display — both biplanes and monoplanes — which enthralled me, was looking through the rear turret of a Wellington and being surprised to find that I could see right out through the front! The Dragon Rapide G-AEPE, *The Luxembourg Listener*, was giving joyrides — but that was too much to ask! My first display was behind me but it was to be many years before I would see another.

We now come to the 1940s and, although I lived in an area surrounded by aerodromes (Kenley, Croydon and Redhill) I was to see surprisingly few aircraft flying over during the war. My first memory was of the Battle for Britain, with the contrails of the fighters whirling about in the clear blue skies over Surrey and towards Kent during that August and September. Two events come to my mind: one of a parachute descending over the village at the height of the battle, and the other of a Lysander chasing an errant barrage balloon across the fields behind my house, while firing its machine guns in its direction in what appeared to be a vain attempt to shoot it down before its trailing ropes became entangled in something on the ground! This 'circus' unfortunately disappeared behind the trees at the bottom of the garden before I could see the outcome!

Then came the nightly air raids with everybody sleeping under the stairs for safety. My grandmother had been to Portsmouth to see one of her sons shortly after the famous raid on the port and came back with stories of whole streets of houses demolished but for the staircases, and so we felt that there would be the best place to sleep; we had no faith in the partially-buried Anderson shelters in the gardens, which were cold, damp and smelly places.

Now, what I am about to recall may make no sense, and may even cast serious doubts as to my sanity, but this is what an 11-year-old boy saw — or thought he did. This lad thought he was good at spotting, having studied all *The Aeroplane* books of aircraft recognition that he could get his hands on. The first of two 'strange' incidents concerned his first close-up view of a German aircraft — a Henschel Hs.126 flying low from south to north in front of his house! It was painted grey and, bearing in mind that Merstham is some 33 miles north of Brighton on the coast, the pilot must either have had a death wish or was more than somewhat lost! The question remains however: what was it doing so far inland and why was it not shot down? One thing is for sure: I didn't confuse it with a Lysander — and I have yet to see a 'Lizzie' with swastikas!

The second mystery incident is almost as strange as the first: I was walking along Frenches Road (past the school of the same name) on the way to Redhill one afternoon, when I heard a strange noise, and on looking up I claim that I saw a Heinkel He.115. It was flying at a reasonable height — low enough to be able to see the floats, anyway — when suddenly I noticed something falling from it. This object turned out to be a bomb, but I didn't stop around long enough to see where it was going to fall; in fact it fell on a house in a row next to the school and demolished it. What this was all about must forever remain a mystery, unless there is someone out there who can put me out of my misery!

My next memorable sighting must have been about 1943/44 when, in a clear blue sky, I saw six 9th USAAF Curtiss C-46 Commandos in close formation (of two rows of three aircraft each) flying across from west to east: they were towing what appeared to me to be Waco CG-13A gliders (although I suppose they could just conceivably have been CG-4As) on short 'solid' tow-bars. This in itself was something of a rare treat, even if they were CG-4As, but I still think that they were CG-13As as I never saw any American aircraft over Merstham, as none were based anywhere near us. It would, however, be interesting to see if anyone could throw any light on these mystery sightings of the wartime period.

However, the final two memories are straightforward, with no mystery other than why in the first place two very new-looking Coastal Command aircraft were flying across Merstham, quite low, in about 1945; the first was a Catalina and the second was a Sunderland and their flights were separated by a few weeks.

One day during the war, while I was shopping in Reigate, a civilian furniture van passed through heading towards Dorking with a dismantled Cessna Crane in the back, painted yellow overall with RAF roundels like the ones in service with the Royal Canadian Air Force. As with the earlier German aircraft mystery spottings I am still trying to work that one out as, to the best of my knowledge, the RAF had none in this country and, if they had, it would not have been in those colours, and no, I didn't dream it!

Some time before D-Day I was cycling along Gatton Bottom, just outside Old Merstham, on the northern boundary of the Gatton Park Estate near Redhill (the prewar home of the Colmans — of mustard fame), when I was very surprised to find a very large number of khaki & black-camouflaged vehicles, all wearing RAF roundels on the mudguards, and including many radio vans, parked under the coppice which lined the whole length of the south side of the road. There were literally hundreds of vehicles and they stretched for what seemed miles along this relatively straight stretch of road which ultimately climbed to the top of Reigate Hill. The fact that they had been there for some time was confirmed by the brick-built 'above-ground' vehicle servicing pit amongst the trees!

However, the reason for their presence defeated me completely at the time — what were the RAF doing so far away from an aerodrome? It was to be some 50 years later that I found the reason in Christopher Shore's & Chris Thomas' most excellent book, *2nd Tactical Air Force Volume One*; here, on page 12, it was written that:

"The nucleus of the Group (No.83 Group within Fighter Command, which had been formed on 1st April 1943) comprised an advanced and rear headquarters at Gatton Park, Redhill, which had been expanded by 15 May to incorporate formations which came to be regarded as permanent elements of the Group. These included 121 Airfield Headquarters at Middle Wallop, 122 at Eastchurch, 123 at Stoney Cross and 124 at Lasham. Other ancillary units included an Air Stores Park, a Transport Company, a Supply and Transport Column, a Mobile Field Hospital, Mobile Operations Room Unit, a Mobile Air Reporting Unit, an Air Ministry Experimental Station and Mobile Signals Unit. All these mobile units had been gathered at Gatton Park on 5 April and a PBX line put in. Early in May, meteorological personnel were allocated to the Group by Air Ministry."

My wife is presently reading Eric Sykes' autobiography and, by a strange coincidence, she recalled my interest and drew my attention to the fact that Eric had been in the RAF as a signaller and was based at Gatton Park in 1943-44. It would also appear from what he wrote that by 1943 the Canadian army had moved out and the RAF had in fact taken over the whole estate. Problem solved! I had, unknowingly, witnessed the ancillary units in operation soon after they had become established there, but by D-Day they had all gone and only the tyre marks amid the trees and the above-ground inspection pit remained.

Then, on 13th June 1944, came the dreaded V-1 *Vergeltungswaffer 1* — Revenge Weapon No.1. After then things were never quite the same: I witnessed far too many of these monstrosities flying over Merstham and landing (although probably 'exploding' would be a more accurate word) all around the vicinity, thanks to the massive balloon barrage and anti-aircraft gun belt just to the south of us. Both the balloons and the guns soon became very adept at knocking bits off the 'Doodlebugs' (as they soon became known), and after that these infernal devices chose the area around Merstham as their target instead of London, where they were originally intended to drop. Now, while the V-1s weren't designed to be very effective by diving into the ground, they certainly came into their own when arriving in a glide with a dead engine to inflict the most possible blast damage. However, it was still quite astonishing just how much damage they could also inflict on the immediate locality by in fact diving into the ground at full power. I was once far too close to the receiving end of one of these 'dive bombers' and can therefore confirm this categorically — strangely enough I was in class at early morning prayers in school when it struck close by and I thought just how prophetic that was as I saw the wall in front of me crack from top to bottom from the vibration just before the thing actually hit the ground!

My father and I then took on the job of erecting Morrison shelters for the ladies in the locality whose husbands were away serving in the forces, in order to give them a little peace of mind. These indoor shelters had undoubtedly saved many lives elsewhere, and we all felt secure in these at night and on the occasions during the day when the V-1s got too close to stay outside and watch them!

We also made and erected a large-scale scratch-built model of a Mosquito on the 'Cottage of Content' public house in Old Merstham, for a 'Wings' appeal. This was hauled up by a rope with its wing leading edges marking the amount collected to date, and this created a great deal of interest in the village.

Apart from the sight of the pilotless V-1s flying across our home at low altitude, mostly after they had had lumps knocked off them, at least they could be seen — unlike the V-2s, which arrived later. A few of these frightening devices fell in the locality and the explosion was followed soon after by the sound of them arriving — most uncanny. I distinctly recall one incident when one fell a couple of miles up the road at Hooley and we couldn't understand what had happened, as the great whoosh which followed the big bang was new to us at the time. I also witnessed a V-2 exploding in a clear blue sky one afternoon over the North Downs, although I didn't realise what it was until later.

Then there were the two interesting visiting aircraft (brought in by road) during the latter stages of the war. The first was a very early mark of Spitfire whose serial, from memory, began with 'W'; this sported yellow panels on its fuselage sides and was fully assembled on the recreation ground at Redhill. The other one was a Spitfire PR.Mk.XI, which appeared one day on the forecourt of the *Embassy* cinema at Dorking. Both were being used to encourage people to part with their money for the 'Wings' appeal.

We now come to September 1944; my father, who by profession was a carpenter and joiner in a family business, had had a long hard war repairing bomb-damaged houses in order to make them at least partly habitable again, and he was finally persuaded by an aunt and uncle of mine (who lived in North Bersted, just north of Bognor Regis in Sussex) to take a week's holiday with them. This in itself was something of an achievement, as I distinctly recall that Dad was a workaholic!

We hadn't had a holiday since before the war and I looked forward to a change of scenery with great interest. It had been a long war and I had lost quite a bit of schooling, mainly due to relocating parts of the school to the local village hall, spending considerable time in the shelters during air-raids and finally also being bombed out after the V-1 attack. Then there was the gardening — *Dig for Victory* — on top of the above-ground air raid shelters in what had been the playground, and the potato picking at a local farm which we somehow got volunteered for! This was a back-breaking job if ever there was one, but at least we got paid for our labours!

What I didn't know, however, before we left for Bognor Regis, was that there were to be two surprises waiting for me! The first was soon after we had left Horsham on the train, when I suddenly realised that we had stopped at a small railway station called Faygate; there was a siding alongside with open wagons filled with scrap aluminium, so you can imagine my surprise when I spotted the reason for this in the field alongside the railway track and next to a Bellman hangar by the railway station: it was filled with broken aeroplanes some twenty feet deep and supported around the edges by what appeared to be Wellington wings! What surprised me even more, though, was the sight of a fully-rigged Airspeed Oxford standing outside the hangar on a concrete apron! It should be mentioned here that Faygate was the home of No.49 Maintenance Unit and had no airfield. Unbeknown to me at the time, however, was the fact that I was also soon to meet with members from this unit, whose main task was to recover crashed aircraft of all nations from all over Sussex and salvage the best bits, the rest being sent for scrap by rail. This, presumably, was the reason for the fully-erected Oxford: perhaps they had found enough salvageable bits to make a complete one and assemble it as a trial run!

The second surprise came soon after we had settled in at my aunt & uncle's house, when I was invited by my uncle to "come and see my aerodrome!" In my ignorance of the location of aerodromes outside my sphere of cycling range in those days, I had no idea of what was he was talking about, but was very keen to learn more, nevertheless. 'His aerodrome' turned out to be Bognor Advanced Landing Ground and although I could not recall the date when I had actually visited the ALG until much later, I was able to remember that it was in the late summer of 1944. However, unbeknown to me at the time, it must have been made just before the ALG was finally vacated for good on 26th September: it had been a close call!

I distinctly remember much activity, including Spitfires of various marks, Typhoons and Ansons coming and going, as the ALG was then occupied by No.83 Group Support Unit, 2nd TAF. This unit was responsible for holding stocks of reserve aircraft and pilots for the 2nd TAF; it had been moved from Redhill in June 1944 due to the V-1s flying over that aerodrome and the fears that, if one had landed amongst them, it would have done our reserves no favours at all. In consequence, ferry pilots of the Air Transport Auxiliary from No.1 FPP White Waltham and

No.9 FPP Aston Down were flown to Redhill to ferry as a matter of the utmost urgency all the Spitfires, Mustangs and Typhoons to Bognor ALG. My uncle Syd told me that the week before I arrived there had been a very nasty accident on the airfield which resulted in the death of one pilot. Apparently this had been caused by a Mustang landing with an engine fire and colliding with an aircraft waiting to take off. Air traffic control at Bognor ALG was a bit crude in those days: a controller stood on a box in a corrugated structure and waved an Aldis lamp at the aircraft on the ground or in the air — green for 'OK to take off or land' and red for 'stop or go away'! However, on that particular day he must have got things horribly wrong as the wing of the aircraft coming in to land sliced into the cockpit of the one waiting to take off, with fatal results.

Whilst walking along the footpath to the ALG we passed a large circular hole in the ground just outside the northern perimeter of the airfield. This was the size of a large propeller and contained the remains of the Typhoon Mk.IB MP202, from No.83 GSU which had suffered structural failure of the rear fuselage while on a test flight from Bognor ALG on 11th September, just a few days before my visit. The tangled remains of the aircraft, which had fallen back from the hole, were in the process of being recovered by an RAF crew from No.49 MU, Faygate. These airmen had a couple of 'Queen Mary' 60 ft transporters, a Coles crane and a radio truck, and spent their lives scouring the countryside recovering crashed aircraft. We got chatting to the crew who, like me, were very surprised that there had been no fire, even though the hole had petrol and live ammunition in it!

The Operation Record Book (ORB) for the Unit recorded that the Typhoon had "lost its tail recovering from dive 1 mile NE of Bognor Regis". The pilot was one of the very lucky few (only three, I believe,) to have actually managed to bale out from a tailless Typhoon at just 300 ft and survive! However, it was this crash which subsequently helped me to date our holiday more accurately.

A notable movement I recall during my stay (apart from the comings and goings of the Spitfires and Typhoons) was an Anson which landed and disgorged a French officer wearing one of those pillbox-type hats — surely not the dreaded de Gaulle I thought! However, there is no record in the ORB of any French officer visiting Bognor ALG, so perhaps not! Then there was the afternoon when I was standing by the boundary hedge looking over the airfield towards Air Traffic Control when I realised that I was being waved at by the man with the Aldis lamp! I thought about waving back but then I noticed that his waving was getting somewhat more agitated. I couldn't see anything amiss, but something made me turn round, and it was just as well I did because I just had time to duck to let an Anson pass over my head before it touched down very close to the hedge!

I now consider myself to have been very lucky and privileged to have been able actually to witness an ALG in operation, but thanks only to the 'Doodlebugs', as Bognor ALG closed for good very soon after my visit. No.83 GSU then moved to Thorney Island on 25th and 26th September 1944, and soon after that the Sommerfeld tracking was taken up and the site returned to agriculture.

During that September of 1944 it is recorded in the ORB that 170 aircraft were received by the unit and 212 aircraft were despatched. This was no mean feat, but unfortunately the movement of aircraft to and from No.83 GSU was so rapid that their details were not recorded on the individual aircraft record cards, and so it has not been possible to identify all of the aircraft that were handled by the Unit.

For more details of Bognor ALG, see the book *It Started with a Map* by Sylvia Endacott, published in November 2005, copies of which may be obtained from the author.

Recently I visited the site in connection with the research for the above book — in which I happily became involved (like you do!); this was to see if I could recall the times and places where I had once stood all those years ago, so I was pleasantly surprised to see that the ALG hadn't really changed much at all. The gaps in the hedges along Chalcroft Lane (to the south) and the Lower Bognor Road to the west, always a sure sign of the presence of an ALG, and Morrels Farm, once the HQ building, were both still there, although by the look of it the farm is now used only as a second home. The four blister hangars had long gone, but there were no other permanent buildings on site, so to the untrained eye there was really little to distinguish it from any other large field. Only a few bungalows have been built to the south of Chalcroft Lane where once the end of one of the runways had been.

I actually found the spot where I had once stood on a sunny Sunday afternoon 61 years ago and memories of the ground crew trying to start a 'Tiffy' on a nearby dispersal came flooding back. The crew were not having much luck and had gone through a complete set of Koffman starter cartridges while I watched with interest. However, after they had reloaded the starter, the mighty 24-cylinder Napier Sabre engine eventually fired and then the inevitable happened: a fire in the carburettor intake! This was promptly extinguished by one of the ground crew by the simple expedient of stuffing his hat into the intake, and from this simple but apparently not uncommon act came the now famous expression: "You can always tell a 'Tiffy' fitter by his hat!"

Merston airfield, just a short distance up the Chichester road from the ALG, was deserted at the time of my visit, but apparently an American B-17 Flying Fortress had tried to land shortly before our visit after returning from a raid with a hung-up bomb — with disastrous results: my uncle said that you could have put a double-decker bus in the hole that it made.

Tangmere however, yielded some interesting Lancasters and Mosquitos, all of which were, from memory, camouflaged in light and dark earth, but I have never found the reason for this unusual colour scheme. The only movement that I can recall during my visit was a visiting USAAF Republic P-47 Thunderbolt taking off, and this was in natural metal finish with a green cowling.

From the top of the Trundles, near Goodwood Racecourse, I could just make out a Royal Navy Hellcat in midnight-blue colours standing out on Westhampnett airfield far below to the south. This, I later discovered from the log book of Hugh Kendall, must have been from the RN Fighter Interception Research Unit which was based there at the time.

We now come to Redhill Aerodrome, of which I have so many happy memories, but I will start at the beginning of my interest in the aerodrome. The last two RAF Squadrons to be based at Redhill aerodrome were No.116 and No.287 Sqdns. No.116 Sqdn. was equipped with Anson Is and XIIs, Oxford IIs, Tiger Moths and Hurricane IIs and had arrived from Gatwick on 5th September 1944, its main task being the calibration of predictors and anti-aircraft radar used by anti-aircraft gun batteries. The squadron painted an unofficial crest on one of the hangar doors which survived into the late 1950s. When the hangars were finally repainted, this crest was photographed by the author in about 1954, but what has intrigued me ever since was the inscription 'Foo-Foo' which was written underneath (see photograph): what this referred to is now probably lost in the mists of time. No.116 Sqdn. left for Hornchurch on 2nd May 1945, where they disbanded on the 26th.

While they were at Redhill, a detachment from No.42 MU moved in, whose main task was to repair Spitfires, Mustangs, Typhoons and Tempests, although other aircraft they worked on included Ansons and Austers. However, other larger aircraft which were on charge to this unit included Bostons and Mitchells, and I recall seeing, from a gap in the hedge by Nutfield church opposite the main hangars, an assortment of silver-painted aircraft outside the hangar (which was later to be used by Field Aircraft Services Ltd., F.G. Miles Ltd. and later still the Tiger Club) including a Boston, all of which were in natural metal finish and could have been from this unit. Years later, when I managed to look in this hangar for the first time, I noticed boards around the inside walls bearing the names of the different types of aircraft which had been worked on in those particular places — including Spitfire, Mustang and Typhoon.

No.287 Sqdn was equipped with Oxford IIs, Martinet Is, Beaufighter Is, VIs and Xs, Tempest Vs and Spitfire Ixs, and they moved from Gatwick to Redhill on 20th January 1945. They provided detachments at numerous airfields in Southern England for target-towing and gun-laying exercises until the end of the war in Europe and, although I recall seeing the odd Oxford flying around, I do not recall seeing any of the other types with which they were equipped. No.287 Sqdn left for Hornchurch on 3rd May 1945.

Following the departure of the last two squadrons, No.1 Aircraft Delivery Flight moved in but departed for Andrews Field on 4th June 1945 with their Ansons, Dominies and Proctors, where they disbanded on 9th October 1945.

It was probably during early 1945 that I remember seeing a Spitfire IX with its undercarriage down on the final approach to land at Redhill Aerodrome. In the still air of a spring evening, probably during April and with the sun getting low on the horizon, I was cycling along the lane at the western end of the east-west runway with my father. We had heard of a farm selling fresh eggs in the area and were off to investigate when the Spitfire appeared from behind the trees with its Merlin spluttering and banging — as they did when throttled back — to come in to a perfect landing; it was a sight and sound to savour.

At some time, probably just before the end of the war, I was surprised to see parked on the overshoot at the eastern end of the east-west runway a Martin B-26 Marauder of the USAAF 9th AF; it was painted olive drab and had, I believe, a yellow marking on the fin. It had likely force-landed after a raid but, probably due to the imminent ending of the war in Europe, it was decreed that it wouldn't be repaired to enable it to be flown out, and was later broken up on the spot. Try as I may, however, I have not been able to establish its identity or the reason for it landing at Redhill.

The entry for 14-15th June 1945 in the ORB for No.36 MU RAF Station Charlwood (which had originally been formed in a quarry at Snodland in Kent on 8/7/40), recorded that there were sub-sites at Snodland and Redhill but that the latter sub-site had already been inspected on 25/5/45 (Ref: Air 29/999). From that time Redhill ceased to be an airfield and became the site for the storage of many tons of bombs and small arms ammunition, which was stacked in square heaps all along the east-west runway. Geoffrey Tait and Paul Smith, in their delightful little book *Redhill at War – The Lighter Side,* note that:

"For the first time as an RAF Station it was no longer possible to keep the aerodrome clean and tidy, with the result that it became a wilderness, providing a haven for pests of various sizes, necessitating the use of violence as shooting parties stalked the vermin. It was not until December 1946 that the last of the stores were removed from the aerodrome, prior to it being returned to its owners in January 1947."

In fact, No.36 MU did not disband until 31st January 1947, although a small party was left behind to do the final tidying up. However, while this

Unit remained at Redhill, I continued to make many fruitless journeys there in the certain hope that one day the aerodrome would be restored to its former owners, British Air Transport Ltd. Always the eternal optimist, even in those days!

I made one of my frequent Saturday morning visits to Redhill Aerodrome in late 1945, as was my wont, probably more in hope than in anger as the main east-west runway was still covered in heaps of ordnance along its full length! However, on this occasion it turned out that I must have been even more optimistic than usual, as the whole aerodrome was fogbound right down to the deck. I was standing by the emergency exit at the eastern end of the east-west runway on Crabhill Lane, contemplating whether to go round to the main entrance in King's Mill Lane to look at the hangars or go home, when the sound of a large aircraft passing overhead attracted my attention. I could see nothing, though, and as the aerodrome was well and truly closed I decided that it must just have been overflying to another destination and went home.

On the following Monday I was told by one of my fellow students at the Redhill Junior Technical Institute that a Liberator had crashed at Redhill on the previous Saturday: I had been at the wrong end of the runway and had missed all the fun! I promptly cycled over there to find out what it was all about, and discovered to my amazement a Liberator GR Mk.VI, with a broken nose-leg, just off the perimeter track in the south-western corner of the western end of the runway! Looking back along its landing 'furrow' which the broken nose had ploughed across the grass, you could see that it had landed diagonally from the north-east and had somehow managed — miraculously — to slice through the heaps of bombs without hitting any of them! However, what made this find even more interesting was the fact that the aircraft, still painted in RAF Coastal Command camouflage, was wearing full national Czechoslovakian Air Force markings.

When recently I visited the National Archives to find out more about the wartime occupation of RAF Station Redhill by No.36 MU, I was pleased to find that the scribe who kept the ORB had faithfully recorded details of this incident. This enabled me to date the incident accurately and also the identity of the aircraft involved. The entry for 30th October 1945 read: *"Liberator aircraft EV994 crashed on Redhill Airfield. No injuries to crew and stocks undamaged."* (Ref: AIR 29/999). This enabled me to establish that the aircraft was with No.311 (Czech) Sqdn, which by then had transferred to Transport Command and had relocated to Prague on 13th August 1945. The Liberator had probably been returning to Prague when it presumably ran into the bad weather which caused it to crash-land at Redhill. For the record, No.311 Sqdn transferred to Czech control on 15th February 1946 and the individual aircraft record card just has the note 'SOC 7/11/47', so the RAF appeared not to be keeping records of this 'foreign' squadron by this time.

Redhill was then occupied only by a skeleton staff of RAF personnel. It transpired that, although they had heard the noise of an aircraft apparently landing, it had taken them some time to locate it due to the fog, and by that time the crew had departed; so had most of its radios and instruments — the locals had been even quicker in locating it! It also transpired that someone had also (mis)appropriated the bomb aimer's panel; this large laminated piece of Perspex had been pushed back into the fuselage following the collapse of the nose leg and, being very heavy, had obviously been dragged to a safe spot nearby until it could be recovered later. Perspex was at a premium in those days, but for some reason it was not collected by the miscreant and was presumably found and recovered by the RAF. Many years later when I was working at Redhill Aerodrome, I discovered this panel in the old pyrotechnics store at the base of the control tower! I tried to lift it but it was so heavy that I could hardly move it and I realised why it had been left for the RAF to find! Shortly after the incident I saw the dismantled remains of the Liberator on RAF 60 ft Queen Mary transporters heading north through Redhill.

Talking about aeroplanes on lorries reminds me that I saw a newly refurbished, silver-painted Royal Siamese Air Force Spitfire on a Queen Mary travelling eastwards through Redhill town centre one day, presumably *en route* to the London Docks.

The owners of Redhill Aerodrome, British Air Transport Ltd., started operations at Kenley in May 1946 (while they were waiting for Redhill, which was still covered in bombs, to be de-requisitioned), and from there they operated two Auster J/1 Autocrats (G-AHAY and 'HCK) and two Airspeed Consuls (G-AHEH and 'HFS) on passenger and freight charters from Croydon. In October 1946 three more Consuls (G-AIDY, 'IDZ and 'IEA) were purchased; all five were finished in a blue and gold colour scheme, and very smart they looked too. Then in May 1947 they finally received permission to return to Redhill Aerodrome; there they then based their operation and at the same time reopened the Redhill Flying Club (which they also owned and operated) and closed their base at Kenley. The club operated three ex-RAF Hawk Trainer Mk.IIIs (Magisters to us old 'uns!), G-AIYB, 'IYC and 'IYD), which had been civilianised by BAT Ltd. at Redhill (having arrived there earlier by road, it is believed,) and four Auster Autocrats (G-AGVJ, 'HAY, 'HCK and 'JED).

In August 1947 BAT Ltd. purchased a number of ex-RAF Anson 1s in order to operate a twice-daily newspaper service to the Channel Islands and Paris, and the first of these entered service the same month. These were all converted by BAT Ltd. at Redhill and comprised G-AHKH,

'IWW, 'IWX and 'KVW. Two Anson Xs, 'IWV and 'IXU were also acquired and converted. It was also about this time that they leased a hangar to Southern Aircraft (Gatwick) Ltd, and it was in this hangar that I first saw and photographed the famous Miles M.12 Mohawk after it had been refurbished by Southern Aircraft (Gatwick) Ltd, either at Gatwick or Redhill.

The large BAT fleet was then joined by the famous DH Flamingo G-AFYH, flown in from Gatwick on 25th May 1947. This lovely aircraft had been impressed with the Royal Navy as BT312, was named *Merlin 27* by them and had been purchased by BAT from Southern Aircraft (Gatwick) Ltd. after refurbishment at Gatwick. Southern Aircraft had previously acquired it from the Royal Navy at Gatwick 'as is' after its abandonment there following a flight from — I believe — its base at Donibristle: apparently it had developed a snag which they couldn't be bothered to fix!

It was also about that time that BAT had grand plans for rebuilding about four of the old Flamingos which had once served BOAC in the Middle East. They had been returned to the UK by sea and then dumped at Croydon round the back of the Bourjois scent factory; the fuselages of G-AFYF, 'FYJ, 'FYK and 'FYL were brought down from Croydon by road and could be seen for a while in the blister hangar off the far eastern end of the aerodrome, where Rex Nicholls took the photographs shown. They were later moved into Tiltman Langley Laboratories' hangar, where work commenced on stripping them down preparatory to carrying out a complete refurbishment and modernisation programme. Unfortunately, however, plans changed, probably due to the prohibitive cost of the project and the lack of guaranteed contracts for their utilisation, and the work was abandoned; the fuselages that had been stripped were later moved into what later became F.G. Miles Ltd's hangar, where they lingered for a while before disappearing.

All these twins made a pleasant sight at Redhill and Croydon, from where they regularly flew on charters and the newspaper runs, until in 1949 the services were run down and the newspaper contract was passed to Transair Ltd of Croydon. BAT sold off the aircraft, apart from the Flamingo which they put into storage, and then concentrated its activities on running the aerodrome, the flying club and No.15 Reserve Flying School, which was formed at Redhill on 1st April 1948. Soon, the sky was full of 36 RAF Tiger Moths and the odd Anson and Oxford, all silver-painted with yellow bands, and the Redhill Flying Club aircraft, all — with the possible exception of the Ansons and Oxfords — without radio: great fun for the Air Traffic Controller. Three other 'Maggies', P6382, L8288 and L5921, were kept in store in one of the hangars, presumably against attrition or possible expansion of the club, and although they were later registered G-AJRS, 'JRT and 'JRU it was to be many years before they were finally civilianised. P6382 was later reregistered G-AJDR, which caused some considerable confusion amongst spotters for many years thereafter as the remains of the true Maggie G-AJDR were still on Redhill aerodrome at the time! However, this still survives to this day to fly with the Shuttleworth Trust at Old Warden (as P6382, G-AJRS!). A few private owners with Miles and Percival aircraft were also taking up residence and the place was coming to life again with a vengeance and beginning to buzz with activity.

British Air Transport Ltd. also acquired two Miles M.19 Master GT.Mk.IIs: these were DL224 (purchased on 4th December 1946) and EM374 (which was sold to them as scrap on 13th January 1947). Both were roaded in to Redhill and kept in a blister hangar opposite the main hangars, but were both scrapped there later after the ARB had refused to grant them Certificates of Airworthiness. The reason for these purchases is still not clear but it may have been in connection with plans to teach advanced flying to potential pilots.

In 1949, Tiltman Langley Laboratories Ltd. obtained a Ministry contract to modify ETPS Mosquito B.35 RS721 for the forthcoming RAF Display at Farnborough in 1950. Mike Randrup, Napier's test pilot, used to fly down in the Proctor G-AHWV, and was often accompanied in the Mosquito by Brian Buss (a design draughtsman at Tiltman's) as operator of the equipment. Unbeknown to me at the time I was later to work with Brian in the Drawing Office at Tiltman's from about 1952 and we have remained good friends ever since.

One day, while grovelling in the dump on the opposite side of King's Mill road behind the main hangars, I discovered some fragments (including the odd instrument) from the Seagrave Metor G-AAXP, but how they had got there remains a mystery.

Other oddities, seen parked at the northern end of the north-south runway at Redhill after it reopened (and for a considerable time afterwards) were Walrus IIs HD925 & HD929; both had been sold as scrap on 10th March 1947 but were then registered as G-AKJE & G-AKIA on the 8th January 1948. In addition, Sea Otter IIAs JM826 & JM764 were sold on 11th & 10th March 1947 respectively and registered G-AKIC & G-AKID on 8th January 1948 to Ciro's Aviation Ltd. The entrepreneurs Sidney and H.S. Rubin of Ciro's Club in London were behind the purchase, as they had ideas of beating the licensing laws of the land. But they must have been somewhat optimistic: their scheme involved mooring ships to be used as gambling dens outside the three-mile limit off the coastline, and then flying the punters out to them in these ancient amphibians. However the scheme never 'got off the ground'; one of the Sea Otters had the paint stripped off it later, but it is recorded that both were broken up as spares for the Dutch Navy before the remainder of the airframes and engines were eventually taken to the eastern end of the aerodrome and scrapped there by the local gipsies.

However, while they were still parked outside the hangars, I witnessed a Redhill Flying Club Auster (which had been fitted with towing gear to assist the glider schools also based there), coming in low from the north to drop the towline before landing. This was flailing about in its normal fashion and as I watched with interest I noticed the hook get caught in the top wing of one of the Walruses! There was an almighty clanging noise and the Auster seemed to momentarily stop in its tracks until something gave way and it continued on to make a safe landing!

Then, in December 1948, F.G. Miles arrived and took over No.1 hangar with his new company, F.G. Miles Ltd.; they soon began to receive a number of Miles aircraft for C. of A.s and modifications. This was to be the start of an enterprise which moved to Shoreham in the early 1950s and soon expanded into the Miles Group of Companies.

* * * * * * * * * *

However, let us return to April 1945. The War Office de-requisitioned the prewar bungalows and houses on the beach at Pevensey Bay, near Eastbourne. One, a small bungalow, was owned by a cousin of mine, and another of my uncles volunteered to go and officially take it back on his behalf, and invited me to go along with him to help. After we had completed the necessary formalities with the Army Officer in charge of the proceedings, we went to inspect the damage that the Army had inflicted upon it during their five years of occupation and to take an inventory of missing items of furniture etc. While we were busily engaged in the task of making the bungalow habitable again, I was suddenly distracted by a loud noise coming from the eastern side of the bay. On rushing outside to investigate I was surprised to see a stream of B-17 Flying Fortresses and B-24 Liberators heading out to sea at low level. We later discovered, thanks to the late Roger Freeman, that this was the 8th USAAF's very last mission of the war in Europe. The B-17s were *en route* to bomb the Skoda Armament Plant and nearby airfield at Pilsen in Czechoslovakia, and the B-24s were *en route* to attack rail centres at Salzburg, Bad Reichenhall, Hallstein and Traunstein. As we looked up at the wonderful sight of the never-ending stream of aircraft, most in natural metal finish with the morning sun glinting on them, we thought that there must have been at least a thousand, as they seemed to be going across for what seemed like hours. However, and thanks once again to Roger Freeman, I have now found that there were in fact 307 B-17s and 282 B-24s, but this was still a very large number of heavy bombers, and the sight they made was impressive and definitely one which will never be forgotten. The date was 25th April 1945.

I will now note other aviation reminiscences from 1945 to 1949, but these will follow in no particular order!

During June 1945 I went to see the Exhibition of British Aircraft which had been arranged (by the Ministry of Information in conjunction with the Ministry of Aircraft Production) in the heart of London, on a bombed site lent for the occasion by John Lewis and Company in Oxford Street. This event, which was opened by Lord Beaverbrook, has already been described in detail by Mike Stroud in another chapter.

On the 8th May 1946, Victory Day and Victory Week was marked in London by three events; the one I managed to attend was the exhibition of 22 representative aircraft used by the RAF & RNAS during the past six years, held in Green Park from then until 16th June 1946; this has also been described elsewhere by Mike Stroud.

I was also lucky in having an aunt and uncle living in Gosport, and sometime during 1945 I stayed with them for a week's holiday. They lived near to Gosport Aerodrome, where I can recall seeing just one interesting aircraft, a camouflaged Bristol Buckingham transport, on the apron in front of the hangars. Unfortunately, not having binoculars, I could not see its serial but apart from this the only other activity in the vicinity was a Naval Tiger Moth flying around. I found Fleetlands Naval Aircraft Repair Yard almost by accident, as I had set out for Lee-on-Solent on the bus! However, whilst it was not possible to see what was going on in the workshops, I did see some very interesting aircraft parked behind the grey-painted storage sheds that backed onto the road and the tall iron railings by the footpath that marked the boundary of the site. Among these were some Spitfires painted khaki overall with square black markings in place of the roundels, which could have been waiting for a ship bound for Turkey; also a complete Mosquito painted PR blue but with a red tailplane, fin and rudder and USAF markings. While the presence of the Spitfires made some sense (even if their markings didn't at the time), the presence of an American Mosquito completely baffled me then and, for that matter, still does! Firstly how did it get there fully assembled, and was the towing route from Lee-on-Solent (the road from Lee-on-Solent Aerodrome was clearly signposted) really wide enough to have taken a Mosquito without folding wings? Secondly, why was it there at all?

While it is well-known that a large number of PR Mosquitos were transferred to the USAAF in this country during the war, a tantalising and possible solution to this mystery was recently discovered in James Halley's *RAF Serials* books; therein it is recorded that the Mosquito Mk.18 PZ467, which DH had earlier converted from a Mk.VI, "*went to USA 9/4/45 with the US Navy Bu.No. 91106*". I have no idea if this machine was painted in PR colours or not, but the connection between Fleetlands (which had a jetty for lighters to collect and deliver aircraft from carriers in Portsmouth) and the US Navy surely cannot be overlooked? However, I'm still a bit worried by the fact that the aircraft was fully rigged.

Portsmouth Airport, however, was a different matter altogether. If only I had had a pair of binoculars! Between Airspeed's factory and Portsmouth Aviation were a great number of RAF Oxfords: they were all camouflaged and one had full Royal Danish Air Force markings. While the majority were presumably awaiting conversion to Consuls, one (possibly BG175, which was relegated to ground instruction with the maintenance serial 5444M in 7/45) was sold to the Royal Danish Air Force on 20th March 1947. By the fence, also again between Airspeed's and Portsmouth Aviation's factory, was the remains of 'Air Min 27', the Focke Wulf Fw.189A-3 which had been sold to Portsmouth Aviation Ltd as salvage on 12th December 1946; this aircraft must presumably have been acquired by them in connection with the design of their Aerocar, a light twin-boomed and twin-engined aircraft of similar layout.

I recently visited Portsmouth for the first time in many years and approached the city via the road which once ran alongside the eastern edge of the aerodrome and Airspeed's factory. This was the first time I had been there since the famous two Channel Airways Avro 748 fiascos of about 1968, which I happened to witness on the day they both came to grief while landing on the wet grass! Although knowing that the airfield had been covered in houses some time ago, I was still somewhat surprised to find that all traces of the factory had gone. In their place stood a typically modern large car showroom and new, light industrial units: so much for our once glorious aviation heritage!

Soon after the war, I've forgotten when, I met and became good friends with David Freeman and his friend Don Pearman. I have remained good friends with both of these enthusiasts ever since, but in those days we three used to cycle to as many aerodromes in the Home Counties as possible on Sundays. These 'grand Sunday tours' usually encompassed a 150-mile round trip taking in Fairoaks, Wisley, Brooklands, Farnborough and Blackbushe where, on one visit, we saw and managed to photograph Dominican Air Force thimble-nosed Beaufighter X309; this was one of a pair which had been purchased by them (the other was, I believe, 310) and was standing on a dispersal while waiting to be ferried to Dominica by a crew from Airwork Ltd., the occupiers of the hangars on the airfield side of the main road.

Sometimes we would head north for Woodley, where there wasn't much to be seen at weekends apart from the RFS Tiger Moths orbiting. Then it was back on to the A40 to White Waltham, where once we discovered the Anson G-AHUD 'guarding' the entrance to six or seven Robin hangars which had once been the Air Transport Auxiliary's Technical School. These hangars were situated in a line alongside a specially constructed road on the opposite side of the road to the large wooden hut that had once been the HQ of the ATA Technical School and which is now home to the West London Aero Club. It is of interest to note that the Robin hangars, long since gone, contained dismantled Fairchild Argus aircraft, which had once been used as taxis by the ATA.

Then it would be off to London Airport (Heathrow), Northolt and Langley. At the latter we didn't see many Hawker aeroplanes, although many of Don Bennett's BSAAC Tudors were in evidence. On the way to Airwork's hangar, which was at the foot of the railway embankment and where we saw a Beechcraft Traveller being worked on, we passed an open shed, literally on the roadside, which contained a number of dismantled Dagling-type gliders. Then it was back to London Airport, followed by Hanworth Park — where there was not much to be seen at weekends as General Aircraft were closed and Field Aircraft Services in the other hangar very rarely seemed to work at weekends either — and then home! By this time we were pretty filthy, starving hungry and in need of a bath, but we were happy and contented after another good day's spotting. Well, we were young and fit in those days and there wasn't the traffic about!

It was about early 1947 that I acquired my first drop-handlebar racing cycle and after that there was no stopping me! Croydon, Gatwick and Redhill suddenly became my oyster and what follows is but a brief resumé of some of the rarer specimens which were seen during the course of these excursions. I also found Horne ALG, between Redhill Aerodrome and Gatwick Airport, where just one blister hangar remained, the Spitfires having long departed, never to return . . .

One Sunday afternoon in 1945, after the end of the war in Europe, I made one of my irregular cycle rides to Croydon Airport. Here I was pleasantly surprised to find a Boeing B-17 fuselage, in natural metal finish, residing on a 60 ft Queen Mary trailer alongside the old Rollason hangar to the north of the aerodrome on the Purley Way. Nearby were parked three USAAF P-51D Mustangs, also in natural metal finish; two were named *Charlot's Chariot* and *Dayton's Demon* respectively, but the third was unnamed. An American 'erk' was preparing them for flight and I distinctly recall that, as he completed the fastening of the last panel, he carelessly threw away what appeared to me to be a brand-new screwdriver into a heap of bomb damage rubble by the side of the road. If only I could have climbed over to retrieve it, as it seemed such a waste, but the Yanks were like that — easy come, easy go! All too soon the three Mustangs taxied out to the north-west corner in preparation for take-off up the hill towards the south-east end of the Purley Way. I cycled back to get a better view as they came over the road and, as they roared across the grass towards me — but almost before they became airborne — I recall that they retracted their undercarts and then departed at high speed. I often wonder what they were doing at Croydon or, for that matter, where they had come from and what became of them.

On another Sunday in August 1945, I saw 'Air Min.19', the massive Junkers Ju.352D which had landed at Croydon on 10th August 1945, having gone unserviceable whilst *en route* from Farnborough to Fassburg. It left Croydon on 23rd August to return to Farnborough. Other weekend visits to Croydon produced such rarities as a French Air Force Martin Maryland in natural metal finish and a similarly-finished Liore et Olivier Leo 45. Caudrons and numerous Ju.52/3Ms of the French Air Force and Air France, as well as many interesting C-47s from various air forces and airlines, including Czechoslovakia, Sweden and Russia, were also to be seen in those days, although the latter one may have been an Li-2.

BOAC were still occupying the large hangar (later to be used by Rollasons) on the south side by the Purley Way and this gave good opportunities for spotting. On one visit in the spring of 1945, I was pleased to find the Mosquito FB Mk.VI G-AGGC and two Lockheed Hudson Mk.IIIs, G-AGDC and 'GDK, both of which were returned to the RAF in August 1945 and given serials VJ416 and VJ421 respectively; these were all parked on the grass alongside the Purley Way, with Lancastrians and Yorks both inside and outside the hangar.

Then I found Hamsey Green on the North Downs, once Chas E. Gardner's private airfield in prewar days. By the time I found it, it was deserted save for the Blackburn Bluebird G-AATE, nominally owned by C. & L. Aircraft Ltd. This was in the locked hangar, but could be seen with its tail propped up on a trestle through the high windows by standing on a collection of old boxes etc. It was said that this had come from Heston for a C. of A. in 1938, but it doesn't reconcile with reports of a fuselage of an aeroplane with the registration G-ADZD (this was a Miles Hawk Trainer II and almost certainly would not have been at Hamsey Green) hanging in the rafters in 1942/43. The fact that two ATC Squadrons had used the field during the war means that surely they would have used the hangar for their gliders (No.143 Gliding School formed in 1/43 at Hamsey Green and No.162 Gliding School by 11/43).

Outside, lying beside an old brick hut, were a number of wings from various light aircraft of the Moth variety with only the 'G-A' or 'G-E' part of their registrations showing! I also found, amongst some papers blowing about, the genuine original American Certificate of Airworthiness document for a Piper Cub, which I still possess to this day although, like so many other bits and pieces, I cannot lay my hands on it at the moment!

Southern Aircraft (Gatwick) Ltd. had their premises near Lowfield Heath, and this could easily be seen from the road which ran from the A23 London-Brighton road to the main entrance by the old Southern

Railway Airport Station. Having finished their wartime work as a CRO, they were then busily engaged in 'civilianising' ex-RAF Proctors, Dominies and 'Maggies', but what intrigued us was their dump of scrapped aircraft round the back of the hangars between the road and the buildings. This contained the last mortal remains of many wondrous relics, including Porterfield 35/70 G-AEOK (less wings), Monocoupe G-AADG, a naked Puss Moth fuselage frame which had a label tied to it purporting it to have been 'AX869' (which would have made it G-ABRR previously), Simmonds Spartan G-ABXO and the fuselages of Moth G-AFWX and Stinson SR.9D Reliant W7984; the Reliant had once been G-AEVY, but by then was just a bare frame with the fin still attached, although complete with RAF fin stripes (of the post-January 1942 type) on the camouflaged background still visible. This is recorded as having been SOC as Cat.E1 11/9/44, probably while it was at Southern's for repair. There were also a lot of wings from light aircraft scattered around, but most of these were covered by the long grass and had obviously been there a long time, probably relics from Hamsey Green before the war.

Then on one occasion NP671, one of the very rare General Aircraft GAL.55 Training Glider prototypes, suddenly appeared fully assembled by the hangars, although I have yet to find out how and why they acquired it — it was scrapped later.

Although I do not intend to list 'telephone numbers' in this chapter, Southern's handled a considerable number of ex-RAF aircraft after the war which haven't been covered elsewhere before to the best of my knowledge so, as this is a 'nostalgia trip', I hope that you won't mind me listing these as they were presented to me by Don Wylds, an ex-employee of the firm:

DH Dragon Rapides: G-AJTU (sold abroad), 'KOM, 'KON (sold abroad) and 'KOO (the latter was C. of A.'d and then crated by R.J. Parks for shipping to South America).

Percival Proctors: G-AJGO, 'JTS, 'JTT (damaged, no engine, not C. of A.'d and scrapped in 1949), 'KEX (not C.of A.'d but sold 'as is' in November 1949 and roaded out).

Avro Anson Mk.I: G-AKEW and 'KUD (although 'KUD was registered on 31/3/48 it was returned to the RAF with its previous serial VM373 in April 1949).

Miles Magisters: G-AIZJ (not C. of A.'d and scrapped in 1949), 'IZK (modified for Skywriting for Aero Publicity Ltd. in May 1948), 'IZL (sold to Midland Flying Club), 'JGK, 'JGL, 'JGM, 'JGN (not C. of A.'d); all, with the exception of 'JGM, were sold to R.A. Short 'as is' in January 1949 and roaded out).

Miles M.19 Master GT.Mk.II: Southern's bought two of these aircraft from the RAF in the hope of getting them airworthy. Although they were registered G-AIZM and 'IZN, the ARB had other ideas! For the record, DM442 was sold to Southern Aircraft (Gatwick) Ltd., Gatwick on 27/11/46 and registered 'IZN to them on 30/12/46, but the registration was not taken up and the aircraft was broken up for spares at Gatwick in 1949. EM300 was sold to Southern Aircraft (Gatwick) Ltd., Gatwick on 4/12/46 and registered 'IZM to them on 30/12/46. An application for C. of A. No.9074 was cancelled, the registration was not taken up and it was broken up for spares at Gatwick in 1949. Apparently, applications for C. of A.s were made for both 'IZM and 'IZN by the company on 2/1/47, but these were cancelled on 9/7/47. Southern Aircraft (Gatwick) Ltd. then placed an advertisement in *The Aeroplane* for 7/2/47 as follows: *'Two Miles Master IIs without C. of A. for £400 each'*, and later in *The Light Plane* for July 1947 as follows: *Miles Master Mk.II Trainers, 2-seaters with dual and blind flying equipment. Without C. of A.*

However, it has since been discovered that the ARB would not have issued C. of A.s for any mark of Miles Master anyway due, apparently, to their record of structural failures in their early service life. The engines and other parts from both aircraft were sold to Sweden later as spares for the Swedish Miles M.25 Martinets.

DH Dragonfly: G-AIYJ (ex-SU-ABW), registered 5/12/46. It was noted as 'dismantled undergoing C. of A.', but was WFU on 17/2/48.

Auster Mk.V: G-AJHV (not C. of A.'d, sold 'as is' in January 1950 and roaded out).

Cierva C.30A Autogiro: G-ACWO (not C. of A.'d and noted as 'sold to Sweden as spares', but also recorded elsewhere as sold to Belgium as spares in 1949).

DH Puss Moth: G-ABKZ fuselage less engine. However, there is some doubt as to whether G-ABKZ was at Gatwick and therefore, were the fuselages of G-ABKZ and G-ABRR swapped at some time (see above)?

Avro 626 Tutor: G-AHRZ (C. of A.'d but sold as a 'children's plaything' to a local farm in 1947.

DH Tiger Moth: N6949, bare fuselage only.

GAL.55: NP671 (see previous page above).

Vultee Sentinel: G-AKYF (received for C. of A. in July 1949 — see comments under Fairoaks).

Miles Gemini: G-AIWS appeared — and then disappeared — during 1949 on its return from crew-ferrying from Israel.

Airspeed Consul: Registration not recorded. This machine would arrive during the afternoon, have a dismantled Cheetah engine stowed aboard and leave during the night!

Miles Mohawk: G-AEKW. This was seen in a hangar at Redhill (and photographed by the author and others), fully refurbished and painted in a lovely maroon & white colour scheme; this was probably the hangar which Southern's had rented for a short time in 1947.

Airwork General Trading Ltd., Gatwick, who occupied the large hangars at the southern end by the main gate, were meanwhile very busy overhauling Seafires and Spitfires, the latter being prepared for foreign air forces, and I recall some Spitfires with Syrian Air Force markings about this time.

Airwork had also previously converted a batch of Coastal Command Liberators into transports for the RAF. These were still parked alongside the Southern Railway line between the Airport and the old Racecourse Railway Stations (the latter is now the main Gatwick railway station and the original Airport Station has now long gone, but how I abhor the modern idiom 'train stations'!). There was a story going about at the time which had it that these large aircraft could take off from Gatwick only when the airfield was frozen. otherwise the excessive drag from this notoriously soggy ground (it was really bad in those days) would have precluded them from leaving *terra firma* before reaching the boundary hedge! However, having had them prepared ready for delivery, the weather inevitably changed for the worse and the airfield became boggy so they couldn't leave; then when the airfield next froze, the aircraft naturally went u/s and vice versa! This state of affairs apparently persisted until in the end the requirement passed and they were all broken up on site! I recall seeing a labourer standing on the wing of one of them with a crowbar, with which he was punching a neat chordwise row of holes which, when joined together (as per *'tear along the dotted line'*), caused the wing to drop off, on one occasion to the detriment of a worker who unfortunately happened to be standing underneath a wing one day when it fell off.

Then, on another occasion, sometime between 16th and 25th February 1946, we were surprised to see the large Savoia Marchetti SM.82 Marsupiale VN163. We discovered much later (courtesy of Phil Butler and his *War Prizes*), that this was its first 'official' flight with the RAF from Celle to Gatwick and so we were lucky to have seen it, because it returned to Celle on the latter date. I also recall seeing VN721, the Junkers Ju.52/3M which had suffered a minor accident there whilst *en route* from Germany to No.6 MU Brize Norton on 24th January 1946.

By 1946 I had left the Redhill Technical Institute and was working as the Personal Assistant to the Chief Engineer of the East Surrey Gas Company at Redhill. This was while I was waiting to be called up for National Service and, in order to get a general — if somewhat 'heavy' — engineering grounding I often accompanied him on his inspection of other gas works in the locality. On one such visit, to the Horley gas works, he decided that as it was about 4 pm we should stop for tea, and this seemed an even better idea when he suggested that we should partake of this delightfully English afternoon pastime at the 'Beehive' at Gatwick Airport, no less! Whilst enjoying the sunshine and welcome afternoon tea break on the balcony of this historic building as a 16-year-old I thought that that was the definitely the life, and while drinking my tea I had the opportunity to witness from that lofty perch a camouflaged French civil-registered Halifax C.Mk.8 starting up just below. This was a truly memorable sight, especially when it came to the ground crew trying to remove the large wooden chocks preparatory to it taxying out for take-off! Unbeknown to all concerned, the pilot had run up the engines during his pre-take-off checks and the chocks had become well and truly stuck between the tyre and the never totally dry Gatwick ground! However, the French captain had the solution: waving the ground crew away he opened the throttles wide and we watched in amazement as the engines reached full power and the chocks slowly began to crumble into matchwood! Problem solved — and away he went!

On one of my many visits to Gatwick I was standing by the main gate trying to persuade a sour-faced Ministry of Civil Aviation policeman into letting us in to look round. A Dakota flew quite low overhead in the general direction of the old Horne ALG, and, suspecting a smuggling operation, the airfield MCA constabulary were galvanised into action; a bunch of them immediately leapt into a Jeep, setting off at high speed in the general direction of the aforementioned airfield. However, I never discovered if the Dakota did actually land there or not in an attempt to beat the Customs & Excise man with its undoubted cargo of contraband!

We were always pleased to see the two DH.86Bs G-ADUH & 'DVJ) of Bond Air Services Ltd at Gatwick in their attractive silver and green finish, and from March 1947 the Halifax C.Mk.8 G-AIOI was added to the fleet. I still marvel at the thought of operating these large aircraft out of Gatwick's relatively small grass (and often boggy) airfield. It is of interest to note that this company name has since been reactivated at Exeter for their helicopter operations and at Henstridge for the Dorset Air Ambulance service.

Then there was the never-to-be-forgotten Miles Aircraft 'Open Day' at Woodley on 20th July 1947. David Freeman, Don Pearman and myself set off early on our cycles, having been made aware of it by the announcement in *The Aeroplane Spotter* and determined not to miss anything. Readers knowing my interest in Miles Aircraft will understand my waxing lyrical about this, because it truly was a remarkable day and one which undoubtedly sparked off my lifetime's enthusiasm for Miles Aircraft and everything that they achieved, both during my childhood and right up to the final end in 1978. To take it all in was the problem though, as there was so much to see: the whole factory was open and tours 'between the white lines' had been laid on. We were able to inspect the assembly lines with the rows of Geminis and Aerovans, and also the Experimental Shop where the prototype Merchantman was nearing completion: and then there was the flying display. This was 'something else': never had a firm put up so many different types before, it really was a remarkable spectacle.

One display in particular, that of the Miles M.39B Libellula, stays in my memory, as with its tandem wing layout it seemed strange at first, but as it flew past it showed off just a little of the genius of George Miles, its designer. It was nearly all too much and eventually, when we could finally tear ourselves away from so many different aeroplanes, we had to face the long cycle ride home — but it had been well worth it! However, to mention anything about it here would develop into a book on Miles Aircraft (thinks — that's what I *have* done!).

In August 1947 I heard a rumour that there was an aeroplane in a yard of a house at Nutfield Marsh near Merstham. So off I went in search and, after peering through many holes in people's fences I finally discovered it in the grounds of the Nutfield Marsh Country Club. What a sorry sight met my eyes as I saw, by the side of a barn just inside the courtyard, Simmonds Spartan G-AAGY; this had once been used by F.G. Miles in Bristol and Wales for joyriding while he was test-flying for Parnall Aircraft in May and June 1932, but was now just a derelict heap with the folded wings warped beyond any hope of restoration and the fabric hanging in tatters.

It was also sometime during 1947 that we decided to cycle to Shoreham Airport for the first time. This entailed a round trip of some 66 miles and, with just one aerodrome to visit, it had to be given some thought! However, it was considered to be well worth the effort, and it was just as well that we did, as this was also to be the start of a lifelong friendship with Fred Lynn. He was walking along the perimeter road by the railway and saw us sitting on the embankment alongside the river, which we felt was an ideal spot for watching the aeroplanes come and go. Fred came over to us and made himself known to us; as it turned out he was a kindred spirit, being very interested in the activities at Shoreham and the other local airfields such as Ford and Tangmere. Fred had also managed to obtain (somewhat illegally, by crawling under the perimeter fence in the long grass) photographs of some of the German aircraft stopping over at Ford *en route* to Farnborough after the war, and he regaled us with stories of other interesting types which he had also seen there. We then debated whether we should in fact also cycle over to Ford while we were on the south coast, but had regretfully to decide against it as it would have entailed a considerable extra mileage and we had still to get home after a hard day's spotting! Shoreham was still without a proper hangar as the original one had been stripped of all its covering in a bombing raid early in the war, but the RAF had constructed a blister hangar within it and in this were often parked broken aircraft recovered from nearby crashes.

Airspeed Horsa gliders abandoned at Thruxton postwar.
Photo: Peter Amos.

J/1 Autocrat G-AHCL is pictured with a young Peter Amos at Elstree
after hs first flight. Photo: via Peter Amos.

Chrislea Super Ace G-AKUW in front of 'The Beehive' at Gatwick sometime in the late forties. Photo: Peter Amos.

Stinson Sentinel G-AKYF was at Fair Oaks postwar. Photo: Peter Amos.

Simmonds Spartan G-AAGY, seen here at Woodley postwar, was scrapped at Redhill in August 1947. Photo: Peter Amos.

Gloster Gladiatior L8032 (later G-AMRK) seen at Eastleigh in the late forties. Photo: Peter Amos.

Vultee Valiant NX54084 arrived at Croydon in August 1949 at the end of an interrupted round-the-world flight with pilot Richarda Morrow-Tait and navigator Michael Townsend. Photo: Peter Amos.

Planet Satellite G-ALOI was at Farnborough in 1948. Photo: Peter Amos.

The remains of Blackburn Bluebird G-AAOG was on the dump at Gatwick with Southern Aircraft Ltd. postwar. Photo: Peter Amos.

Avro Prefect G-AHRZ at Gatwick in the late forties. Photo: Peter Amos.

Bücker Bestmann G-AKAX was seen at Denham in the late forties.
Photo: Peter Amos.

This mysterious wartime artwork on a hangar door at Redhill survived
until about 1954. Photo: Peter Amos.

The Brookside Flying Group was a non-profit making group at Shoreham at that time, as recalled in 'Benjy' Benjamin's chapter in this book. Many years later I was to meet 'Benjy', another Miles Aircraft enthusiast, and we became good friends. 'Benjy' later went on to become a very active member of The Tiger Club at Redhill, and published a couple of books on its history *(a few still available from Cirrus Associates! — Ed.)*

Denham aerodrome was at the extreme end of our range for a Sunday's cycling, and I recall that we only visited it on one occasion, probably during August 1948: I should have kept notes! But the visit was well worthwhile as we saw G-AKAX, the Bücker Bü.181C-3 Bestmann, parked on the grass by a blister hangar. However, Fairoaks was another matter and we often called in there on our Sunday outings. On one visit I was allowed to peep through the crack between the closed and locked, hangar doors to see Stinson L-5 Sentinel LG552 in RAF camouflage. This surprised me, as I didn't think that the RAF had ever used them in Europe: in fact I soon discovered that they hadn't! This specimen had apparently been 'acquired' from the US Army (probably when nobody was looking) by an RAF officer on the Continent near the end of the war; it was then flown to his local airfield near his home in Cobham and we were told that the serial number was in fact his home telephone number! This was later found not to be the case as it had apparently previously worn the US Army serial 42-98552; however, I suppose that his initials may well have been 'LG'! It was later registered G-AKYF. There was the famous Tiger Moth, *The Old Hag of 1935,* still in use with the reserve school, also the two red and silver Tigers (G-AIIZ & 'IJA) of The London Transport (Central Buses) Sports Association Flying Club, which had opened on 20th July 1947, operating from a blister hangar near the road.

On another occasion we stopped to have a look at Wisley in the ever-optimistic hope of seeing something, although we knew that Vickers rarely seemed to fly at weekends in those days. However, to our surprise there was a RAF Harvard lying on its belly in the middle of the grass runway! While we were observing this novelty another Harvard appeared overhead which, to our utter astonishment, had a propeller strapped to its port side just below the cockpit! While this was in the circuit some Vickers ground staff moved a gantry out to the stricken aircraft, jacked it up, lowered the undercarriage and wheeled it off the runway so that the second one could land! The second Harvard then landed and a quick propeller swap was carried out. There couldn't have been much damage however — although we never found the reason for its predicament in the first place — as it then took off and departed with its mate! I don't doubt that this highly illegal episode was promptly hushed up back at base before work started the next day!

Then one Sunday someone kindly left the back door of the flight shed open and to our great surprise we saw the Me.163B VF241 inside. It was fully painted in RAF camouflage and markings, but the reason for its presence at Wisley remained a mystery for many years. The problem was solved much later when Capt. Eric Brown wrote of his experiences flying the actual aircraft; it was normally based at Farnborough but the grass runway at Wisley was deemed more suitable for its 'glider'-like operations. For the record, EN498, the Spitfire Mk.IX, which normally towed it to altitude before casting off, had been modified with glider-towing equipment by Miles Aircraft Ltd. at Woodley.

On another weekend, unofficial RAF visitors to Wisley included an Anson C.19, whose pilot obviously lived nearby! While looking at a pile of abandoned fabric-covered wings on another occasion, we found a camouflaged one with 'G-A' on it, which presumably could only have come from one of the old BOAC Warwicks. However we soon gave up calling on Brooklands on a Sunday because never once did we see an aeroplane there!

A fortuitous visit to Croydon on 24th March 1948 enabled me to see and photograph the two Miles M.57 Aerovan Mk.4s before they departed to their new owners, the Iraqi Aeroplane Society, Baghdad. Their first Aerovan, YI-ABV, had arrived from Broxbourne, where Harry Smith recalled (in his book *One Foot on the Ground)* that this and their second, YI-ABW, were first loaded with new spare Cirrus engines, a compressor, spares and 'other bric-a-brac'. The pilot of one of the two Aerovans was said to have been Freddie Bosworth, manager of the Iraq Aeroplane Society, later to found Gulf Aviation Co. in Bahrain, and other ferry pilots for Herts & Essex at the time were Peter Ayles, Dr. H. da Costa and Victor Ercolani; both aircraft departed from Croydon later that day.

Later that year there was an International Rally at Gatwick, well reported in the aviation press at the time. Then on 10th July came the never to be forgotten *Daily Express* Air Pageant at Gatwick, again well reported, but I would just like to mention a couple of memorable items. Mr. B.I. 'Benny' Lynch OBE, a Martin-Baker employee, carried out the first live public demonstration of a Martin-Baker seat ejection from a specially converted two-seat Gloster Meteor; this was quite a novel item for an air display, even in those heady days, and one which would doubtless be frowned upon in today's 'nanny' state. I cannot resist the temptation to reproduce an extract from *The Aeroplane* for 16th July 1948:

"Then came the next thrill, though, in point of fact, it represents a great feat of engineering and to many fighter pilots one which must seem as much as a morale-raiser as the introduction of the Irvin parachute. This was the first public demonstration of the Martin-Baker Ejector Seat. To make the display more tantalizing the two-seat Meteor

disappeared into cloud just as Mr. Lynch was timed to pull the blind over his face. We heard the bang as the ejecting cartridges fired and then there was a pause. Next came a shout as the seat and its parachute came through the clouds. It was soon vacated by Mr. Lynch who dropped some way before his own chute opened. While both parachutes were in the air a pair of Sea Hornets arrived for the next item. They not only rolled in formation but did it with one airscrew feathered . . . ."

And so it went on, more and more daring feats, including a landing by three Horsa gliders and then a demonstration of the Fulton Roadable Aircraft, a novel, if somewhat impracticable, idea which never caught on — even though F.G. Miles produced a scheme for such an aircraft probably even earlier than the Fulton; what a day!

The next day, 11th July, Redhill held a 'Tea Patrol', their first since the war, but the weather was awful with a cloud base down to 400 ft! *The Aeroplane* reported on the event thus:

"Even so, some visitors 'pressed on regardless' and got through. The LPTB busmen arrived with a brand-new Tiger, built from Queen Bee spares; the Chrislea Super Ace and the Newbury Eon arrived earlier; two Fairey Juniors buzzed around like dodgem cars at a fun fair. It was at a later one of these popular 'patrols' that G-AKLG, a civil registered Percival Prentice, which was painted yellow with black registration, gave a demonstration before departing to its home base at Luton.

Then there were the famous 'Dawn Patrols' and 'Tea Patrols' at Redhill, hosted by the Redhill Flying Club. These were really wonderful events and attracted many different light aircraft from all over the country, all hoping to get in without having their registration letters being 'taken' in order to get a free breakfast or tea! This was not an easy task, though, as the local defenders included a number of private owners with good spotters on board! I am afraid that I could go on and on (and probably have — sorry!) about Redhill, so I'll have to try to curb my enthusiasm for the place.

To my eternal regret I could not attend the second and last *Daily Express* Air Pageant at Gatwick, held there on 23rd July 1949, as I was by then helping my King to defend his country. The Commanding Officer of the REME camp at Sutton Veny, near Warminster, Wilts, where I was stationed, decided that he was going to hold a 'Sports Weekend' over that same weekend and, try as I might, I just could not get out of it and, being the 'sportsman that I ain't' — apart from a *penchant* for long-distance high-speed cycling — I was not best pleased. However, I had to make the most of it and so I entered for the cycle race around the square — what a let-down from Gatwick! I had my bike sent down by train and came in a creditable second, and had to be content with that, but of course all I could think about was what I was missing at Gatwick. This major event was duly reported on at some length in *The Aeroplane* for 29th July and I have to just reproduce an extract here as the missing of it still rankles!:

"Thanks to the Daily Express quite a large slice of the British Public were able to show last Saturday that even if they do not want an Air Force, they do want to see flying. The organizers tell us that some 90,000 people travelled and sweated miles, 40,000 of them by train, in the broiling weather on July 23, to Gatwick".

They may have enjoyed it, but I wasn't one of them!

Now we come to the great Cycle Tours of July 1948. David Freeman and I joined the Youth Hostels Association early that year so that we could obtain cheap overnight accommodation while we cycled around the countryside in search of aerodromes and aeroplanes. We planned our routes very carefully to take in as many aerodromes as possible which were also within striking distance of a Youth Hostel. Some Youth Hostels provided evening meals, and we chose these in preference to the others as we were travelling light and did not wish to have to cook a meal when we arrived after a long hard day's cycling and sightseeing. The routes, of which there were three, were also carefully planned so that each one cunningly crossed at our homes at the end of a few days in order that we could get a good night's sleep in a decent bed and also get a change of clothing! We took only a minimal amount of gear, but this included my handwritten copy of the British Civil Register so that we could check and enter the types seen in our travels. We then wrote to the managers of all aerodromes we intended to visit and were pleasantly surprised at the mostly friendly replies we duly received.

Tour No.1 — 291 miles: Monday 12th July 1948. First stop Tangmere, where there was little to see, similar to Thorney Island, which couldn't be seen easily from the road anyway. That night we stayed at Soberton in an old barrack hut in what had once been a Royal Navy camp during the war. This was to be our first taste of what we termed 'service' life, as part of the exercise was also to prepare us for the rigours of National Service, which was to follow soon after I achieved my 18th birthday in August.

Our next day took in Portsmouth, Gosport and Lee-on-Solent, but between Fleetlands Royal Naval Aircraft Repair Yard and Lee-on-Solent airfield, we passed several road signs proclaiming that this was still an 'Aircraft Towing Route'. Aircraft which had been flown off aircraft carriers to Lee-on-Solent before they returned to Portsmouth then had their wings folded preparatory to being towed along this road to Fleetlands for overhaul. Before we arrived at Lee-on-Solent however, we stumbled across a Royal Naval Aircraft Dump by the roadside! This contained a number of interesting naval aircraft in various stages of decomposition, including a prototype Firefly (which could possibly have been either the F.Mk.I Z1838 or the NF.Mk.II Z1875, both of which were 'awaiting scrapping at the beginning of 1945' — but where?). There was also an Avenger as well as many other unrecognisable bits and pieces in the dump, which was guarded by the inevitable unfriendly-looking Ministry policeman.

That night we stayed at Burley in the New Forest, and the next day we spent a very pleasant one at Hamble, but if only we had known about it, Hamble had held an Open Day on the 3rd July. Nevertheless, amongst the multitude of No.14 Reserve Flying School's and Air Service Training Ltd.'s Tiger Moths and Oxfords were a few Royal Navy Ansons painted yellow overall with large radomes under their noses. The Bristol Beaufort IIA transport conversion, ML672, which was still in Coastal Command colours and which had been used only by Armstrong Siddeley and, latterly, by AST, was still at Hamble where it was SOC on 26th December 1946. The Miles M.19 Master GT.Mk.II, EM323, sold to AST on 16th December 1946, either as a possible advanced trainer or for ground instruction, was also outside the ground instruction hangar in the long grass, where it languished for many years before being broken up. We were then shown around the ground instruction hangar and this contained many ex-RAF aircraft, including (from memory) Tiger Moths, Austers and Proctors all with fictitious registrations, e.g. G-ARBO, G-ERTY, G-RETA etc, which were being used for ground instruction by the engineering students.

We were also shown around Eastleigh, and were pleased to see in the Hampshire Flying Club hangar the now-famous Gladiator (later G-AMRK) which I had seen previously in Green Park, London in May 1946, together with another one in pieces and the Supermarine S.6B hanging in the roof. As we were making our way out, a very nice MCA policeman suggested that if we would like to have a look inside a BEAC 'Pionair' (Dakota) which was on the tarmac awaiting its next service, he would keep a watch for the returning crew; this was a surprise and way outside his jurisdiction, but who were we to argue?

There followed a short journey to Winchester, where we stayed at the mill on the river at the entrance to the city, near the statue of King Alfred. More memories! On asking the warden where the washing facilities were, he took us a down a flight of steps to a quay below the building by the river. Here he showed us a row of shining buckets on the wall with lengths of rope attached — you can guess the rest — but boy, was it cold!

Then we made our way home, looking in on Chilbolton (where nothing was to be seen) and then on to Thruxton, where the sight that met our eyes as we cycled up the road leading to the main entrance and the control tower literally took our breath away! In a field behind the tower were about 50 Horsa gliders: their job done, they had been abandoned by the RAF and were to be seen in various stages of decay. Needless to say we just had to wander through this wonderful collection and actually sit at their controls and try to imagine what it must have been like to fly them. However, by then the ply of the wooden control wheels had separated due to the weather to which they had been exposed over the previous three years getting through their broken Perspex canopies. We didn't know it at the time, or we would have undoubtedly been round there like a shot, but an aerial photograph of Thruxton, discovered much later, shows not only the site of the abandoned Horsa gliders at the western end of the airfield but also two other sites of about 50 Horsas each, just off the perimeter track at the eastern end of the airfield. On reflection, I now find this most surprising as we had cycled around the southern part of the peri-track to see a camouflaged ex-RAF Dominie in a blister hangar which had the registration letters G-ALAX (previously RL948 and only registered on 27/5/48) crudely painted on the fuselage sides. The one Bellman hangar contained a goodly collection of newly civilianised ex-RAF light aircraft and a few Miles types, and the nearby sheds also contained many parts of 'Maggies'.

Then on to Blackbushe, where we relaxed for a while in a grass-lined ditch by the side of the A30; from here we could watch the comings and goings on the main runway which ran almost parallel with the road. It was on one of the stops that we heard over the Tannoy that 'Dove George Able Item Willy Fox' (if I have remembered the old phonetic alphabet correctly!) was about to land! In those days the airfield was still intact, with the two Bellman hangars on the south side being occupied by civilian operators and the traffic having to be stopped on the busy A30 in order to let aircraft cross from and to the airfield.

Our last stop on the way home was Farnborough, where very little could be seen from the road at the best of times. But there was an interesting scrap yard at North Camp, which we always checked as many of the German aircraft which had been tested at Farnborough had been dumped there. Most were unrecognisable heaps of junk but I do recall seeing an Me.109 in Lufwaffe markings.

Tour No.2 — 263 miles: Friday 16th July 1948. First stop Biggin Hill, then on to Rochford (Southend) after which we stayed the night at Hockley. The next day we went to Southend Corporation's 'At Home', which was reported on in *The Aeroplane* for 13th August as follows:

"The Southend Corporation's 'At Home' on July 17 commenced with home-based aircraft defending the aerodrome against visiting aircraft. Twelve visitors managed to evade the defence and arrived without having their registration letters taken. Out of thirty arrivals, seventeen took part in the competitions arranged. Mr. B. Collins, the Aerodrome Manager, amused the crowd with a fine exhibition of aerobatics in a

Miles Magister, and Mr. Barnes, the School CFI, scared everyone to death with his crazy flying in a Tiger."

We returned to Hockley for the night and next day set off via North Weald for Broxbourne. After being shown around the hangar we were then taken, very surreptitiously, by the Chief Engineer (W.S. 'Jock' Ogilvie) behind a curtain at the back of the hangar to see his pride and joy, the prototype Dart Kitten G-AERP, which he had purchased in the autumn of 1947. It was very near to completion, having been restored by two DH students in their spare time; as I was to discover much later, these students were none other than Desmond Norman and John Britten, of later B-N Islander fame!

After a night at Nazeing, Essex, we then moved off to Hatfield and Luton but do not recall seeing anything at either aerodrome worthy of note. Following this we stayed at Hemel Hempstead overnight before setting off for home the next day via Elstree, where we both had our very first flight, courtesy of London Aero Motor Services Ltd and Auster J/1 Autocrat G-AHCL.

"Would you like to see the 'new' London Airport at Heathrow being made?" asked the pilot.

"Not half!" we said (or words to that effect), and so off we went for a circuit of that muddy, tented airfield! Nobody seemed to mind and I don't recall him having a radio: ah, the sweet nostalgia of it all, you'd probably have half the Air Force after you if you tried it today! We then called in at Northolt, when we were lucky enough to spot a Boeing B-17 landing. This in itself was a rare enough sight at a civil airport in those days, but when David had focused its registration (written vertically down the fin in small letters) through his binoculars we could hardly take it in! We later discovered that this aircraft, EP-HIM ('His Imperial Majesty') was the personal aircraft of the Shah of Persia, who was making a short trip to Britain in July 1948, and contained only his entourage, the Shah having arrived at London Airport in a RAF York with a fighter escort sometime earlier. We, however, had seen and photographed the best bit! London Airport again, from the ground this time, seemed tame after that bit of excitement, with its usual airliners plying their trade, but then it was home again for a bath and another change of clothes!

Tour No.3 — 222 miles: Wednesday 21st July 1948. First stop Blackbushe, then back to Farnborough and onwards to Oxford where we stayed the night. Next day we went on to Thame, where we had a most enjoyable time, and Airtech Ltd., the resident occupiers of the airfield, who were into Halifax C.Mk.8s in a big way at the time, very kindly provided a guide who showed us around the hangars. They also took us into an ex-BOAC Halton parked outside, but I pitied the poor passengers having to climb up the steep cabin in the narrow aisle to get to their seats. Then there was the mainspar, which the crew had to climb over to gain access to the cockpit! It was then on to Kidlington, where we were pleased to find the one and only British-registered Fleet 7C G-AEJY in one of the hangars. Although there were also a number of other Bellman type hangars there, these contained (from memory) little of interest in the way of complete aircraft, being mainly filled with RAF spares etc.

Culham was the next stop and, being an RNVR base, this meant that flying usually only took place at the weekends and therefore we saw no aircraft, but that night we stayed in Oxford again as we had more airfields to visit in the vicinity. Next day it was off to Benson, Blackbushe, Farnborough and then home again.

The total cost of the three tours on Youth Hostels, food and the joyride had been £4-10s, not bad for 12 days! We had just one mechanical breakdown when a chain link on my cycle broke and one near-major accident when approaching a main road junction in Newbury; I screamed to a halt but David, being a fixed-wheel enthusiast (I was a gear man myself) and rather close behind me, seemed to have trouble stopping, so the next thing I knew was that he was flying over the top of me, cycle and all! In the ensuing crash, we all finished up in a big heap just a few yards short of the junction, somewhat bruised, battered and scratched but no bones broken! When we eventually returned home we found we had covered a total distance of 776 miles, and had thoroughly enjoyed ourselves . . . .

What can I say about the SBAC Show of 1948 that hasn't already been said? This was the first one to be held at Farnborough and it was the first that I attended. Well, one thing which does remain firmly embedded in my memory is the never-to-be-forgotten sight of the jet-propelled Avro Tudor Mk.8; this sat on the end of the runway by the black sheds awaiting take-off clearance before departing like the proverbial rocket with a trail of blue smoke behind it — most impressive!

The Battle of Britain Air Display at Biggin Hill in September 1948 also produced an interesting aircraft in the shape of the light blue-painted Fieseler Storch of AVM Sir Harry Broadhurst. This had his personal code 'HB' on the fuselage but no serial (it later became VX154) and carried out a very slow flypast in front of the crowd.

On 6th January 1949 I reported for National Service basic training with the Royal Electrical and Mechanical Engineers at Blandford in Dorset. This was a rather rude awakening, even after my earlier basic YHA experiences! However, there is just one lovely memory of that dreadful place and that was shortly after arriving in the wooden hut of first World War vintage which was to be my home for the next six weeks. I looked out of the window to take stock of my surroundings and to confirm that there was still a civilised world out there and saw, to my utter amazement, a couple of Lancastrians, shining in the winter sunshine, standing atop the hill on the horizon! I could hardly believe my eyes: what were they doing in this God-forsaken place? It soon transpired that the airfield on which they were standing was none other than the famous Tarrant Rushton; from here many Hamilcar and Horsa gliders had been towed off for the Normandy landings on D-Day during the night of 5th June 1944, and it was now the home of Flight Refuelling Ltd. They had moved to Tarrant Rushton from Ford in 1948 but it was an airfield that I hadn't realised existed when we had carefully— as we thought — planned our tours the year before.

Such a sight gave me hope, however, and I vowed that at the first opportunity I would go and inspect this further; but it was to be a few gruelling weeks, though, before we were deemed worthy enough to be allowed out and seen in the King's uniform. When I did eventually set out one Sunday afternoon, I found to my dismay that, although the Lancastrians had looked quite close from the barrack room, a deep valley separated me from the airfield and, as there were no buses going anywhere near, I had to walk quite a few miles down the valley and then up the other side to get there. But it was well worth it just to be near aeroplanes again: in a corner of the hangar near the main entrance was a red and silver Hornet Moth, G-AESE from memory. The sight of all the Lancastrians, which had been converted to carry fuel for the Berlin Airlift, was one to savour and this helped to keep me sane during my training! I also remember seeing a Lancaster from Tarrant Rushton refuelling a Meteor on one of the early trials of in-flight refuelling.

In February 1949, I was posted to No.27 Command Workshops, Warminster, Wiltshire, another equally God-forsaken 'garrison town', but our camp was at Sutton Veny, a bleak spot about 2½ miles' march from the workshops, unless you were lucky enough to get a lift — sometimes in a 3-tonner. The only thing of even vague interest that happened in an aviation sense, apart from when it snowed one day in May, was the arrival one afternoon of an RAF 60 ft Queen Mary with a Horsa glider on it. I discovered that it was night stopping en route to its destination (which I could not discover), and the crew were being put up in our camp for the night. On reflection, it was a wonder that they didn't get roped in for guard duty — everyone else there did!

In order to relieve the monotony, I later decided that a Blue Coach trip to Bristol might make a pleasant diversion from the interminable marches to workshops and continuous 24-hour guards. So one Sunday morning I walked down to the town and duly arrived in Bristol, from where I got a bus to Filton. I am very glad that I did because, apart from a few engineless and near-derelict Beaufighters, a few Bristol Brigands and the odd Freighter or two, one of the two Bristol Brigands for the Pakistan Air Force was within photographic range. The enormous Brabazon hangars were firmly closed though, so I missed the opportunity of seeing that 'white elephant', which was due to make its first taxying runs in July.

In July 1949 I was posted to the SRDE at Christchurch, where I duly arrived, penniless (some thieving swine had stolen my pay before I left Warminster!) on the 29th. Although I had no idea of where I was going — or what the initials SRDE stood for — as nobody there had heard of a camp at Christchurch, I was very pleasantly surprised to find, when I arrived, that I been posted to the Signals Research and Development Establishment. This was a Ministry of Supply research establishment and they urgently needed Electrical Draughtsmen. This was nearly my downfall as my trade in the regiment was *Mechanical* Draughtsman — a typical army dis-organisation! This, I thought was *it* — and before I had even got my feet under the table, so to speak! After the usual unprintable words from the duty corporal regarding the incompetence of 'the idiots in the postings department', some very hard talking followed regarding my knowledge of electrics. This had been gained from previous Technical College and night school experience while studying for the Ordinary National Certificate, and so I was allowed to stay; phew, that had been a near thing, as the thought of going back to Warminster did not grab me one little bit!

I soon discovered that SRDE was on the edge of Christchurch airfield, where Airspeed's were testing and producing the Airspeed Ambassador; joy of joys, I just could not believe my luck! I then moved from the austerity of a typical army camp 'brick hut' into a delightful old mansion known as Bure Homage — by then nearly derelict — but situated just off the eastern edge of the airfield and connected to a perimeter track of sorts by a dirt track. Bure Homage had last been home to the officers of the 409th FG, 84th FW of the USAAF 9th Tactical Air Command, who had once flown (and crashed) Thunderbolts from Christhurch in 1944. Undoubtedly Bure Homage (which had been a stately home) must, when in its prime, have been a delightful place in which to live, but by the time I arrived it was in a pretty poor state (not helped by 'us lot'), but from that moment it became my second home! With all that Christchurch offered I no longer had the desire to escape to my home at every available opportunity, and in fact it wasn't long before I decided that I should learn to fly (on 28/- a week); well, you nearly could in those days, and for further gruesome details of this episode in my life, including the memorable visit to Tarrant Rushton in early 1949, the Surrey Air Pageant at Kenley on 12th June 1949, Hurn and all the activities at Christchurch during this period, see Chapter 5 of *Tails of the Fifties.*

By this time, where I went my cycle went too, and I soon took the opportunity to visit all the New Forest airfields, most of which were deserted but full of atmosphere. I also tried to imagine what I had missed, by just a few years. During one such Sunday morning trip to

Stoney Cross airfield, where the last occupants had used Stirlings on the transport run to India, I was enjoying a cycle ride down the main runway to get to a Bellman hangar on the other side to see what it held. Then I detected a strange noise coming from the clear blue sky above, and this unnatural phenomenon soon manifested itself as VN799, the blue-painted prototype Canberra, probably on a very early test flight from Boscombe Down; it had made its first-ever flight from Warton only in May.

As the Canberra got ever closer I soon realised that the pilot, probably 'Roly' Beamont, either had every intention of scaring the living daylights out of me, as the dive was lining the aircraft up nicely with me on the centreline of the runway, or that he was in some kind of trouble and was going to belly-land the thing on the main runway: although, on reflection, at that speed he would have been hard pressed to have got away with the latter choice. However, it appeared that the former was his intention, and in that he certainly succeeded, as I was off that runway *toute de suite* to join the cows grazing peacefully alongside!

I cannot remember now if this excitement spoilt my Sunday morning revelry or enhanced it, but having finally recovered from the shock of having been beaten up by one of the very latest RAF jet-propelled bomber prototypes, I reached the Bellman hangar only to find that it was filled with surplus Auxiliary Fire Service trailer pumps! A search of the ditch to the rear of the hangar revealed an instrument panel (less instruments), but from what aircraft it had come I could not tell. Nothing else remained to see from the days when Stoney Cross had been a very active aerodrome. On occasions when I visit Bournemouth, I often stop off at Stoney Cross to have a sandwich and try to recall those far-off days

. . .

Holmsley South airfield, on the other hand, was very quiet and it was difficult to imagine my cousin arriving there in a York from the Far East shortly after VJ-Day after serving in the REME behind the Jap lines in Burma for much of the war. Apart from the new civilian residents of the Nissen huts there was little to be seen and certainly no beat-ups by new jet bombers!

Air Races were again held at Thruxton on 21st August 1949, and another chapter in this book describes the 1948 event from the point of view of one of the entrants. *The Aeroplane* for 2nd September 1949 reported on the event and I can do no better than reproduce this for old time's sake:

"Thruxton Air Races: A crowd of some 6,000 spectators were present on August 21 at Thruxton Aerodrome for the annual air races and display run by the Wiltshire School of Flying, in conjunction with the Royal Artillery Aero Club. The main event was the Thruxton open handicap race over a 72-mile course from the aerodrome to Totland

Bay, Isle of Wight, and back. The winner, out of a field of 23 aircraft, was D. Jemmett in a Miles Magister, which averaged 140 mph; second was Tommy Rose flying a General Aircraft Cygnet at an average speed of 116¾ mph, and third was Flt. Lt. J. Thompson in a Miles Magister averaging 112½ mph. The fastest time was set up by R.R. Paine in his Miles Hawk Speed Six, clocking an average of 188¾ mph, and runner-up was Ian Forbes in a Miles Nighthawk at 155¾ mph. The winner of the race for Auster Autocrats was Sqdn. Ldr. L.H. Cliff, followed by J. Vine, second, and G.G. Plank, third. The winner of the race for Auster Is was entered by the Earl of Cardigan and flown by Sdqn. Ldr. L.H. Cliff; second was Capt. D.M. Spenser Smith. There were only two entrants for the Auster 5 (Lycoming) race. The winner was Mr. G.P. Shea-Simonds' aircraft, flown by Mr. Wade-Palmer, and the other entrant was disqualified for cutting across a turning point.

There was also a Magister race, won again by Ron Paine, with Sqdn. Ldr. L.H. Cliff second, and Mr. K. Combes third. The races were judged by Brigadier G.G. Mears, CBE, DSO, MC, ADC, GOC Southern Command, and Group Capt. C.F. MacPherson, and the prizes were presented by Mrs. Mears, wife of Brigadier Mears. Also present was Air Commodore C.A. Stevens, CB, CBE, MC, Officer Commanding RAF Maintenance Command. Flt. Lt. Peter Gush was Clerk of the Course.

The air display that followed included a parachute descent by Gwynn Johns from 1,700 ft, with a delay to 800 ft before opening his parachute and landing on the tarmac. H.A. Marsh, test pilot of Cierva, demonstrated their Skeeter and a Sikorsky Hoverfly was flown by an army pilot. W. Jennings performed in an Olympia sailplane and Ranald Porteous gave his usual demonstration of aerobatics and cross-wind landing in Auster's demonstrator fitted with Goodyear wobble-wheels.

A Vampire demonstration should have formed part of the next item on the programme, but the aircraft was unable to arrive because of undercarriage trouble, so the Spitfires of No.41 Group, flown by Sqdn. Ldr. Cree, DFC and Flt. Lt. Hibbert carried on alone. A simulated dog-fight was part of their exhibition and they were hooked up by VHF via amplifiers to the spectators. Sqdn. Ldr. J.E. Doran Webb was Secretary of the meeting."

An interesting snippet on the same page of the same copy of *The Aeroplane* has reminded me:

"*Christchurch. — A member of the South Hants Ultra Light Air Club* (the Christchurch club I joined a few months later!) *was fined for flying less than 1,000 ft over Bournemouth. As this altitude is quite considerable for an ultra light* (probably the Autocrat G-AIPX, as the club didn't have any ultra-lights at the time! – author), *it seems that little craft must always go round towns. By a coincidence club members* leaving the police court saw a Sunderland making low-altitude banked circuits over Bournemouth on a civic occasion." There ain't no justice!

Realising that the Airborne Forces Experimental Establishment (AFEE) at Beaulieu were going to hold what was to be their last "At Home" to the public on 17th September 1949 in commemoration of the Battle of Britain, I naturally decided to attend, as it was only a short cycle ride from Christchurch! This event was very well covered in *The Aeroplane* for 23rd September 1949 and I can do no better than to reproduce this below — purely for nostalgic reasons, you understand!

"Standards of showmanship and entertainment vary from station to station, but the Airborne Forces Experimental Establishment at Beaulieu has established a high reputation for what has been organized at previous "At Homes." This year a very ambitious programme indeed was staged and once again people came in thousands from far and wide to see it.

The main functions of the Establishment are: to test and develop methods of transporting and delivering airborne forces and equipment; to investigate the suitability of aircraft for Airborne Forces' use; to advise on relevant technical matters; and in a somewhat different field, to test rotary-wing aircraft and prototype helicopters. As a result of the final function an "At Home" at Beaulieu becomes a red-letter day for the Helicopter Association and a special exhibit of these aircraft is put on show.

But that is far from all, and at the show this year were a large proportion of exhibits from the SBAC Show at Farnborough. Air Marshal Sir Alec Coryton was a guest, as was also Sir Hew Kilner, who came with a party from Weybridge in a Viscount. Sir Frederick Handley Page, whose Hastings aircraft played a large part in the programme, was there as well. As many of the guests brought their ladies and families, the special enclosure took on the happy atmosphere of prewar gatherings at Hendon.

Highlight of the whole performance was the airborne forces action, which began with an attack on a stage coach by a party of Indians, mounted it seems on New Forest ponies; the coach was only able to escape by virtue of the superior speed of its tractor! However, the Indians, having 'asked for it', 'got it' in a most satisfactory manner. After a preliminary softening up by low-level attacks made by assorted aircraft, including a Devon in this somewhat unusual role, the heavens opened and not only parachute troops but guns and equipment rained down to join those who had already been put down by Hamilcar and Horsa.

After the white flag had been raised exactly on schedule a Westland-Sikorsky helicopter came in to evacuate a casualty. This part of the performance was only made possible by the close co-operation of the Army with whom the Establishment works very closely.

Then came the Command flypasts, Yorks, Lincolns and Meteors, before the American Superfortresses arrived. Sqdn. Ldr. Cable showed what could be done with a Bristol helicopter, including engine-off landings. Seen for the first time in public was the new technique developed by Flight Refuelling Ltd. After coming over linked together, the Meteor broke away from the Lancaster right overhead.

Bill Huggins and his circus of performing helicopters are becoming an annual event. They deserved to be so. At the end of the turn the Air Horse arrived and disgorged a herd of pantomime ponies which, after amusing the crowd with their antics, were lassoed and taken round to collect for the Benevolent Fund. During the next part of the programme high-speed aerobatics by Meteor and Vampire were contrasted with slow-speed aerobatics by Hawker Tomtit and Comper Swift.

We had to leave before the Indian's forest set itself on fire and was duly dealt with by airborne fire-fighters, but not before we had had time once more to see Mike Lithgow put the swept-wing Supermarine 510 through its tremendous paces. Some precisely-made jumps were done from the static balloon, including one right on to the signalling square in front of the control tower. Here were the headquarters of B.J. Hurren and Norman Hill, responsible for the well-informed and spoken commentary. Group Capt. Hamblin and his officers and men have every reason to be satisfied with the results of their efforts. Their guests certainly were. — T.J."

I can but echo these sentiments, as a wonderful day was indeed enjoyed and it had been well worth the cycle ride.

Then one day the RAF crews of a couple of 60 ft Queen Mary aircraft transporters stayed the night with us. They had come to collect the fuselages of a Lancaster and Halifax which had been with the Military Engineering Experimental Establishment (MEXE) at Christchurch for some time; these could easily be seen from the bus to Bournemouth but no explanation for their presence at MEXE has ever been found, however they were duly taken away (and probably scrapped) in early 1950.

We have now reached 1950. I remained at Christchurch, thoroughly enjoying myself, until being demobbed in June of that year. I could have signed on but the thought of possibly being posted away from my new home did not appeal to me, so I regretfully said my goodbyes and left. By then I had got to like the place so much that I applied for a job as a junior draughtsman with Airspeed's, but unfortunately they had no vacancies at that time; this was a great disappointment as I would so dearly loved to have stayed as there was so much going on — and, who knows, I might even have gained my PPL with the Christchurch Aero Club!